I0816227

PADMA'S ALL AMERICAN

Also by
Padma Lakshmi

COOKBOOKS

Easy Exotic

Tangy Tart Hot & Sweet

MEMOIR

Love, Loss, and What We Ate

CHILDREN'S

Tomatoes for Neela

ANTHOLOGIES

Best American Travel Writing 2021 (editor)

Best American Food and Travel Writing 2024 (editor)

REFERENCE

The Encyclopedia of Spices & Herbs

With Chris Kajioka, cutting sugarcane in Hawaii

ALFRED A. KNOPF
New York
2025

PADMA'S ALL AMERICAN

TALES, TRAVELS, AND RECIPES FROM *TASTE THE NATION* AND BEYOND

PADMA LAKSHMI

Photographs by Charity Burggraaf

A BORZOI BOOK
FIRST HARDCOVER EDITION PUBLISHED BY ALFRED A. KNOPF 2025

Published by Alfred A. Knopf, a division of Penguin Random House LLC, 1745 Broadway, New York, NY 10019.

Knopf, Borzoi Books, and the colophon are registered trademarks of Penguin Random House LLC.

The recipes for Maheecheh and Yogurt Tahdig on pages 235 and 120 are adapted from *Bottom of the Pot: Persian Recipes and Stories* © 2018 by Naz Deravian. Used by permission of Flatiron Books.

Photos on pages 2, 5, 42, 76, 97, 122, 129 (bottom), 197 (bottom), 237, 238, 263, and 264 courtesy of Anthony Jackson.
Photos on pages 152, 153, and 156 courtesy of Padma Lakshmi.
Photos on page 109 courtesy of Kamal Attara.

This book contains a QR code. Penguin Random House collects and processes your personal information. See our Notice at Collection and Privacy Policy at prh.com /notice.

Library of Congress Cataloging-in-Publication Data
Names: Lakshmi, Padma, author.
Title: Padma's all American : tales, travels, and recipes from *Taste the Nation* and beyond / Padma Lakshmi.
Other titles: All American
Description: First edition. | New York : Alfred A. Knopf, 2025. | Includes index.
Identifiers: LCCN 2024047158 | ISBN 9780593535325 (hardcover) | ISBN 9780593535332 (ebook)
Subjects: LCSH: Cooking, American.
Classification: LCC TX715 .L2145 2025 | DDC 641.5973—dc23/eng/20241205
LC record available at https://lccn.loc .gov/2024047158

penguinrandomhouse.com | aaknopf.com

Some of the recipes in this book may include raw eggs, meat, or fish. When these foods are consumed raw, there is always the risk that bacteria, which is killed by proper cooking, may be present. For this reason, when serving these foods raw, always buy certified salmonella-free eggs and the freshest meat and fish available from a reliable grocer, storing them in the refrigerator until they are served. Because of the health risks associated with the consumption of bacteria that can be present in raw eggs, meat, and fish, these foods should not be consumed by infants, small children, pregnant women, the elderly, or any persons who may be immunocompromised. The author and publisher expressly disclaim responsibility for any adverse effects that may result from the use or application of the recipes and information contained in this book.

Printed in China

9 8 7 6 5 4 3 2 1

The authorized representative in the EU for product safety and compliance is Penguin Random House Ireland, Morrison Chambers, 32 Nassau Street, Dublin D02 YH68, Ireland, https://eu-contact.penguin.ie.

Book design by Shubhani Sarkar, sarkardesignstudio.com

For all our participants
who shared their lives with me on this journey.

And for my mother, Vijaya Lakshmi,
who has always encouraged my curiosity about others.

CONTENTS

INTRODUCTION xiii
HOW I COOK xix
Tools xxiii
Pantry xxiv

RADEEM 2
KAMAL 108
BJ 130
TWILA 194
ROSA 214
HAMID 236
SAIPIN 262

SMALL PLATES AND SALADS

Som Tum / **Green Papaya Salad** 5
Romaine Heart Salad with Za'atar and Herbs 6
Kale-Pomegranate Salad 9
Plum Chaat / **Spicy Fruit Snack** 10
Ramp Salt [ACCOMPANIMENT] 12
Muhammara / **Roasted Red Pepper and Walnut Spread** 13
Pickled Peanuts 15
Kuku Sabzi / **Herbed Frittata** 19
Aushak / **Leek and Scallion Dumplings** 20
Butternut Squash Bolani / **Stuffed Flatbread** 23
Red Onion Chutney [ACCOMPANIMENT] 24
Papas a la Huancaína / **Potatoes in Ají Amarillo Sauce** 27
Pakori / **Vegetable Fritters** 28
Mint and Cilantro Chutney [ACCOMPANIMENT] 31
Tostones / **Fried Green Plantains** 32
Mushroom Tacos Campesinos 35
Spicy Coleslaw 36
Latkes / **Biracial Latkes / Fried Potato Pancakes** 39
Whipped Spam with Toast Points 41
Chowchow / **Pickled Garden Vegetables** [ACCOMPANIMENT] 42
Sach Ko Jakak / **Kreung-Infused Beef Skewers** 43
Asun / **Spicy Goat Bites** 45
Pork Dumplings with Water Chestnuts and Dates 46
Dumpling Sauce [ACCOMPANIMENT] 49

SOUPS AND STEWS

Essential Chicken Broth 54

Vegetable Broth 56

Tomato Rasam / **Spicy Tomato Broth** 57

Sambar / **Tamarind Lentil Stew** 59

Tomato Egg Drop Soup 62

Tomorrow's Borsch / **Beet and Vegetable Soup** 65

Tom Yum Goong / **Hot and Sour Soup with Shrimp** 66

Tadka Dal / **Yellow Lentil Soup** 68

Ribollita / **White Bean and Vegetable Stew** 71

Pork and Kimchi Soondubu / **Soft Tofu and Pork Stew** 72

Aash / **Hearty Noodle Soup** 74

Savory Minced Meat Sauce [ACCOMPANIMENT] 77

Garlic Yogurt Sauce [ACCOMPANIMENT] 78

Avgolemono / **Chicken Lemon Soup** 79

VEGETABLES AND LEGUMES

Sabzi / **Sautéed Greens** 84

Zucchini with Sun-Dried Tomatoes 87

Blackened Corn with Suya Spice 88

Peppery Sweet and Sour Red Cabbage 90

Cabbage Poriyal / **Stir-Fried Cabbage** 91

Braised Leeks 93

Calabaza con Mojo / **Roasted Squash in a Citrus-Garlic Sauce** 94

Saag and Grits / **Greens and Grits** 96

Grits [ACCOMPANIMENT] 98

Chile Vinegar [ACCOMPANIMENT] 99

Podimas / **Potatoes with Turmeric and Fried Lentils** 101

H&H-Style Breakfast Burritos with Homemade Pinto Beans 102

Salsa Macha / **Chile Oil with Nuts and Seeds** [ACCOMPANIMENT] 103

Holishkes / **Sweet and Sour Stuffed Cabbage** 104

Fatteh Batinjan / **Roasted Eggplant Layered with Chickpeas, Yogurt, and Pita** 112

GRAINS AND NOODLES

Yogurt Tahdig / **Rice with a Crispy Top** 120

Congri / **Moros y Cristianos / Rice and Black Beans** 123

Coconut Rice 124

Southeast Asian–Inspired Risotto / **Rice Porridge with Shrimp and Coconut Milk** 126

Jollof Rice / **Rice with Roasted Tomatoes and Peppers** 128

Crab Fried Rice 137

Rice "Stuffing" with Chinese Sausage and Shiitake Mushrooms 138

Krishna's Upma-Style Sriracha Butter Couscous 141

Uova in Trippa / **Egg "Noodles" in Tomato-Basil Sauce** 142

Pasta all'Amatriciana / **Rigatoni and Pork Cheek Pasta** 147

Spaghetti alla Carbonara / **Pasta with Eggs and Pancetta** 149

Spicy Noodles with Sesame Chutney and Mint 150

Sesame Chutney [ACCOMPANIMENT] 152

Dosas / **Savory Fermented Crepes** 155

Coconut Chutney [ACCOMPANIMENT] 160

SEAFOOD

Tuna Larb / **Tuna with Herbs** 166

Peruvian Ceviche / **Fish Marinated in Citrus and Onion** 171

Shoyu Poke / **Rice and Tuna Bowl** 173

Pickled Onions [ACCOMPANIMENT] 173

Pad Thai Fish / **Tamarind Steamed Fish with Spinach** 176

Amok Trei / **Coconut Curry Fish** 178

Fish Simmered with Potatoes and Lemon 180

Nam Banh Chuk / **Fish and Noodle Soup** 181

Mussels with a Rasam Vibe / **Mussels Simmered with Tomatoes and Spices** 182

Sweet and Sour Shrimp with Cherry Tomatoes 185

Shrimp and Grits 186

CHICKEN

Chicken Larb / Ground Chicken with Herbs 192

Yogurt Chicken 193

Desert Chicken / Chicken Thighs with Sumac and Agave 200

Arroz Caldo / Chicken and Rice Porridge 203

Fried Shallots [ACCOMPANIMENT] 204

Chicken Adobo / Braised Chicken in Coconut and Vinegar 205

Jerk Chicken / Spicy Marinated Chicken 206

Chicken Tikka Masala / Chicken in a Creamy Spiced Tomato Sauce 208

Tagine-Inspired Chicken / Spiced Chicken Stew with Lemon, Apricots, and Olives 211

Fesenjan / Braised Chicken with Pomegranate and Walnuts 213

Amazonian Tamales / Tamales Stuffed with Chicken 218

Rosa's Green Sauce [ACCOMPANIMENT] 221

MEAT

Saltimbocca di Casa Mia / Beef Rolled with Prosciutto, Pecorino, and Sage 226

Chile Verde / Pork in Green Chile and Tomatillo Sauce 230

Salsa Verde [ACCOMPANIMENT] 230

Schnitzel / Fried Veal Cutlets 231

Ropa Vieja / Braised Beef 232

Maheecheh / Braised Lamb Shanks 235

Beef Koobideh / Ground Beef Kebabs 241

Mast-o Khiar / Yogurt-Cucumber Sauce [ACCOMPANIMENT] 243

Passover Brisket 246

Sisig / Pork with Chicken Livers 247

Pernil / Roast Pork with Crispy Skin 249

Pineapple Salsa [ACCOMPANIMENT] 250

Qabuli Pulao / Lamb and Rice Pilaf 253

SWEETS

Sholeh Zard / Rice Pudding with Saffron and Rose 260

Khao Niao Mamuang / Sticky Rice with Mango 266

Mysore Pak / Buttery Sweet Chickpea Squares 268

Decolonized Halo-Halo / Tropical Fruit and Crushed Ice Sundae 271

Black Sesame Maple Ice Cream 273

Ruiz's Pieces / Peanut Butter–Mesquite Treats 274

Eric Nam's Quick Hotteok / Sweet Pancakes Stuffed with Nuts and Cinnamon 276

Banana Lumpia / Sweet Fried Spring Rolls 279

Blackberry Slump-ish / Fruit Dessert with Cornmeal Dumplings 280

Strawberry-Cardamom and Cream Cake 283

DRINKS

Rose Water Limeade 288

Chicha Morada / Iced Purple Corn Tea 291

Horchata / Sweet Rice and Almond Milk 292

Masala Chai / Spiced Tea 294

Hot Toddy Tea 295

Red Chile Hot Chocolate 296

Emergency Mojito / Rum and Sprite Cocktail 298

The Company Cocktail / Spicy Tequila-Citrus Punch 301

FEASTS 304

ACKNOWLEDGMENTS 309

INDEX 311

INTRODUCTION

Dear Reader,

The book you have before you is a personal one, a record of my last seven years of eating, traveling, and exploring. Much of this time was spent in cities and towns all over America, eating my way through our country as I filmed the shows *Top Chef* and *Taste the Nation*.

Through this work I've had the pleasure and luck of meeting people who create and evolve the cuisine of the United States every day. They include Michelin-starred and James Beard Award–winning chefs, dance teachers and healers, gas station owners and restaurateurs, and foragers, musicians, artists, educators, historians, farmers, and city council members, to name a few. Most of them are immigrants or children of immigrants. This book is my love letter to them—and to all immigrants who have made a life here and, in turn, made America what it is.

A few months after the 2016 election, I began working with the American Civil Liberties Union (ACLU) as an Artist Ambassador for immigrants' and women's rights. I was motivated by the vitriol coming out of the White House and the way President Donald Trump was demonizing and vilifying immigrants, not just in speech—despicable enough—but in action: separating families, caging children, and prosecuting asylum seekers. As I write this, he is back in office.

My mother arrived here as an immigrant in 1972 after a turbulent arranged marriage to my biological father. Seeking a better life for us, she worked hard to establish herself in America. With a steady job as a nurse and a cute little apartment on the Upper East Side of New York City, my mother brought me to America two years later when I was four years old. The journey from New Delhi to New York City took nineteen hours. I made the flight alone, my mother's contact info printed neatly by my grandfather on a small sheet of laminated paper, pinned to my red coat. Not only am I an immigrant (and the child of an immigrant), but I also came of age in immigrant communities, first in

Above: Me and Mom
Opposite: With Brandon Jew in Marin County

With Michael Twitty at Middleton Place in Charleston

New York City, and later in the San Gabriel Valley in Los Angeles. My experience of immigrant life in working-class neighborhoods was completely at odds with Trump's claims that we were "rapists" and "criminals."

While his spurious and dehumanizing claims about immigrants made me angry, I didn't want to combat his lies by reinforcing the idea of "the good immigrant"—the hard worker who contributes to his or her community and is therefore "acceptable." The truth, is most immigrants have little choice but to work hard. Regardless of how hard we work or how well we assimilate, our lives are meaningful. We are integral to this country. Where is that story in the media?

Could I combine my advocacy for immigrants with my professional life in food? Given my background as a food writer and making television shows such as *Top Chef,* I wondered if I could use food as a vehicle to expose the contradictions in how conservative media and politicians perceive and treat immigrants. Food would be my Trojan horse and serve to inspire curiosity about our fellow Americans and our shared history. And so, my producing partner, David Shadrack Smith, and I began developing a show about immigration.

We began exploring "American food" and what that looks like today. Americans purchase more salsa and sriracha than ketchup. And pad Thai, sushi, bubble tea, burritos, and bagels are as American as apple pie—which, by the way, contains not one single ingredient indigenous to North America! If I think about what's *really* American, it's desert pack rat cooked with sumac and agave. It's the Appalachian ramp salt that I now sprinkle on top of my Indian plum chaat.

The way we eat today is so different from the way we ate even a generation ago. Just look through any recent "What's for dinner?" cookbook: Fish sauce, turmeric, gochujang, and chipotles are all now commonly used in recipes designed for average home cooks. This is American food now. But why don't we know more about the provenance of these ingredients—and about the people who introduced them to this country? And how might we see ourselves, one another, and our culture differently if we did?

Taste the Nation was conceived as a show for immigrants to tell their own stories, as they saw fit, and its success owes everything to the people who invited us into their communities, their homes, and their lives. I am forever humbled by how much trust and generosity they showed us.

I am lucky to have been able to go deep into these communities, eating and learning from the people I met and interviewed. They inspired me to be braver in the kitchen—before making the show, I had never made tamales, pad Thai, or tahdig at home. Despite how much I love these dishes, I was too intimidated.

Taste the Nation brought me back to my roots. It reminded me of the skill and resourcefulness of home cooks. I saw my mother in the faces of the women who spent all day on their feet, working as nurses or dance teachers, and who then came home to cook the foods of their origin countries so that their children would have a stronger connection to their heritage. I saw that same intrepid courage—born of necessity, sure, but brave nonetheless—it takes to start over, to strive for more for their families.

With Ali Wong in San Francisco's Chinatown

I have always felt Indian *and* American, but I've never felt that others considered me just as American as they were. I've always felt like an outsider. This feeling will be nothing new to most immigrant kids. But in making *Taste the Nation,* I felt more American than I ever have. Getting to know the vast diversity of people who also call America home only reinforced my belief that this is still one of the most unique countries in the world.

I've called this book *Padma's All American* because it's *my* vision of what it means to be—and eat like—an American. This is a book for how we eat now—a chronicle of cultural exchange and adaptation. A book both faithful and freewheeling, with reverence for the immigrant and Indigenous histories behind the deliciousness.

This book is also a scrapbook of my travels. A journal of what I've eaten and how I (re)make it in my kitchen. I wrote it for the average American eater—someone who eats a variety of foods in any given week, who maybe didn't grow up with a dish or cuisine but who wants to share in its delights. But especially, I wrote it hoping that cooks who recognize a dish from their heritage will find that its beloved essence remains intact. I am not claiming to make the most traditional or authentic version of anything, including my own Indian food. For generations, immigrants—the heroes of this book, along with Indigenous Americans—have had to adapt the dishes of their homelands to the constraints of time and American grocery stores. I present these recipes with that same inventive spirit. Consider these third culture recipes.

If you're reading this book, then you love food and cooking. Like me, you're probably a passionate spelunker of hyperlocal food culture and all its delights. You know where the best poke spot is and who serves the most delicious dumplings. But have you tried making them yourself? Growing up, many of us learn how to cook at the side of a parent or caregiver. The dishes they teach us—their ingredients, their techniques—become *familiar.* We don't think of them as "too hard" to make at home. I grew up making Tomato Rasam (page 57). I know how easy it is to heat oil and fry spices. And yet, many competent home cooks who adore Indian food and eat it regularly at restaurants wouldn't make it at home. Because the ingredients are unfamiliar—what's asafoetida?—a dish can *seem* intimidating. Here's the thing: With a sharp knife, a pan, and a fire, we are all starting from the same place. Home cooks from other cultures don't possess special powers—they possess knowledge, *familiarity.*

I promise, all it takes to understand an ingredient is to try using it. These recipes are designed to get you familiar with the flavors you love (or will love) but may have never tried cooking at home. They were written for and tested in a home kitchen—in many home kitchens, by cooks of all different backgrounds.

The recipes in these pages are drawn from Afghan, Gullah Geechee, Cambodian, and Greek culture, from Cuban American and Chinese American families, from people who are of Nigerian and Arab and Thai and Ukrainian heritage. But the road that brought me to this food took me to kitchens from Dearborn to DC, from Miami to Milwaukee, from Houston to San Francisco. I never had to leave the country to taste the world's flavors—and neither do you.

Wherever you live, come along with me.

This is a book for how we eat now—
a chronicle of cultural exchange and adaptation.
A book both faithful and freewheeling,
with reverence for the immigrant and
Indigenous histories behind the deliciousness.

HOW I COOK

Welcome to my kitchen! The recipes in this book are filtered through my palate and my way of cooking at home. I am not a chef. You will not read about fancy techniques or be asked to do anything but apply some time, focus, and elbow grease—for most of cooking is indeed prep and chopping. I am a home cook, a curious and voracious eater who seeks to bring all the flavors of my fellow Americans home.

My North Star in adapting and developing these recipes has been loyalty to the essence and spirit of what these dishes represent for someone from within the culture of their origin. With that commitment at the forefront of my mind, I have also tried to adapt these recipes so that they are as accessible to as wide an audience of home cooks as possible. Inevitably, in my adaptation of these dishes, I may have omitted or changed an ingredient or a step you consider crucial. Forgive me. I want those of us who did not grow up making these recipes to be successful. My great hope is that each of you will discover at least one dish, flavor, ingredient, or technique that's new to you—and that you will use that as a launchpad to explore other recipes.

Let your curiosity lead you. Don't be afraid to try a recipe because you can't source all the ingredients. Use what you have or is easily found, as immigrants have always done. These recipes are in your hands now. Make them your own.

MY KITCHEN RULES

Now that you know what to expect in my kitchen, I should probably warn you about how things actually go down. I'm detail oriented. You're going to quickly see that in these recipes, I expect *you* to be detail oriented, too. I'm particular about when to salt food and what size to chop your vegetables. I guarantee you that these small details are vital to the outcome of your dish. I don't want your cooking to be good. I want your cooking to be extraordinary. I want the people at your table to feel lucky to be there. I want these recipes to become regular favorites in your rotation. I want you to marvel at your ability to re-create them in your own kitchen. When you've made one of these recipes once or twice, the details will become second nature to you. So, let's get into it.

Read every recipe all the way through twice: Before you start cooking, before you chop an onion or mince even a clove of garlic, take your time and read your recipe from start to finish. Knowing what to expect—what tools you'll need, how long different steps may take, et cetera—is key to avoiding mishaps along the way.

Gather your ingredients: Before you even turn on the stove, assemble everything you will need on your counter. There is nothing worse than hunting through your produce drawer for that knob of ginger you could swear was there last night, or rifling through a crowded cabinet for smoked paprika while your aromatics burn in the pan.

Mise en place for the win: Chop everything that needs to be chopped and set it out in the order that you'll use it. Prepping vegetables (meat, too) always takes longer than you think it will. I, too, fall prey to this at times. By preparing your veggies beforehand, you'll set yourself up for success, especially the first time you're making a recipe. As you become familiar with a dish, you may realize that, yes, you can mince the garlic while the onion sweats. But the first time? Nah. Save yourself from stress. Just do the work beforehand.

Chop consistently: I'm specific about the size I want you to chop your veggies. Note that the smaller you chop something, the quicker it cooks. Also, things that are cut unevenly will cook unevenly. This means that you want each piece of carrot to be cut about the same size so that they cook uniformly.

Volume: My recipes usually include both the approximate number of vegetables you'll need and the volume you should end up with when they're chopped. I do this because I believe a potato is not just a potato—your "small" potato may be smaller than my "small" potato, so providing these details sets you up for the best possible result.

Cooking times: What I've given you here is merely a guide. My times are approximate; your stove or oven may vary from mine. Your pots and pans may be thicker or thinner than mine. I tend to prefer my vegetables on the crisper side, and I will often give them shorter cooking times—especially in soups—to retain that crunch. If you like your vegetables more tender, cook them longer. The point is to pay attention to controlling your heat source and understanding the nature of your equipment.

Salting: I salt in stages. Here's why: Salting at different times changes the texture and the moisture balance of ingredients. Salting as you go is insurance against oversalting your food as well. It allows you much more control over the final product. These recipes contain the amount I prefer. We all have different salt preferences: My mother likes less; my daughter likes more.

Chiles: Warning: Some of these recipes are downright spicy. This is not meant to intimidate you but to preserve the essence of what makes the recipe a cherished one. When a recipe calls for a substantial amount of chiles, that's because the original recipe has a lot of heat to it. Rather than skip a recipe you might otherwise try, adjust the heat to your own preferences. These are your recipes now. You do not need to use all or any of the amount indicated—this is why I provide a range.

Acid: My daughter, Krishna, often reminds me of my strong preference for tart flavors; with this in mind, I've given ranges of lemon or lime juice in many cases, to suit your own tastes.

Roasting whole spices: To roast whole spices, add them to a dry pan and set it over medium heat. Swirl and shake the pan occasionally to prevent burning and toast until fragrant—usually 1 to 2 minutes—and then remove them from the pan. This is the easiest, fastest game changer you can make in your cooking, right this minute. With very little effort, you can extract an abundant amount of flavor by dry-roasting whole spices, heating up the oils that lie deep within, waking them up and bringing them to the surface. I grew up doing this in my grandmother's kitchen, in South India, the birthplace of spices. However, many people in the West—some even in the culinary industry—scoff at this practice. To them, I say, you have no idea what you're missing. And I challenge you to an experiment: Take ½ teaspoon whole cumin seeds, stir-fry them in a dry hot pan for 1 minute, then grind them into a powder using a mortar and pestle. Now compare the result with some store-bought ground cumin. Taste them side by side. Your freshly roasted cumin will pack so much more punch and nuance, with just a bit of tart funk. Also, your kitchen will smell amazing.

Washing rice: I always wash my rice, because you never know where that rice has been or what it's gone through to get to you. I grew up picking stones out of rice. Washing rice also gets rid of excess starch, which can make rice sticky. With rice like basmati, it's imperative to wash the rice several times so the grains remain fluffy and separate. Don't worry about whether the water runs *completely* clear; what's important is to just do it a few times to rinse most of the starch off.

Recipes labeled

ACCOMPANIMENT

Each of these recipes goes with the recipe that precedes it. However, many of them, such as the Mint and Cilantro Chutney (page 31), Garlic Yogurt Sauce (page 78), Red Onion Chutney (page 24), and Fried Shallots (page 204), are great paired with a variety of dishes. It's fun to mix and match them to suit your tastes.

TOOLS

I'm not a big gadget person. I think most kitchen gadgets don't really deliver enough value to justify their taking up precious real estate on my counter or in my drawers. What follows are the indispensable tools I reach for day in and day out.

Candy/Deep Fry Thermometer

When dissolving sugar at high heat or deep-frying foods, this is an invaluable tool. It clips to the inside of a pot and ensures that you don't burn your sugar or that you've brought your oil to the proper temperature (and helps you keep it there), leading to crispy bliss. Frying food in oil that's not hot enough leads to a sad, soggy, and greasy outcome. It's a must-have for making Mysore Pak (page 268).

Coffee Grinder

This is critical for grinding larger amounts of whole spices. Buy an inexpensive one and use it only for spices, otherwise your coffee will be spiced, and your spices will taste like coffee.

High-Powered Blender

My Vitamix high-powered blender (any brand is fine) is indispensable in several recipes, including the tough job of grinding lentils and rice for Dosas (page 155), emulsifying sesame seeds in Sesame Chutney (page 152), and transforming rice into the sweet milky drink Horchata (page 292).

Immersion Blender

This small, handheld blender (also called a stick blender) has blades you submerge in liquids or other ingredients while they're in a container (such as a soup pot). It is very helpful for quickly emulsifying, beating, or pureeing without having to pour ingredients out of a hot or heavy pot into a blender. Bonus: Immersion blenders fit easily in a kitchen drawer.

Microplane

Vital for the finest dusting of Parmesan, lemon zest, and nutmeg, a Microplane grater is something that won't take up much space in your utensil drawer but can add great aroma and nuance, vastly elevating the flavor and appearance of your food.

Mortars and Pestles / Molcajetes

These date back to ancient times, and many cultures still use them to crush, grind, puree, or mix ingredients and flavors. I use them to grind spices and large salt crystals. I crush garlic and ginger into a paste, which is sometimes faster than chopping. My grandmother made dosa batter using a huge one. I love a deep Thai-style one made of wood or metal. For larger whole spices, like star anise and black cardamom, I often prefer a molcajete, commonly used in Latin kitchens, with its rough surface usually made from basalt or volcanic rock.

Small Food Processor or Blender

While doing things the old-fashioned way never hurt anybody, when time or your own fatigue is a factor, a small blender, such as a Ninja, comes in handy and is much easier to clean than the bigger high-powered blender. You'll find it makes quick work of many chutneys and sauces in this book.

Spider

A spider is useful for straining food from any hot liquid like boiling water or oil, especially when needing to remove larger batches and tongs won't do.

PANTRY

My pantry reflects my evolution as a cook. A decade ago, I might have flung a dollop of harissa into a stew that needed heat. Now I might reach for gochujang. We are lucky to live in an age where once hard to find ingredients are now more widely available. What follows is by no means a comprehensive list of every pantry item in this book. Instead, think of this as a super starter kit, a curated pantry that will equip you to make most of the recipes here and elevate your cooking. When storing dried herbs and spices be sure to keep them in a cool, dark space such as a drawer or cabinet so they don't lose their potency. If you'd like to stock your pantry with all these ingredients in one fell swoop, below is a QR code for ordering them all at once from Kalustyan's in New York, a shop I've loved and trusted my whole life.

Chiles

Aleppo Pepper Flakes

Originally from Syria, this treasure has an earthy, mild heat, which makes it great on delicate vegetables. Commonly used in Middle Eastern cooking, it's wonderful on kebabs and roast chicken or as a garnish for dips, and I love it in creamy egg salad. Its flavor is similar to that of Urfa biber, a Turkish chile. If you're trying to save money or space, just buy one or the other.

Anchos (Whole or Ground)

Ancho chiles, which are dried poblanos, are the middle path between mild and hot. Anchos have some heat but a lot of earthy depth and sweetness. Great when you want heat that doesn't obscure delicate flavors. Try anchos in soups, stir-fries, or salsas like Salsa Macha (page 103), and try using them in place of hotter chiles when making food for those sensitive to heat.

Chipotle Peppers in Adobo (Canned)

Chipotle peppers are smoked, dried jalapeños. But when they are rehydrated in an adobo sauce and canned, they are a whole 'nother story. My love of these smoky, saucy peppers dates way back to my high school days among many Mexican classmates. I prefer La Morena brand, which I blend into homemade barbecue sauce and add to stews. When I don't have harissa, I've even added chipotles in adobo to a tagine. I use them in Spicy Coleslaw (page 36) and love them in potato salad, too.

Gochugaru

A type of coarse ground red chile, gochugaru is integral to kimchi, soondubu, and many other Korean dishes. Moderate in heat level, it has smoky and sweet notes.

Gochujang (Paste)

This Korean condiment is a fermented blend of gochugaru, glutinous rice, and other ingredients. It has a medium heat level and is quite savory with an edge of sweetness. It is integral to Korean dishes but useful in many others.

Indian Dried Red Chiles (Whole)

I always keep these around, and you'll find them in many recipes, sometimes in addition to fresh chiles. I prefer the Indian long variety for medium heat, but you could also pick up a bag of the milder Szechuan chiles or the much hotter Thai bird's eye chiles.

Kashmiri Pepper (Ground)

I adore this chile powder's beautiful, bright red-orange color, its finely ground texture, and its gentle heat. It's less angry than cayenne and can be a good gateway to hotter chile powders. Its vibrant color makes it ideal as a finishing spice, but I also use it in rice, curries, and pasta sauces. Need a quick dip? Try whisking it into plain yogurt with za'atar, sumac, and salt.

Morita Chiles (Whole or Ground)

Smoked, dried red (ripe) jalapeños. Because they are smoked for less time than chipotles (also smoked, dried jalapenos), they are sweeter and fruitier.

Spanish Smoked Paprika

You know that secret flavor in barbecue potato chips that is hard to imitate? Say hello to this endlessly useful ingredient, which comes in handy anytime something feels a little too one-note. It is crucial to buy Spanish smoked paprika, which is softer and more round in flavor than the more jagged but equally delicious Hungarian paprika.

Herbs and Spices

Amchur

I use this sawdust-colored dried mango powder as an all-purpose flavor amplifier with predominantly tart notes. It's not salty, but it does intensify flavors the same way salt does. Try sprinkling some on bland fruit or adding to dry rubs, ground meat, salad dressings, gravies and curries, or breading such as for Schnitzel (page 231). Sumac is a good substitute when you want to add tartness without moisture and don't have amchur.

Asafoetida Powder

This spice, also known as hing in Hindi and perungaium in Tamil, is integral to Indian cooking, and is thought to aid digestion. Do not be turned off by its pungent smell. A little goes a long way to give your dishes a necessary depth and funk that is hard to pinpoint and recognize but easy to note when missing.

Bay Leaves

I prefer the stronger flavored fresh bay leaves, when possible. Dried bay leaves can be swapped. In this book, I use Mediterranean bay or laurel leaves, not the Indian kind, which are milder in flavor.

Black Garlic
This indispensable pantry ingredient is merely garlic heated slowly to concentrate and sweeten the garlic flavor without any of the bitterness that can come when one overcooks garlic. Peel and slice or chop the sticky cloves and use them to give depth to broths and stews. I often turn to black garlic when seeking umami flavor without using an animal product.

Black Mustard Seeds
Integral to Indian cooking and present in everything from Cabbage Poriyal (page 91) to Coconut Rice (page 124), as well as wet curries and soups like Tomato Rasam (page 57), mustard seeds bring an undeniable flavor to well-rounded dishes. They have a slightly bitter edge and funk and are often added at the beginning of cooking. They burn easily, so fry them cautiously: Heat oil over medium-high heat, add a few seeds, and when they sizzle, turn the heat down to medium and add the rest of the seeds. Remove from the heat or add the other ingredients as soon as the seeds begin to pop like popcorn.

Black Peppercorns
Freshly ground dry roasted peppercorns are seriously underrated. There is no better way to enhance almost any savory dish. If you really want to get fancy, try making a black pepper brown butter (see page 68). My favored peppercorns are Indian Tellicherry or Malabar, and Cambodian Kampot.

Cardamom, Black
This is what you'd get if green cardamom and star anise had a baby; it tastes like menthol without the mint, medicinal almost. It's generally used to add a deep, woodsy undertone to savory dishes, such as Asian curries. You'll need this spice only for Chicken Tikka Masala (page 208) in this book, but I've also ground and rubbed it on roast pork for an Indian-style pernil, and sautéed the pods for rice pilaf.

Cardamom, Green
This lovely, pungent, floral spice is delicious in both savory and sweet preparations: Use it anywhere you would use cinnamon. Try it in tea or coffee; throw a few pods into curries, meat braises, or saucy vegetables. It's available in pods, seeds, and ground form: I like to buy the pods or seeds and grind them myself for the best flavor. When a recipe in this book calls for cardamom, it is this type of cardamom, unless it is labeled black cardamom.

Cumin
Cumin is integral to many cuisines: You'd be surprised how many of your favorite foods contain this spicy, warm ingredient. You should have both seeds and powder on hand, as both have different textures and tastes: I dry-roast cumin seeds and grind them myself for optimal flavor.

Curry Leaves
These are essential to South Indian cooking: There is no good substitute for their fragrant herbaceousness. Buy them at any good Indian grocery store. If making a special trip, stock up: You can freeze them. Immediately wash and dry them well, and place them between paper towels, then in a plastic ziplock bag, pushing as much air out as possible.

Fennel Seeds
From the same family as caraway and cumin but with a distinctive sweet licorice-like flavor, fennel seeds are found in Italian sausage, Indian curries, liqueurs such as ouzo, and many cookies and cakes. Indians also often nibble candied fennel seeds as a digestif.

Galangal
This is a rhizome like ginger, but it has its own distinct taste: more peppery and piney. It's common in Thai and Cambodian recipes. It often keeps for at least a few weeks in the fridge and longer in the freezer.

Garam Masala
A defining spice blend of North Indian cuisine, this spice mix can vary greatly from cook to cook but often includes green and/or black cardamom, cinnamon, cloves, and black peppercorns. It's best to buy this in small batches, online or from an Indian store that has good turnover. It can be used near the start or the end of a recipe: I like to use it to season kebabs and vegetables, sprinkle it on stir-fried potatoes, and add it to curries that have a tomato, nut, or cream base.

Lemongrass
Fresh lemongrass has an incomparably clean, lemony aroma that defines many Southeast Asian cuisines. You can unlock it by stripping the thin stalks of their tough outer layers, then chopping and pounding the fibrous insides: The thicker lower parts of the stalks have the most flavor. Save the greener tough tops for tea. Avoid dried lemongrass: It has much less flavor.

Makrut Lime Leaves
These shiny, dark green leaves lend a powerful citrusy aroma to Southeast Asian recipes. They can be hard to find in stores but can be mail-ordered, and they freeze impeccably. They are also called kaffir lime leaves, an outdated term from colonial times that is offensive. Try not to substitute dry leaves for fresh.

Mexican Oregano
I encourage you to buy this if you like to cook a lot of Latin dishes. It has a more intense, spikier, less floral note than the more common Mediterranean oregano that is probably already in your spice drawer. Dominican oregano is an alternative option.

Rosemary
I always recommend buying this woodsy herb in its fresh form for the best flavor.

Saffron
Known as the King of Spices because of its traditionally high cost, saffron is common in Mediterranean, Middle Eastern, and South Asian cooking. Its flavor is very much dependent on its smell. I prefer Spanish or Iranian saffron, if you can find it. These tend to be more fragrant.

Star Anise
I love its complex, restrained flavor, akin to licorice, and its elegant beauty, which gives any dish—from pho to biryani—a little panache. I fry whole star anise in oil for pilafs, or use it to flavor broth, sangria, and cider. I toss it into boiling water for rice, which adds a subtle aroma to the grains. I also use ground star anise to impart flavor to stews and roasts.

Szechuan Peppercorns
These are not from the pepper or *Piper nigrum* family of plants but come from a citrus plant. They are such fun to have around, delivering a eucalyptol tingle that is less spiky than that of black peppercorns, though still somewhat piquant, and of course they famously can numb your tongue. I love using them in Pickled Peanuts (page 15), soups, chicken wings, noodle dishes, and spicy oils and chutneys.

Sumac
Common in Native American and Middle Eastern cooking, sumac comes from drying and grinding sumac berries. Sumac is useful when you want to add tartness to a dish without adding moisture. The beautiful vermillion-red color makes for a gorgeous garnish. Try sprinkling sumac on flatbreads with olive oil, or using it in salad dressings, dips, and barbecue sauces, or on simple grilled fish or chicken as a garnish.

Turmeric
Fresh turmeric adds a bright yellow hue and a slightly bitter, astringent flavor to many South Asian recipes. Its dried ground version has been a part of Indian cooking and Ayurvedic tradition since ancient times. The fresh version is now trendily ubiquitous in Western (juice) bars.

White Pepper (Ground)
White pepper has a flavor distinct from that of its black counterpart, packing an earthier, less spiky heat. These *Piper nigrum* peppercorns are picked off the vine later than those harvested for black pepper, with the dark husks removed.

Za'atar
I reach for this bright, herbaceous, and toasty spice blend, originally from Palestine, at least once a week in my kitchen. Mix it with olive oil and brush on warm flatbreads or toss with croutons, whisk it into salad dressings and dips, and use it to garnish anything, from yogurt to white beans. While blends vary, they often include sumac, wild thyme, salt, and toasted sesame seeds. The name za'atar refers to both the herb wild thyme (a relative of oregano) as well as the blend itself.

Lentils/Dal

Green Lentils

They're great for holding their shape, for salads, stuffed cabbage, and lots of stews.

Chana Dal

Often labeled "desi chickpeas," these are great when fried, adding crunch and a nutty flavor to any stir-fried dish. They may have escaped your attention if you don't come from a South Asian background, but are great for those who are allergic to nuts but want a similar crunch and texture.

Masoor Dal

Often called red or orange lentils, they actually turn yellow when cooked. They boil quickly and are the base for comforting dishes like soups and Tadka Dal (page 68).

Urad Dal

This small legume is actually not a lentil but is commonly referred to as such. The legume is split and peeled and can be labeled white gram. The skin-on (unpeeled) legume is called black gram. I use urad mostly in its skinless and split form in this book. I fry it in hot oil until golden and add it to stir-fries and rice dishes, like I do chana dal. For Dosas (page 155), however, you will need whole skinless urad (often labeled urad gota).

Oils

Extra-Virgin Olive Oil

I use this frequently but don't consider it a substitute for neutral oil: It is best used in lower-heat cooking, salad dressings, and dishes that are enhanced by its distinct flavor, such as those from the Mediterranean or the Middle East.

Neutral Oil

A neutral oil is a cooking oil that does not impart any or very much flavor to a dish, used mainly for frying or sautéing. These oils have a high smoke point. This is the temperature at which oil starts to burn and produce smoke, potentially imparting an acrid or bitter taste to foods, beneficial nutrients in the oil are destroyed, and compounds harmful to health are released. Use your choice of vegetable, grapeseed, avocado, sunflower, or untoasted sesame (I like Idhayam brand, found in Indian grocery stores). All should work in these recipes.

Sesame Oil (Toasted)

Not to be confused with the lighter, untoasted sesame oil, this dark brown finishing oil adds a nutty, faintly smoky taste to Asian noodles and stir-fries.

Rice

Basmati

My default rice: There's nothing like its long, elegant grain. I didn't grow up eating it regularly because of its price, but today, it's usually my choice, particularly with Indian and Persian dishes.

Jasmine

My choice when making other Asian dishes: It's stickier than basmati and makes a great bed for saucy dishes like Pad Thai Fish (page 176). It breaks down much easier than basmati, making it essential for porridge-like dishes such as Arroz Caldo (page 203).

Parboiled Rice

Parboiled rice, also called converted rice, is rice that is partially cooked while still in its husk. Though it's not my everyday pick, there are times when parboiled rice comes in handy, such as in Congri (page 123) and Jollof Rice (page 128). I find Ben's Original foolproof and hard to overcook. Note: For making dosas, you will need something called "idli rice," which is also parboiled but is of a different variety than Ben's.

Rice Flour

Useful to give fried foods that extra crunch, and helpful for those eating gluten-free.

Sushi Rice

Fun to eat, with a tacky, chewy texture that is indispensable in Southeast Asian–Inspired Risotto (page 126) and Rice "Stuffing" with Chinese Sausage and Shiitake Mushrooms (page 138).

Thai Glutinous (Sticky) Rice

When ground, this rice gives texture to Tuna Larb (page 166) and Chicken Larb (page 192), and when soaked overnight, steamed, and mixed with sweetened coconut milk, it makes the beautiful dessert Khao Niao Mamuang (page 266).

Salt

Flaky Sea Salt

I like Maldon, a game changer as a finishing salt, especially on salads or raw fish, adding just a bit of crunch. Try smoked flaky sea salt, which is wonderful, too.

Fleur de Sel

This is a coarse sea salt that is grittier and wetter than Maldon but dissolves less quickly and is great when you want pops of crunchy salinity in a dish.

Himalayan Pink Salt

Its savory mineral quality comes from deep in the earth, and I find it amplifies sour notes. It's often used as a finishing salt.

Kosher Salt

I use Diamond Crystal kosher salt, a great all-purpose salt that meets most of my cooking needs. It's fine to use another brand of kosher salt; just go slow and taste frequently. (It's important to note that regular table salt and kosher salt are not interchangeable, as they differ in salinity.)

Sea Salt

I use La Baleine brand in pasta water, because it gives the pasta a subtle marine flavor, along with that ephemeral quality when you know something tastes just a little bit better, but you don't know why.

Sauces, Sweeteners, et cetera

Aash Noodles

These Afghan wheat noodles will come in handy to add to soups or as a bed for stews in place of rice. Try them in the recipe for Aash (page 74). Linguine or udon are acceptable substitutes.

Agave Syrup

A sweetener made from the agave plant.

Barberries

Dried barberries are smaller, less sweet, and more delicate than dried cranberries and are great when you want a burst of color and tartness. I discovered these beautiful jewels of bright flavor from cooking Persian food, like the frittata Kuku Sabzi (page 19), but since then, I have tossed them into chicken salad, sprinkled them over rice pilafs, and garnished leafy green salads with them.

Besan Flour

Besan, also known as gram flour, is made from chana dal and is used in many South Asian and Caribbean dishes and to thicken some curries. Nuttier than conventional chickpea flour, the two are not interchangeable.

Fenugreek Leaves (Dried)

Also known as kasoori methi, dried fenugreek leaves are used in many cuisines, and are often found in Indian food. They are great when you want a touch of bitterness in either spice blends or rich soups and stews. Not to be confused with ground fenugreek, used in Dosas (page 155), or fenugreek seeds.

Fish Sauce

This umami bomb is life-changing when used in restrained amounts, giving food a deep, oceanic salinity and a fermented funk that cannot come from simply adding sea salt. I always have a bottle of Red Boat 40°N on hand, and not just for Thai dishes: I use it in many sauces, soups, and stir-fried dishes, too.

Jaggery

I grew up using this brown Indian palm or cane sugar as a sweetening agent. It has a deeper flavor than light brown sugar but isn't as molasses-y as dark brown sugar. Use it to balance tart notes in dishes like Tomato Rasam (page 57). You can also swap it with Thai palm sugar, if that's what you have.

Pomegranate Molasses

What a joy it is to drizzle this sweet-tart vermillion-hued secret weapon atop yogurt or hummus. Taste a dab before you pour it into any recipe. Brands can vary wildly in fruitiness, sweetness, and tang: I prefer Cortas. It's wonderful in dips, salad dressings, barbecue sauce, marinades, curries, and stews.

Preserved Lemons

I always have a jar of Moroccan preserved lemons in the refrigerator to chop, seed, and add bright flavor to dishes like tagines, stews, pilafs, vegetables, fish, and chicken. Traditionally, only the rind is used, but I use the whole fruit. Sometimes I use the brine, too. Look for darker lemons: This indicates they've been preserved for longer, and they'll have the most developed flavor and the least amount of bitterness.

Rose Water

Common in a lot of Middle Eastern and South Asian dishes, a little truly goes a very long way. Too much can make a dish overly perfume-y, but in small amounts, it elevates sweets and drinks, such as Rose Water Limeade (page 288) and Sholeh Zard (page 260).

Tamarind

I grew up munching on tamarind pods that I pulled off trees in India, and my love for this sweet and sour fruit has not waned one bit. It comes as a jarred concentrate, which can vary quite a bit in intensity and sweetness between brands (I prefer Swad and Laxmi), but it's easy to use, and you can keep a jar in your fridge for weeks in case something needs a little tang. It also comes as compressed bricks of pulp, which require soaking in hot water. These tend to be less sweet and more sharply sour, making them ideal for soups such as Sambar (page 59) and Tomato Rasam (page 57).

Yuzu Juice

Yuzu is a citrus cultivated primarily in East Asia. Yuzu juice is the most floral citrus juice I've ever had, even more so than calamansi or Meyer lemon. It typically comes in tiny bottles and can be expensive but will keep a long while in your fridge. Try it as a swap for lime or lemon juice, especially in salad dressings, raw fish preparations, and cocktails.

Vinegar

Apple Cider

Use this for a sweeter, less intensely acidic flavor than white vinegar.

Balsamic

This sweet, tangy Italian vinegar is great on salads and vegetable dishes. Also, a good substitute when I'm out of tamarind concentrate.

Black

This is wonderful in all kinds of Asian dishes: Use it to marinate tofu or to whisk into dipping sauces and marinades (it would make a great addition to sticky sauces for ribs). It's essential for Pickled Peanuts (page 15).

Red Wine, White Wine

Use these in salad dressings when you want to add some mellow acidity.

Rice

Used mostly in Asian recipes, it is the sweetest, most gentle of all the vinegars. Be sure to buy plain, not seasoned, rice vinegar, which includes salt and sugar.

White

I favor distilled white vinegar in many instances, particularly pickling, when I want a purely sharp, neutral vinegar.

PADMA'S ALL AMERICAN

SMALL PLATES
AND
SALADS

RADEEM

With *Taste the Nation*, we built each episode around a different Indigenous or immigrant community. Early on, we knew that though many of these communities experienced similar issues, each had its own stories to tell. Our episode on the Thai community in Las Vegas is one of my favorites. The episode is centered on women and focuses on starting over in a place where no one understands you, but it is also very much about love.

And not just romantic love, but friendship. Female friendship.

Early Thai immigrants to the United States were predominantly women: From 1968 to 1977, almost fifteen thousand Thai women immigrated to America as wives of servicemen. They were known as war brides. Three of those "war brides," Radeem, Saithong, and Karn, first became friends in the early '70s, when they were all young women working as waitresses at a Royal Thai Air Force base mess hall. Each would end up marrying an American GI stationed there during the Vietnam War. Radeem arrived in the United States first. Eventually she moved to Las Vegas with her husband, who was stationed at Nellis Air Force Base. The three women kept in touch via phone calls and letters until Saithong's and Karn's husbands requested and received transfers to Nellis so that the friends could be together. These women had to be everything to one another. Though their husbands were remarkably supportive—especially given that they must have been nursing their own psychic war wounds—there was still so much they couldn't relate to in their wives' lives.

Now, as these lifelong friends chat with me in a spotless suburban Vegas kitchen, they recount the difficulty of their early days in this strange new land. When Radeem speaks of waiting by the mailbox for a letter from her mother, Saithong and Karn nod in agreement. "We were so young," Karn murmurs. I imagine that for these women, loneliness was a constant devil in the shadows. They knew to keep it away with work; by building a temple and cultural center; and by creating,

together, a space in which they would be seen and understood, and feel at home. Their love is just as profound to me as that of an enduring marriage.

One of my favorite love stories in *Taste the Nation* is the marriage between Radeem and her husband, Steve. Radeem was a twenty-nine-year-old divorced mother of four when she caught the eye of Steve, an eighteen-year-old American GI stationed at the base. Despite their age difference, it was love at first sight—for Steve. Initially, Radeem rebuffed him, but Steve persisted. At every meal, he would sit only in Radeem's section. After two years of courting, he proposed and Radeem said yes. But Steve's captain wouldn't allow him to marry without first calling home for his parents' permission—he was still so young. Once they married and were back in the United States, they moved in with Steve's parents. I imagine it must have given them pause when their young son returned with a much older bride who also had four children from a prior marriage.

Radeem, however, speaks lovingly of the way her mother-in-law welcomed her with open arms. Though Radeem struggled with extreme loneliness her first months in America, her mother-in-law accepted her as a daughter and helped her navigate her new culture with patience. Eventually, Steve and Radeem were able to bring her kids over, with Steve raising them as his own. I love their story both because it's so unconventional and because Radeem's relationship with her in-laws, especially her mother-in-law, defies expectations. Even in an era that was much more culturally conservative, it shows how welcoming Americans can be.

When I ask Karn why so many GIs married Thai women, her answer is an unexpected gut punch. "Most of them were young boys, they had been drafted, they were far from home," Karn answered. "And we were young, too. We grew up together." It's easy to forget, meeting these seventy-something men now, that they were just boys then. Boys forced to serve in a war they did not choose to fight, lonely, and far from everything and everyone they had ever known. I feel a deep but bittersweet admiration for those young women and men. They sought and found love even amidst the chaos and horror of the Vietnam War. Half a century has passed—a lifetime, really—and they have sustained that love in friendship, in marriage, across continents, across cultures and time.

They sought and found love amidst the chaos and horror of the Vietnam War. . . They have sustained that love in friendship, in marriage, across continents, across cultures and time.

Som Tum

GREEN PAPAYA SALAD

To soothe her longing for Thailand, Radeem Ramsay did her best to re-create in her American kitchen the foods she grew up with. The dish Radeem missed most was som tum. Her beloved green papaya was nowhere to be found back then, so she used Granny Smith apples instead to make a modified version. As a nod to her resourcefulness and because *it's delicious,* I use both. Green papaya can be tricky to shred; using a box grater often results in a wet, smashed mess. Instead, I recommend cutting the papaya with a knife into long, thin julienned strands, or carefully using a shredding/julienne blade on a mandoline. You can also use a special handheld shredding tool, such as the Kiwi Pro Slice peeler. Traditionally, the green beans are served raw, and I like that crunch, but feel free to give them a quick blanch in salted boiling water if you prefer.

SERVES 4 TO 6

2 to 3 fresh jalapeño, serrano, or Thai chiles, to taste
1 dried Thai red chile
¼ cup fresh lime juice (about 2 limes), plus more to taste
4 large garlic cloves, roughly chopped (2 tablespoons)
3 tablespoons fish sauce (I like Red Boat 40°N brand), plus more to taste
2 tablespoons turbinado sugar, plus more to taste
About 12 ounces green papaya, peeled and julienned (about 4 cups)
2 cups cherry tomatoes, quartered
8 ounces green or long beans, trimmed and cut into 2-inch pieces (about 2 cups)
1 Granny Smith apple, cored and shredded, tossed with 1 teaspoon fresh lemon juice
2 to 3 tablespoons salted dry-roasted peanuts, roughly chopped

1. In a small blender or food processor, combine the fresh chiles, dried chile, lime juice, garlic, fish sauce, and turbinado sugar and blend into a dressing.

2. In a medium bowl, combine the green papaya, tomatoes, beans, and apple. Add the dressing and toss to combine. Taste and season with more lime juice, fish sauce, and/or turbinado sugar if it needs it. Sprinkle with the peanuts and serve at room temperature.

Children at the Wat Pa Temple in Las Vegas

Romaine Heart Salad
with Za'atar and Herbs

This tangy, creamy, herbaceous salad is a riff on a romaine salad I love at La Mercerie, a favorite French restaurant in New York. I've adapted their dressing by adding feta, an abundance of fresh herbs, and savory za'atar, the fragrant herb blend that typically includes sumac, wild thyme, toasted sesame seeds, and a little salt. Garnishing with barberries makes for a salad that is a punchy delight.

SERVES 4

- ⅔ cup whole-milk or low-fat yogurt
- ½ cup extra-virgin olive oil
- ¼ cup plus 1 tablespoon fresh chives
- 2 tablespoons red wine vinegar
- 1 tablespoon Dijon mustard
- 1 tablespoon mayonnaise
- 2 teaspoons za'atar
- 1 teaspoon sumac
- 1 teaspoon Kashmiri chile powder
- ½ cup crumbled feta cheese
- ¼ cup plus 1 tablespoon chopped fresh flat-leaf parsley
- ¼ cup plus 1 tablespoon chopped fresh dill
- ¼ cup plus 1 tablespoon torn fresh mint
- 2 medium heads romaine lettuce, top 3 inches of the leaves cut off and saved for another use, quartered lengthwise
- 2 tablespoons dried barberries, rinsed and patted dry (optional)
- Freshly ground black pepper

1. In a medium bowl, whisk together the yogurt, olive oil, ¼ cup of the chives, the vinegar, mustard, mayonnaise, za'atar, sumac, and chile powder until emulsified. Stir in ¼ cup each of the feta, parsley, dill, and mint.
2. On a large serving platter, arrange the romaine quarters in a single layer. Pour the dressing over the top. Sprinkle with the remaining 1 tablespoon each chives, parsley, dill, and mint, then top with the remaining ¼ cup feta, the barberries (if using), and several healthy grinds of black pepper. Serve immediately.

Originating in Palestine, za'atar is a star player in the cuisines of many countries in the Levant. The most delicious version I've ever had comes from the incredible women of the Burj el-Barajneh refugee camp in Lebanon. The thriving food truck business they began was the subject of a documentary named *Soufra.* The women produced a great cookbook they were planning to give out for free at the film's premiere. I encouraged them to self-publish and sell copies to raise money for their fledgling catering business. As a thank-you, they sent me their homemade za'atar. And I excitedly started sprinkling it on many dishes.

Kale-Pomegranate Salad

While the bulk of this salad is kale, it's really my ode to the pomegranate. I grew up eating this fruit my grandmother painstakingly peeled on her veranda, from a bowl she filled to the brim. Years later when I discovered pomegranate molasses in a Middle Eastern market, I thought I'd hit the jackpot. The dressing for this salad is a great, simple three-step template for any salad dressing: something sweet-tart (in this case pomegranate molasses), something acidic (in this case, fresh lime juice), and olive oil. I add spikes of heat from a serrano chile and freshly ground black pepper. Kale can be wiry, so I tenderize it by massaging the dressing into the finely cut leaves. The pomegranate seeds, underscored by the molasses, lend a fruity flavor that contrasts well with kale. You can substitute a syrupy aged balsamic if you don't have pomegranate molasses. Slice the apples just before tossing them in so that they don't brown, or toss them in some extra lemon juice to preserve their color. Add the salt just before serving as well so that it does not fully dissolve and imparts a gentle briny crunch to each bite.

SERVES 4

1 bunch of lacinato kale, stemmed and finely shredded (about 4 cups)
1 cup pomegranate seeds
1/2 cup torn fresh mint
1 small serrano chile, thinly sliced into rings
2 tablespoons extra-virgin olive oil
1 tablespoon pomegranate molasses (I like Cortas brand)
1 tablespoon fresh lime juice, fresh lemon juice, or yuzu juice
Freshly ground black pepper
1 small green apple, cored and thinly sliced
1/2 to 3/4 teaspoon fleur de sel, Maldon salt, or another flaky sea salt

1. In a large bowl, toss together the kale, pomegranate seeds, mint, and serrano chile.
2. In a small bowl, whisk together the olive oil, pomegranate molasses, lime juice, and several grindings of black pepper.
3. Pour the dressing all over the salad and toss to combine. Use your hands, or a spoon, to work the dressing into the kale. (This can be done up to 2 hours ahead.)
4. Right before serving, add the apple, sprinkle the salt all over the salad, and toss. Serve at room temperature. (This will last in the refrigerator for up to 2 days.)

Plum Chaat

SPICY FRUIT SNACK

I grew up sprinkling salt and chile on fresh fruit, just as many shake Tajín, a Mexican chile-lime seasoning, on fresh mango. Years later, I visited Chandni Chowk market in the old part of New Delhi, and took chef Rajeev Goyal's eye-opening food tour. I had never visited that part of town. Chef Goyal led us to all kinds of eateries with fantastic food. One vendor sat on a ledge, beside a big basket of apples and green guava and a bowl of chopped onion and cilantro. Holding the fruit in his hand, he made quick work of slicing it with an ultrasharp paring knife. This vendor's mixed-fruit chaat was the most delicious of the tour, and inspired this plum chaat recipe.

Serve this in a dainty ice cream dish as a first course in hot weather, as a condiment for fish, or as a palate cleanser after a big meal. While filming the Appalachia episode of *Taste the Nation,* two Cherokee elders taught me how to make Ramp Salt (page 12), a great way to harness the flavor of the fleeting wild aromatic all year, and it's divine in this chaat. You may end up with extra spice mix; save it to sprinkle over any fresh fruit or salads.

MAKES ABOUT 4 CUPS

1/2 teaspoon cumin seeds
1/2 teaspoon Himalayan pink salt or Ramp Salt (recipe follows), plus more to taste
1/2 teaspoon amchur (dried mango powder)
1/2 teaspoon Kashmiri chile powder
4 firm red plums, pitted and sliced or cut into bite-size pieces (about 2 cups)
4 firm black plums, pitted and sliced or cut into bite-size pieces (about 2 cups)
1/4 cup fresh lime juice (about 2 limes)
1/4 cup torn fresh mint leaves

1. Heat a small dry pan over medium heat. Add the cumin seeds and toast until just smoking and fragrant, 30 to 45 seconds. Transfer to a mortar and pestle and grind into a powder. Measure out ½ teaspoon and add it to a small bowl (you may have some left over).
2. Add the salt, amchur, and Kashmiri chile to the bowl and mix well. This spice blend is your masala: you may not use all of it.
3. In a medium bowl, combine the plums, lime juice, mint leaves, and 2 teaspoons of the masala.
4. Taste and add additional reserved dry-roasted cumin powder, and/or more salt to taste. Serve at room temperature or cold.

(Continued)

Ramp Salt

Ramps, delicately flavored alliums, always produce a flurry of excitement at the green market in New York because they sprout for a short time in the spring and then disappear until the next year. While filming the Appalachia episode of *Taste the Nation,* I learned a beautiful way to preserve their flavor: dry and grind with sea salt. The result tastes like a more floral version of onion salt and makes a lovely accent for Plum Chaat (page 10) or tomatoes, eggs, or raw sushi-grade fish. Use it as you would onion salt.

MAKES ABOUT ¼ CUP

¼ pound wild ramps, roots trimmed, washed and patted dry

1½ teaspoons coarse sea salt

1. Preheat the oven to 200°F. Line a large sheet pan with parchment paper.
2. Strip the leaves from the ramps and spread on one side of the sheet pan. Chop the bulbs and spread on the other side.
3. Bake until dry and brittle, 1 to 1½ hours. The time will depend on how much moisture is in the ramps. The leaves may dry first; feel free to remove them before the bulbs.
4. Cool completely. Place in a mortar and pestle or spice grinder with the salt and grind until a coarse powder forms.

Muhammara

ROASTED RED PEPPER AND WALNUT SPREAD

Full of roasted red peppers, toasted walnuts, and tart pomegranate molasses, this rich, nutty dip is intensely flavored, and packed with umami goodness. This luscious spread served with toasted pita, sliced vegetables, and feta cheese makes a sumptuous appetizer. You could also add it to a charcuterie board. I adapted this version from a recipe by my friend Kamal Attara (page 108). He grew up in Lebanon. Kamal roasts his vegetables whole. I prefer to cut them before roasting so that I can more easily remove the seeds. Feel free to slightly alter the amounts of pomegranate molasses, sumac, and lemon juice to achieve a level of sweet tartness that suits you.

MAKES ABOUT 3 CUPS

- 8 large red bell peppers (about 4 pounds total), halved or quartered and seeded
- 1 poblano chile, halved and seeded
- 3 tablespoons unsalted butter
- 1½ cups walnuts
- ½ cup plain dried bread crumbs
- ¼ cup extra-virgin olive oil, plus more for drizzling
- 2 tablespoons pomegranate molasses, plus more to taste (I like Cortas brand)
- 1 tablespoon Aleppo pepper, plus 1 teaspoon for garnish
- 1 teaspoon sumac, plus more to taste
- 1 teaspoon Spanish smoked paprika
- Kosher salt
- 1 tablespoon fresh lemon juice (optional)
- ¼ cup pomegranate seeds
- Chopped fresh parsley leaves

1. Preheat the oven to 450°F. Line two sheet pans with parchment paper.
2. Place the bell peppers and poblano skin-side up on the pans and roast until the skin is dark and blistered, about 45 minutes.
3. Remove from the oven and immediately cover the sheet pans with foil, tenting it loosely over the pans but tightly sealing the edges: This will create a steam chamber and will ultimately make the skins easier to peel. Steam until mostly cool, about 30 minutes. Peel the skins off the peppers and transfer the peppers to a food processor.
4. Meanwhile, in a medium skillet, melt the butter over medium-low heat. Add the walnuts and toast, stirring occasionally, until darkened, 4 to 5 minutes. Transfer the walnuts to a plate. Add the bread crumbs to the pan and stir frequently until golden brown, 1 to 2 minutes. Transfer to the plate with the walnuts and cool.
5. Add the walnuts and bread crumbs to the food processor. Add the olive oil, pomegranate molasses, 1 tablespoon of the Aleppo pepper, the sumac, smoked paprika, and 1 teaspoon kosher salt. Pulse until smooth. Taste and add the lemon juice (if using), and more pomegranate molasses, sumac, and salt, if desired.
6. Transfer to a shallow bowl and garnish with pomegranate seeds, parsley, a drizzle of olive oil, and the remaining 1 teaspoon Aleppo pepper. Serve at room temperature.

LEE LUNG SI TONG
ASSOCIATION
李氏青年組
LEE ON DONG ASS'N.
YOUTH GROUP
109
四樓 4TH FL.
文光印
承印:餐牌·中
CULTURE-LITE PRINTIN
SUPPORT
"CHINATOWN STATION"

Pickled Peanuts

My girlfriend Ali Wong came over for lunch while I was deep in testing this recipe. Years on, she still asks for these every time she comes over. If you have only one of the two vinegars, it's fine in a pinch. But the perfect combo is both balsamic and Chinese black vinegars. The Szechuan peppercorns are a must here because nothing else will give you that numbing zing. The peanuts will absorb the marinade and develop flavor over a couple of weeks. This is also one of those unique dishes that works well both in summer (out of the fridge, with a beer) and slightly warmed in winter.

MAKES ABOUT 3 CUPS

2 cups raw red-skinned peanuts
1/2 cup minced red onion (about 1/2 small onion)
1/2 cup chopped fresh cilantro
1/4 cup balsamic vinegar
1/4 cup Chinese black vinegar
1/4 cup soy sauce
1 tablespoon Szechuan peppercorns, roughly ground
2 teaspoons toasted sesame oil
1 teaspoon ground white pepper
1 teaspoon Szechuan chile flakes, or 3/4 teaspoon red chile flakes
1/2 teaspoon Himalayan pink salt or fine sea salt, plus more to taste

1. Heat a large skillet over medium heat. Add the peanuts and stir constantly, until darkened and toasted, about 2 minutes. Transfer to a sheet pan to cool.
2. In a large bowl, stir together the onion, cilantro, balsamic vinegar, black vinegar, soy sauce, Szechuan peppercorns, sesame oil, white pepper, chile flakes, and pink salt. Add the peanuts and toss well to combine. Add more salt to taste.
3. Transfer to an airtight glass container and refrigerate. The peanuts will be ready after 2 weeks and will keep for at least another month in the fridge. Make sure to never use a wet spoon in the container, which could cause spoilage!

OPPOSITE: With Ali Wong in San Francisco's Chinatown

Kan's
Kan's
EASTERN
Asian Renaissance
JUNO
EMBROIDERY TRANSFER & SCREENPRINTING
T-SHIRTS SWEATSHIRTS JACKETS CAPS
KIMONO & CHINESE DRESS
HANDBAGS BACKPACKS LUGGAGE
廣東商場
廣東
酒

廣東商場
CANTON
BAZAAR
廣東商場
CANTON
BAZAAR
BAZAAR
unique treasures from the orient
廣東
sale
ON SELECTED ITEMS
UP TO 60% OFF

Kuku Sabzi

HERBED FRITTATA

I'm constantly in search of portable, make-ahead dishes, and this herbaceous frittata is a particularly beautiful one to leave on the counter and eat one wedge at a time. Slice and pack it for picnics and playgrounds or add it to a buffet: It's great at room temperature, warm, or chilled. It also sums up so many highlights of Persian cuisine: the copious amounts of herbs, the delightful tang of barberries, and generous dollops of cool yogurt and cucumber sauce called mast-o khiar. Do not skip the barberries, which are worth seeking out for their unique pop of tartness. They'll be great in your salads or to garnish rice pilafs. You can save a lot of time by finely chopping the greens in a food processor (use about 1½ cups packed whole leaves of each if you do, as the greens will break down more than if cut by hand). I still recommend cutting the leeks by hand for the best texture.

SERVES 6 TO 8

6 tablespoons extra-virgin olive oil
3 large leeks, white and light-green parts only, finely chopped (about 3 cups)
Kosher salt
6 large eggs
1 teaspoon baking powder
1 teaspoon freshly ground black pepper
1/2 teaspoon ground turmeric
1 cup finely chopped fresh cilantro leaves
1 cup finely chopped fresh dill
1 cup finely chopped fresh parsley
1 cup finely chopped fresh baby spinach
1/4 cup dried barberries, rinsed and patted dry
1 tablespoon dried fenugreek leaves, also known as kasoori methi (optional)
About 3/4 cup crumbled feta cheese (optional), for serving
1 tablespoon dried rose petals (optional), for serving
Mast-o Khiar (page 243), whole-milk yogurt, or sour cream, for serving

1. In a 10-inch broilerproof sauté pan or skillet with straight sides, heat 3 tablespoons of the olive oil over medium heat. Add the leeks, season with ¼ teaspoon salt, and cook, stirring occasionally and reducing the heat if they start to brown, until soft, 10 to 12 minutes. Transfer to a plate and let cool. Wipe out the pan.

2. In a large bowl, whisk the eggs with 1½ teaspoons kosher salt, the baking powder, black pepper, and turmeric. Using a rubber spatula, fold in the leek mixture, cilantro, dill, parsley, spinach, barberries, and fenugreek (if using). The mixture should be thick and very green.

3. Preheat the broiler (this is for browning the frittata at the end).

4. In the reserved pan, heat the remaining 3 tablespoons olive oil over medium heat. Pour in the egg mixture, using a spatula to spread evenly across the top and poking the barberries beneath the surface so they do not brown during cooking. Cover and cook the frittata for about 3 minutes, then reduce the heat to low and cook just until the eggs are barely set, 8 to 10 minutes.

5. Uncover and place the pan under the broiler until the top sets, about 1 minute.

6. Remove and let cool slightly, then run a knife around the edge of the frittata. Transfer to a platter by placing the platter upside down over the pan, then flipping carefully using both hands. Garnish with the feta and rose petals (if using) and serve warm or at room temperature, with mast-o khiar on the side.

Note: Washing barberries plumps them up and makes a world of difference to their taste and texture. Make sure to dry them well between two paper towels before using.

Aushak

LEEK AND SCALLION DUMPLINGS

When the writer Jamil Jan Kochai introduced me to these revelatory dumplings in the Afghan episode of *Taste the Nation*, I moaned with pleasure at first bite. These are so light, with a simple, pure allium flavor and a thin, silky, steamed dumpling skin. This would be a wonderful place to use ramps when they are in season: Swap them for some or all of the scallions. I love drizzling these dumplings with melted butter or Garlic Yogurt Sauce (page 78), but feel free to top them with Savory Minced Meat Sauce (page 77), too, as is traditional during special feasts.

SERVES 4 TO 6

- 1/4 cup extra-virgin olive oil
- 4 large leeks, white and light-green parts only, rinsed well and finely chopped (about 4 cups)
- Kosher salt
- 12 scallions, white and green parts, chopped (about 2 cups)
- 1 teaspoon ground turmeric
- 1 teaspoon Kashmiri chile powder, or 1/2 teaspoon cayenne pepper
- 1 to 2 tablespoons fresh lemon juice
- Flour for dusting
- About 50 store-bought square dumpling (or wonton) wrappers
- 1 to 2 tablespoons unsalted butter or olive oil

FOR SERVING

- Savory Minced Meat Sauce (optional; page 77)
- Garlic Yogurt Sauce (optional; page 78)
- Unsalted butter (optional), melted
- Sumac (optional), for garnish

1. In a large skillet, heat the olive oil over medium heat. Add the leeks and a pinch of salt and sauté until softened, 6 to 8 minutes. Add the scallions and 1 teaspoon kosher salt and sauté until softened, another 2 minutes. Add the turmeric and Kashmiri chile powder and sauté for 2 more minutes. Remove from the heat and stir in 1 tablespoon of the lemon juice. Taste and add the rest of the lemon juice, if desired.

2. Fill a small bowl with water. Cover a large platter or sheet pan with parchment paper and dust with flour. Place a dumpling wrapper on a plate and add a heaping tablespoon of the leek mixture to the wrapper. Dab your finger in the water, dampen the edges of the wrapper, and fold in half to make a triangle, pressing the edges to seal. Set the aushak on the lined platter. Repeat with the rest of the wrappers.

3. Bring a large pot of water to a boil and stir in 1 tablespoon kosher salt. In a large serving bowl, place 1 to 2 tablespoons unsalted butter or olive oil, and keep this near the stove.

4. Working in batches of 5 or 6, add the aushak to the boiling water and boil until tender, 2 to 3 minutes. Use a slotted spoon or spider to transfer the aushak to the bowl with the butter.

5. **To serve:** Top with meat sauce and/or garlic yogurt sauce, or just a little melted butter. If desired, dust with sumac.

Butternut Squash Bolani

STUFFED FLATBREAD

Traditionally, this skillet-cooked Afghan flatbread is stuffed with potatoes. But I was inspired by the beautiful orange blobs of sweet potato in the bolani I made with Afghan journalist Taban Ibraz and her sister in the Afghan episode of *Taste the Nation*. Here I use delicate butternut squash, which I roast to concentrate its natural sweetness and then mix with scallions. This is a great project to try with kids.

SERVES 8

- 1 medium butternut squash (2 pounds), halved lengthwise, seeds and pulp removed
- 2 tablespoons extra-virgin olive oil
- Kosher salt
- 1 to 2 scallions, white and green parts, chopped (about 1/3 cup)
- 1/2 cup tightly packed chopped fresh cilantro
- 1/2 medium serrano chile (optional), minced
- 1 teaspoon sumac
- Freshly ground black pepper
- 3 1/2 cups all-purpose flour, plus more for dusting
- Neutral oil, for cooking
- Whole-milk yogurt or Garlic Yogurt Sauce (page 78), for serving
- Mint and Cilantro Chutney (page 31) or Red Onion Chutney (recipe follows), for serving

1. Preheat the oven to 425°F. Line a large baking dish with foil.
2. Drizzle the squash with the olive oil, sprinkle with pinches of kosher salt, and place cut-side up in the prepared dish. Roast, occasionally brushing any pooled oil over the surface of the squash, until soft and mashable, 1 to 1½ hours. Cool until the squash can be handled, at least 10 minutes.
3. Turn the squash cut-side down and use a paring knife to gently peel the skin off the squash (it should come off easily). Discard the skin, place the squash in a large bowl, and mash roughly with a fork. Mix in the scallions, cilantro, chile (if using), sumac, 2 teaspoons kosher salt, and several grinds of black pepper and mix. Add more salt to taste. Set aside.
4. In a wide bowl, whisk together the flour and 2 teaspoons kosher salt. Slowly add 1½ cups water, mixing with your hands to hydrate the flour. Transfer to a floured surface and knead until smooth and firm, about 5 minutes. Cover the dough with a towel and let rest for 15 to 20 minutes. (This can be done while the squash is roasting.)
5. Meanwhile, line a large sheet pan with parchment paper.
6. Use a bench scraper or knife to divide the dough into 8 equal portions. Shape each portion into a ball. Roll out each ball into a 6-inch round. Spread half of the round with about ⅓ cup of the filling, leaving a ½-inch border around the edges. Fold the other half of the dough over to form a semicircle. Gently use the palm of your hand to push out any air pockets from the center outward and press the edges together with your fingers or a fork to seal the flatbread. Transfer the bolani to the prepared sheet pan in a single layer.
7. Line a plate with paper towels and set it near the stove. Warm a large nonstick or cast-iron skillet or griddle over medium-high heat. Add 1 teaspoon neutral oil and use a paper towel to rub it all over the surface of the pan. Place one bolani in the pan and cook for 1 minute. Brush another ½ teaspoon of oil on the top of the bolani, flip it over, and cook for about 1 minute on the other side. Flip two more times, cooking for another 1 to 2 minutes on each side, brushing more oil only as needed, until browned and blistered, about 5 minutes total per bolani. Remove and place on the paper towel–lined plate.

(Continued)

8. Serve warm. The bolani will probably disappear quickly, but you can keep them warm in a 250°F oven, if necessary. Serve with yogurt and a chutney as a dip.

Note: In a pinch, do as Afghan cook Homayon Karimy sometimes does: Use a flour tortilla instead of the flatbread dough. Spread half of the tortilla with about 1/3 cup filling and fold the other half over the filling. Add a few drops of oil to the pan and cook until browned on both sides.

Red Onion Chutney

ACCOMPANIMENT

When we judges cooked for the finalists of *Top Chef: All-Stars* in Italy, I served this chutney with cheese as a starter course before my Ribollita (page 71). All of it disappeared, and no one told *me* to *pack my knives*. Try serving this tangy condiment alongside goat cheese, young pecorino, sharp Cheddar, or Manchego. It's fantastic on top of grilled steak, chicken, or a roast. At my house, it's typically served with Dosas (page 155) or mixed with butter and hot rice. I've spread it in sandwiches and spooned it over sweet potatoes and roasted squash in the fall. In a pinch, I've even substituted aged balsamic vinegar for the tamarind, and it's still divine. Make an extra batch and keep it on hand in the fridge for impromptu canapés and snacks.

MAKES ABOUT 2 CUPS

1/3 cup neutral oil
4 red onions, thinly sliced (about 5 cups)
4 to 6 dried red chiles, to taste, broken into small pieces
Kosher salt
3 tablespoons tamarind concentrate (I like Swad or Laxmi brands), dissolved in 1 cup hot tap water
1 teaspoon sugar, plus more to taste

1. In a large nonstick skillet, heat the oil over medium heat. Add the onions and chiles and stir to combine. After about a minute, stir in 1½ teaspoons kosher salt. Cover the skillet and cook, stirring often, until the onions wilt and collapse, 7 to 10 minutes.

2. Add the tamarind water and sugar and stir until the sugar is dissolved. Bring to a simmer, turn the heat to medium-low, and cook uncovered, stirring occasionally, until the chutney has a loose, jammy consistency, about 30 minutes. In the last few minutes of cooking, you can use the side of your spoon to mash and break up the onions for a more spoonable chutney.

3. Add more salt or sugar to taste. Let cool and store in an airtight glass jar in the fridge for up to 1 week.

Note: Brands of tamarind concentrate vary wildly in texture, flavor, and pungency. Decrease or increase the amount to your taste.

1

2

3

4

5

6

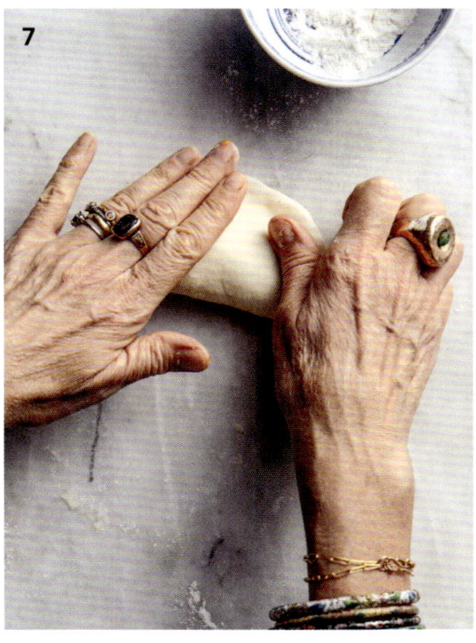
7

8

Papas a la Huancaína

POTATOES IN AJÍ AMARILLO SAUCE

Papas a la huancaína is a comforting dish of sliced boiled potatoes and eggs, smothered in a spicy creamy sauce. *Ají* is what you call a pepper in the Quechua language, spoken by Indigenous peoples in the Andes. *Amarillo* is "yellow" in Spanish. This Peruvian dish is one of my fondest childhood taste memories, thanks to a Peruvian babysitter I had growing up in Queens. Elena was our glamorous, green-eyed neighbor with spiky strawberry blonde hair. I visited her apartment each day for lunch, then again after school until my mother picked me up. I would help her peel potatoes, and I loved the satisfying pleasure of my knife slicing through a boiled egg. I can still remember the soft-on-soft textural pleasure of the dish years later. When I interviewed chef Erik Ramirez on *Taste the Nation,* he mentioned that his mother made this dish better than anyone. He taught me her secret: combining ají amarillo with a touch of habanero. I have adapted it here, for a papas a la huancaína that finally lives up to the warm memory of Elena's kitchen.

SERVES 6

1½ pounds unpeeled Yukon Gold potatoes (4 to 6 medium)
Kosher salt
1 tablespoon neutral oil
2 tablespoons roughly chopped white onion
4 large frozen ají amarillo peppers, thawed, seeded, and chopped (about ½ cup)
2 large garlic cloves, sliced (1 tablespoon)
¼ cup evaporated milk
¼ cup crumbled queso fresco
3 tablespoons extra-virgin olive oil, plus more if needed
2 or 3 saltine crackers
1 habanero chile, seeded and minced (¾ teaspoon)
6 hard-boiled eggs, quartered lengthwise
Flaky sea salt (I like Maldon brand)
6 whole black olives, for garnish
1½ teaspoons torn fresh oregano leaves

1. In a large pot, combine the unpeeled potatoes, 1 tablespoon kosher salt, and water to cover. Bring to a boil and boil until fork-tender, about 15 minutes, depending on the size of the potatoes. Drain. When cooled enough to touch, peel the potatoes and set aside to cool to room temperature.

2. In a small skillet, heat the neutral oil over medium heat. Add the onion and sauté for just 1 minute, then add the ají amarillo peppers, garlic, and a healthy pinch of kosher salt and sauté just until the ají amarillo gets a little color on the peel, 2 to 3 minutes. Cool slightly.

3. Transfer the pepper mixture to a small blender. Add the evaporated milk, queso fresco, olive oil, 2 saltines, habanero, and ⅛ teaspoon kosher salt and blend until smooth and pourable. (If the sauce is too thick, add a little olive oil; if it's too thin, add half a saltine, keeping in mind that you may want to adjust the other ingredients to taste.)

4. Cut the potatoes into ¼-inch-thick slices. Divide the potato slices among six serving plates and add 1 quartered egg to each dish. Sprinkle pinches of flaky sea salt evenly on top of the potatoes and egg. Drizzle 1½ to 2 tablespoons sauce over each dish and garnish each plate with an olive. Sprinkle each plate with ¼ teaspoon oregano. Serve immediately at room temperature.

Note: Ají amarillo peppers are not widely available in the United States, but you can find them frozen in Latin markets. You can also substitute with yellow bell pepper.

Pakori

VEGETABLE FRITTERS

When it rains, we Desis, folks from the Indian subcontinent, make pakori. I don't know why. We just do. It rains and all over the world, we pour oil into kadais or woks and turn whatever vegetables we have into these hot, savory fritters. I've often wondered if there are oil shortages in India during the monsoons. But even when the sun is shining, pakori (which are often called pakoras, though pakori is the correct plural) are an undeniable crowd-pleaser. And while we like ours with Masala Chai (page 294), you should feel free to swap the tea for an ice-cold beer.

You can really use any vegetable, but I prefer red onion. The ingredient here that is absolutely *not* optional is besan flour, which is made from small, dense chana dal. It's naturally gluten-free and is available at Indian grocery stores and online. Do *not* substitute with the chickpea flour you'll find from brands like Bob's Red Mill: The texture and flavor will not be the same. Do as I do and always keep some besan flour on hand to prepare for the next storm. Because as we know, there will always be a next storm.

MAKES ABOUT 2 DOZEN

- 2 cups besan flour, sifted
- 2 tablespoons rice flour, sifted
- Kosher salt
- 1 teaspoon ground turmeric
- 1 teaspoon Kashmiri chile powder
- 1/2 teaspoon asafoetida powder
- 1/2 teaspoon amchur (dried mango powder)
- 1 large red onion, very thinly sliced (about 2 cups, firmly packed)
- 1 cup roughly chopped fresh cilantro leaves
- 1 to 2 serrano chiles, to taste, minced
- Neutral oil, for frying
- Mint and Cilantro Chutney (recipe follows) or ketchup (yes, ketchup), for serving

1. In a medium bowl, combine the besan flour, rice flour, 2 teaspoons kosher salt, the turmeric, chile powder, asafoetida powder, and amchur and stir to mix well. Add the onion, cilantro, and chiles and knead with your fingers to thoroughly combine and extract as much moisture from the vegetables as possible. Really press it all together. This will take 3 to 4 minutes. Add water, 1 tablespoon at a time, as needed, just enough to hold the thick, shaggy mixture together.
2. Line a plate with paper towels and set near the stove. Pour 2 inches of oil into a medium wok or pot and heat over high heat to 350°F on a candy or deep-fry thermometer.
3. Using a tablespoon scoop, or two spoons, gently portion and turn pakori directly into the hot oil, spacing them about 1 inch apart. Fry until deep golden brown and crisp, 2 to 3 minutes per side. Use a spider or slotted spoon to transfer the pakori to the paper towels.
4. If serving a large group, transfer fried pakori in a single layer to a sheet pan and keep warm in a 200°F oven. Serve hot, with chutney or ketchup.

(Continued)

1

2

3

4

5

6

7

8

Mint and Cilantro Chutney

ACCOMPANIMENT

Most Desis have a deep relationship with this all-purpose chutney, which packs heat plus verdant, sweet, and sour flavors into one versatile condiment. It pairs well with rich and fried foods. And there's hardly any chopping, because everything goes in the food processor. For me, eating any Indian snack without this chutney (especially Pakori, page 28) is like eating French fries without ketchup. It shows up in street foods like chaat and deserves a place in your grilled cheese, or whisked with mayo and spread on your turkey sandwich, and as an accompaniment to Latkes (page 39) or Butternut Squash Bolani (page 23).

MAKES ABOUT 3/4 CUP

- 1 cup loosely packed fresh mint leaves
- 3 cups loosely packed fresh cilantro
- 2 to 3 small green chiles, such as Indian or serrano, to taste
- 2 tablespoons fresh lemon juice
- 2 tablespoons whole-milk yogurt
- Kosher salt
- 1/4 to 1/2 teaspoon sugar (optional)

1. In a small food processor, blend the mint, cilantro, green chiles, lemon juice, yogurt, 1 teaspoon kosher salt, and 2 tablespoons water until smooth.
2. Taste, and if the chutney is bitter or too spicy, add the sugar to balance the flavor and blend again. This is better when served immediately but can be stored in the refrigerator for up to 2 days.

Cilantro, the bright, peppery, and aromatic herb critical to Latin and Asian cuisines, may just be the most used fresh herb in my culinary repertoire. I feel sad for the genetically cursed cilantro haters of the world ("it tastes like soap"). Whenever I call for simply "cilantro," I mean leaves and tender stems. This is because cilantro stems add great texture and are packed with flavor. There's no reason not to use them. I call explicitly for "cilantro leaves" when only leaves are appropriate.

Tostones

FRIED GREEN PLANTAINS

When I was in high school, I always looked forward to eating at my friend Louis's house. His parents were originally from Puerto Rico, and his mother made the best tostones ever. Tostones aren't any harder to make than French fries, and there is an unmatched, very specific pleasure to eating them. They have an aggressive outer crunch that gives way to a softer inside. The key to this textural contrast is frying the plantains twice, with a little smash and a quick salt-water bath in between. While there are tools that are made just for flattening plantains, you can use the bottom of any small heavy glass or mug; I like using a smooth stone mortar. Get on your tippy toes, exert your weight evenly, and know this will lead you to fried bliss.

SERVES 4

4 garlic cloves, sliced
Kosher salt
Neutral oil, for frying
8 green plantains, peeled and cut crosswise into 3/4-inch-thick rounds
Mint and Cilantro Chutney (page 31), for serving

1. In a 9 × 13-inch baking dish, mix 6 cups lukewarm tap water with the garlic and 2 tablespoons kosher salt.
2. Pour 1 inch of oil into a Dutch oven or sauté pan and heat over medium-high heat to 325°F on a deep-fry thermometer.
3. Line a large sheet pan with parchment paper. Working in batches, add the plantains in a single layer and fry until lightly golden, 90 seconds to 3 minutes. Remove the plantains with a spider and transfer to the sheet pan.
4. When all the plantains are cooked, cover them with another sheet of parchment paper. Center the bottom of a flat heavy glass or mug on top of each plantain and press to smash it flat. Transfer the plantains to the dish of garlic water and soak for 5 minutes.
5. Meanwhile, return the skillet to medium-high heat and bring the oil temperature to about 375°F. Line a large plate with paper towels and set it near the stove.
6. Carefully remove the tostones from the water and pat dry with a paper towel. (A few may fall apart; don't worry, it's okay!) Working in batches, fry until crisp and deep golden brown, 3 to 5 minutes. Drain on the paper towel–lined plate and immediately sprinkle with salt.
7. Serve warm with the mint and cilantro chutney.

Mushroom Tacos Campesinos

When I was in El Paso, Texas, chef Emiliano Marentes made me tacos with handmade blue corn tortillas and a delectable layer of crispy cheese. As he got all *cheffy* with some microgreens, I told him I was already plotting how to make my own version of the tacos at home, using mushrooms and topped with plain old cilantro. I love searing mushrooms, making sure not to crowd the pan so that there is plenty of room for them to release their liquid and become dense and meaty. Emiliano makes his tacos with quesillo or queso Oaxaca, which is traditional, but I often just use a packaged blend of shredded Jack and Cheddar cheese that, I admit, is always in my fridge. I also top these with a spicy coleslaw.

MAKES 8 TACOS

1 teaspoon ancho chile powder (or cayenne, for those with a higher heat tolerance)
1 teaspoon dried thyme
1 teaspoon sumac
Kosher salt
1/4 to 1/2 cup neutral oil
1 1/2 pounds portobello mushrooms (7 to 10 caps), sliced about 1/2 inch thick
8 corn tortillas (preferably blue, if you can find them)
2 cups shredded Cheddar, quesillo (queso Oaxaca), and/or Monterey Jack cheese
2 cups Spicy Coleslaw (page 36)
1 avocado, smashed with a squeeze of lime juice and pinch of salt (optional)
Salsa Macha (page 103), Sesame Chutney (page 152), or hot sauce of your choice

1. In a small bowl, mix together the ancho chile powder, thyme, sumac, and ½ teaspoon salt.

2. In a large nonstick skillet, heat 2 tablespoons of the oil over medium heat. Working in batches (add 1 to 2 tablespoons of oil for each batch), add the mushrooms in a single layer, leaving at least ½ inch space between them. Sprinkle with the chile-thyme mixture and sear until they darken and shrink, 3 to 4 minutes. Flip the mushrooms over, sprinkle with more of the chile-thyme mixture, and sear until they have darkened and shrunk to half their original size, another 2 to 3 minutes. Transfer the cooked mushrooms to a plate.

3. Wipe out the skillet and place it over medium-low heat. Add a few drops of oil. Add a tortilla and warm it through on one side, about 30 seconds. Flip it over, top with ¼ cup cheese, cover the pan, and cook until melted, about 1 minute. Flip over the tortilla so that the cheese hits the hot pan, increase the heat just slightly, lightly press a spatula down on the tortilla to sear the cheese, and cook until golden brown, about 1 minute. Flip the tortilla cheese-side up onto a plate. Repeat with the remaining tortillas.

4. Cover entire surface of each taco with a layer of mushrooms. Cover each with ¼ cup coleslaw. If using the avocado mixture, divide it evenly over the tacos. Drizzle with the salsa. Serve immediately.

Spicy Coleslaw

This spicy refreshing slaw makes taco night much more flavorful. Just grill some steak, fish, or shrimp, heat some tortillas, and mix up some guac and margaritas. Brands of chipotle in adobo vary wildly; feel free to reduce the amount of chipotles called for here, especially if your heat tolerance is on the lower side. You can use this as a template to make a spicy potato or chicken salad, too. This coleslaw is also delicious alongside chicken dishes, such as Desert Chicken (page 200), and meat dishes, such as Sach Ko Jakak (page 43), Schnitzel (page 231), and Pernil (page 249).

SERVES 4 TO 6

½ large or 1 small head red cabbage, shredded (about 5 cups)
1 large carrot, peeled and shredded (about 1 cup)
½ to ¾ cup mayonnaise, to taste
¼ to ⅓ cup canned chipotle peppers in adobo sauce (I like La Morena brand), to taste, mashed or finely chopped
1 to 2 tablespoons minced jalapeño or serrano chiles, to taste
1 tablespoon fresh lime juice
1 teaspoon kosher salt
Freshly ground black pepper
½ cup torn fresh mint

1. In a large bowl, combine the cabbage, carrot, mayonnaise, chipotle, jalapeño, lime juice, kosher salt, and a few grinds of pepper. Stir in the mint.
2. Let sit at room temperature for at least 10 minutes to allow the flavors to develop. Then keep it chilled in the fridge until serving. Store in the refrigerator for up to 2 days.

Latkes / Biracial Latkes

FRIED POTATO PANCAKES

This recipe is adapted from that of Russ & Daughters, the iconic New York Lower East Side appetizing shop that specializes in Ashkenazi delicacies. They make wonderful traditional latkes, usually served with sour cream and/or applesauce. I couldn't resist a twist on tradition, in honor of my daughter, Krishna, who is half Ashkenazi and, of course, half South Indian. You will see both versions below. Mint and Cilantro Chutney (page 31) and Garlic Yogurt Sauce (page 78) would be lovely pairings here.

SERVES 4

- 2 pounds russet potatoes, peeled
- 2 small yellow onions
- 2 large eggs
- 2 scallions, white and green parts, finely chopped
- 1/2 cup all-purpose flour
- 1/2 cup panko bread crumbs
- 4 tablespoons unsalted butter, melted and cooled
- 1 teaspoon cream of tartar
- Kosher salt and freshly ground black pepper

INDIAN ADD-INS

- 1/2 cup chopped fresh cilantro leaves
- 2 teaspoons minced green chile
- 2 teaspoons minced fresh ginger

- Neutral oil, for frying
- Kosher salt

1. Set a large fine-mesh sieve over a medium bowl. Place a box grater on a cutting board. Using the large holes, grate some of the potatoes, followed by some of the onions, moving the grated vegetables to the sieve. (Alternating the potatoes and onions prevents the potatoes from discoloring.) Repeat until all the potatoes and onions are grated.
2. Squeeze the vegetables, pressing out as much of the liquid as possible. Allow the accumulated liquid to stand in the bowl for 2 to 3 minutes. Pour off the watery part, but leave the thick, starchy paste that has accumulated at the bottom.
3. Use a spatula to scrape that paste into a clean large bowl. Add the potato-onion mixture, the eggs, scallions, flour, panko, melted butter, cream of tartar, 2 teaspoons kosher salt, and 1 teaspoon black pepper and mix well.
4. **For the Indian add-ins:** Scoop about half of the mixture into another large bowl and gently mix in the cilantro, chile, and ginger.
5. Line a tray with wax paper. Scoop out ¼-cup portions and shape into patties about ½ inch thick and 2 to 3 inches in diameter. Arrange in a single layer on the tray. Chill for at least 1 hour and up to 4 hours.
6. Pour ½ inch of oil into a large skillet and heat over medium-high heat until it shimmers and registers about 350°F on a deep-fry thermometer.
7. Line a sheet pan with paper towels and set near the stove. Working in batches, gently place the latkes in the hot oil and fry until crisp and deep golden brown, 2 to 3 minutes per side. Remove to the paper towels and sprinkle with salt.
8. If serving a large group, transfer the latkes in a single layer to a sheet pan and keep warm in a 200°F oven.

Whipped Spam
with Toast Points

I spent time in Appalachia with chef Travis Milton, chopping wood, stringing beans, and eating whipped Spam on fried saltines. Blending the Spam in a food processor results in a rich pâté. When I set out to re-create Travis's dish at home, I pared back the salt by buying low-sodium Spam and soaking it in water, a trick I borrowed from *Top Chef* contestants over the years. I prefer my whipped Spam with a 1:1 cream cheese ratio, lots of fresh dill, and tart notes from lemon juice and sumac, on toast points. I laughed when Krishna came home one day, tried it, and declared, "Oh, Jewish food," given that Spam is made of pork. She must have been reminded of chopped liver, showing us that there are more parallels between cuisines than we realize.

MAKES ABOUT 3 CUPS

1 (12-ounce) can 25% Less Sodium Spam, cut into roughly 1-inch cubes, soaked in cold water for 1 hour and drained
12 ounces cream cheese
1/4 cup chopped fresh dill
1 tablespoon chopped fresh chives
1 tablespoon fresh lemon juice
1 teaspoon sumac
Several healthy grinds of black pepper

FOR SERVING

Toasted sliced white bread, quartered into triangles
Sliced cornichons or chopped Chowchow (recipe follows), for garnish

1. In a food processor, blend the Spam and cream cheese until smooth. Add the dill, chives, lemon juice, sumac, and black pepper and blend until well combined. Refrigerate for several hours to chill.
2. **To serve:** Spread over toasted bread and garnish with cornichons or chowchow.

(Continued)

Chowchow

ACCOMPANIMENT

PICKLED GARDEN VEGETABLES

Chowchow is always on many Appalachian tables. Why throw out those odds and ends of vegetables lurking in your crisper (or growing in excess in your garden) when you can pickle them, turning them into this bright condiment? Chowchow adds crunch and punch to dishes such as Saag and Grits (page 96) and Whipped Spam (page 41). Like its cousins, Italian giardiniera, Anglo-Indian piccalilli, or Haitian pikliz, chowchow can be a great way to coax pickle-loving children into eating vegetables. I prefer mine with a touch of heat, so I add in serranos. While many recipes dilute the pickling liquid with water, I prefer to use undiluted vinegar because I like using the leftover liquid as a condiment unto itself, a more nuanced version of Chile Vinegar (page 99).

MAKES ABOUT 2 QUARTS (8 CUPS) PICKLED VEGETABLES AND LIQUID

4 cups dense vegetables, cut into 1/2-inch pieces (I use equal parts green cabbage, cauliflower, carrots, and daikon)
4 serrano chiles (optional), slit several times with a paring knife
Kosher salt
1 tablespoon sugar
2 (4-inch) sprigs fresh thyme
1 bay leaf, ripped in half
6 black peppercorns
4 allspice berries
3 cups distilled white vinegar

1. In a 2-quart or larger lidded glass jar, or divided evenly between two 28- or 32-ounce mason jars, place the vegetables, serrano chiles, 1 tablespoon kosher salt, the sugar, thyme sprigs, bay leaf, peppercorns, and allspice berries. Pour in the vinegar, seal the lid tightly, and shake.
2. Let sit at room temperature for at least 2 weeks, shaking occasionally. Serve at room temperature.

Sach Ko Jakak

KREUNG-INFUSED BEEF SKEWERS

This skewered snack, marinated in a uniquely aromatic paste known as kreung, is a real crowd-pleaser and a fun way to introduce Southeast Asian flavors to children. Because of the geographic proximity of Cambodia and Thailand, the cuisines share similar flavors; Cambodian food is more delicately flavored and relies less on heat from chiles. I first ate these at a park in Lowell, Massachusetts, while meeting former gang members who are now part of the Every Asian American Ally Stands Together, or EAAAST, movement. You will need to pick up a pack of bamboo skewers for this recipe, if you don't have any on hand.

SERVES 4 AS A SNACK

- 1/2 cup roughly chopped fresh lemongrass, cut from the tender bottom half of the stalk, outer layer removed
- 1/4 cup fresh lime juice (about 2 limes)
- 10 makrut lime leaves, stem and midrib removed, roughly torn
- 3 garlic cloves
- 1 tablespoon chopped peeled fresh galangal
- 1 scant tablespoon chopped peeled fresh turmeric
- 1 tablespoon plus 1 teaspoon fish sauce
- 1 pound flank or skirt steak, cut against the grain into 1/4-inch-thick slices

1. In a small food processor or blender, blend the lemongrass, lime juice, ¼ cup water, lime leaves, garlic, galangal, turmeric, and fish sauce until smooth (a bit of texture is okay). Pour into a long shallow baking dish, add the steak, and gently toss to coat. Marinate in the refrigerator for 2 to 4 hours.
2. Meanwhile, soak 8 to 10 skewers in water for 30 minutes. Drain. Thread the beef onto the skewers (if it breaks apart, freeze for 10 minutes to firm the meat, then try again).
3. Cook on the grill or in a grill pan on the stovetop.

   To grill: Preheat a gas grill on high. Grill the skewers, turning to cook evenly, about 3 minutes total.

   To cook indoors: Oil a large grill pan and heat over high heat until scorching hot. Grill the skewers on both sides, about 90 seconds per side, about 2 minutes total.

All-Clad

Asun

SPICY GOAT BITES

Asun is a beloved Nigerian snack, passed around at parties with toothpicks and cold beers to get things started. This dish had the most heat of anything I ate while filming *Taste the Nation.* I learned how to make it from Tobi Smith and Bethany Oyefaso of Adùn, a mail-order Nigerian food company the couple founded. They took me to a wonderful African market in Houston and introduced me to ingredients I had never experienced before. I did not grow up eating any meat, let alone goat. However, goat is eaten a lot in the Global South, including India and many African, Latin, and Caribbean countries. While it takes a long time to cook, especially if you don't have a pressure cooker, it's really easy and not labor-intensive. Bethany and Tobi demystified the recipe, and I now make it all the time. The best part is the resulting delicious broth, so save that for ramen or other soup. For this, I use goat leg, which is available at my local Latin market, but other cuts would work fine. If your heat tolerance is not high, reduce the amount of chiles. I suggest serving these to start your party, followed by Jollof Rice (page 128), Blackened Corn with Suya Spice (page 88), and Beef Koobideh (page 241).

SERVES 4

- 2 pounds bone-in goat, cut into roughly 3-inch pieces (ask your butcher to do this)
- 2 cups Essential Chicken Broth (page 54), or store-bought chicken broth or stock, or water
- 3 red bell peppers, quartered and seeded
- 2 medium yellow onions, 1 quartered, 1 thinly sliced into rings
- ½ cup roughly chopped fresh parsley leaves and stems
- 4 garlic cloves, halved
- 5 to 6 Scotch bonnet chiles, to taste, stemmed and halved
- Kosher salt
- 2 tablespoons neutral oil

1. In a large pot, combine the goat, 4 cups water, chicken broth, 1 of the bell peppers, the quartered onion, the parsley, garlic, 1 Scotch bonnet chile half, and 1 tablespoon kosher salt. The meat should be fully submerged in liquid; if not, add a little more water. Cover the pot and bring to a boil over high heat. Reduce the heat to low, cover, and simmer, giving it an occasional stir, adding a little more water if necessary to keep the meat immersed, until the goat can easily be pierced with a fork, about 3 hours. (You can also cook the goat in a pressure cooker on high pressure for 45 minutes. Let the pressure release naturally.) This can also be done the day before and stored in the refrigerator.
2. Remove the meat from the liquid. Let the broth cool and save for another use. Let the meat cool enough to touch. Pull the meat off the bones and chop or tear into 1-inch pieces.
3. In a food processor, combine the remaining 2 bell peppers, the remaining chiles, and 1½ teaspoons kosher salt. Pulse until finely chopped.
4. In a large skillet, heat the oil over medium-high heat. Sear the meat until browned on all sides, about 2 minutes. Add the bell pepper/chile mixture, toss, and sauté until most of the juices cook off, about 2 minutes. Add the sliced onions and stir constantly for just 2 minutes, until the onions become pliable.
5. Transfer to a serving platter and serve immediately, with toothpicks.

Pork Dumplings

with Water Chestnuts and Dates

These dumplings are an homage to the platters of wonderful dumplings I wolfed down at Yank Sing, the legendary dim sum house in San Francisco. From their delicate, springy shrimp dumplings to their earthy mushroom dumplings and juicy Kurobuta pork dumplings, I can never have too many dumplings at Yank Sing, where the Chan family has been delighting lovers of dim sum for nearly sixty years.

Krishna and I are obsessed with all kinds of dumplings—vegetarian, soup, meat—and my perfect dumpling is crisp on the outside, moist and soft in the middle. That's why I prefer this sear-and-steam method, which preserves the flavor and moisture of the filling while giving you a crisp, bronzed bottom. I also believe that dumplings should taste good without a dipping sauce, and these do. This dumpling is sweeter than most because of the dates but also has a delicate crunch to it from the water chestnuts. That said, the spicy, umami, and tart dumpling sauce is a perfect counterpoint to the sweetness of the dates.

MAKES ABOUT 40 DUMPLINGS

1 pound ground pork
1/3 cup finely chopped Medjool dates (6 to 12)
1/4 cup (about 5) canned whole water chestnuts, diced
1/4 cup minced scallion greens
2 tablespoons soy sauce
2 tablespoons Chinese black vinegar
2 tablespoons toasted sesame oil
1 1/2 teaspoons minced fresh ginger
1 small garlic clove, minced (about 1 teaspoon)
3/4 teaspoon kosher salt
1 teaspoon white pepper
Freshly ground black pepper
About 40 round dumpling wrappers, 3 to 4 inches in diameter
Neutral oil, for frying
Dumpling Sauce (recipe follows)

1. In a medium bowl, mix the pork, dates, water chestnuts, scallion greens, soy sauce, vinegar, sesame oil, ginger, garlic, kosher salt, white pepper, and a few grinds of black pepper. Use your hands to mix well until the mixture begins sticking to your hands, 1 to 2 minutes.

2. Pour a little water into a small bowl. Lay a dumpling wrapper on a flat surface and top with 1 to 2 teaspoons filling (use a tablespoon scoop and fill it about halfway). Dip your index finger into the water and dab it all over the edges of the wrapper. Close and seal the two halves (you can make pleats, if you want). Repeat with the remaining wrappers and filling. Place the dumplings on a sheet pan upright so there is a flat bottom and the top is the sealed seam.

3. Line a large plate with paper towels and set it near the stove. Working in batches, heat 2 tablespoons of neutral oil in a large nonstick skillet over medium heat (until the dumplings sizzle when they hit the pan). Add the dumplings in a single layer about ½ inch apart, setting them in the pan seam-side up, and sear until golden brown on the bottom, about 1½ minutes.

4. Pour ¾ cup water into a measuring cup. Have a glass lid ready in one hand. With the other hand, position the cup low and carefully pour the water just inside the edge of the skillet to avoid splashing. Quickly cover the pan to prevent splattering.

5. Cook the dumplings undisturbed until the wrappers have darkened, the water has largely disappeared, and the bottoms are a dark golden brown, 4 to 5 minutes. Drain the dumplings on the paper towel–lined plate.

6. Serve warm with dumpling sauce for dipping.

(Continued)

1
2
3
4
5
6
7
8
9

Dumpling Sauce

ACCOMPANIMENT

This dipping sauce is something I whipped up one day with what I had on hand, when my daughter said, "Where's the sauce?" It's versatile and delicious for any fried snack.

MAKES ABOUT 1¼ CUPS

- ¾ cup soy sauce
- 3 tablespoons fresh lime juice (about 2 limes)
- 2 tablespoons finely minced fresh ginger
- 1 tablespoon plus ¾ teaspoon rice vinegar
- About 1 tablespoon finely minced fresh green chiles (1 to 2 Indian or bird's eye chiles, depending on your heat preference)
- 1½ teaspoons toasted sesame oil

In a medium bowl, stir together the soy sauce, lime juice, 3 tablespoons water, the ginger, rice vinegar, green chiles, and sesame oil. Serve with the dumplings.

Note: You can save a lot of time by making ginger paste ahead and using it instead of minced ginger. Simply peel 1 pound of ginger, cut it into big chunks, whiz them in a small blender or food processor, and store the puree in a dry, clean jar in the refrigerator. It will stay good for at least 1 month. Remember: Never add a wet spoon into the jar or you may get spoilage.

SOUPS

AND

STEWS

Essential Chicken Broth

This broth will serve many purposes: You want it to be tasty, versatile, and balanced. I am a firm believer in salting my broth—I prefer it to taste like something you'd want to drink right out of the pot (which is why I refer to it as "broth," since many define "stock" as unsalted). I always start with the best bird I can find, with a pale white to light yellow skin and plump, shiny flesh, as well as a few onions and other aromatics. My secret ingredient: black garlic. These caramelized aged garlic cloves add a punch of umami that cannot be replicated. It's optional, but I highly recommend it! I also prefer sea salt for briny depth to kosher salt, but use what you have. Store the broth in 1-pint containers so you only open and use what you need. Throw in some vegetables, rice, and leftover meat for a quick bowl of soup. Use it for ramen (and discard that flavor packet). Use it to make Ribollita (page 71), Arroz Caldo (page 203), or many other recipes in and out of this book.

MAKES 3 TO 5 QUARTS

- 2 to 3 medium yellow or white onions, peeled, trimmed, and quartered
- 4 celery stalks (with leaves), cut into 4 pieces each
- 4 to 5 large carrots, trimmed and roughly chopped
- 1 fennel bulb, quartered, plus all the stalks and fronds
- 1 bell pepper, any color (red will be sweeter than green), quartered and seeded
- 1 (2-inch) knob fresh ginger, cut into 4 pieces
- 1 head garlic, some of the papery outer skins removed, halved horizontally
- 1 whole chicken (4 pounds), giblets discarded, rinsed and patted dry inside and out
- Fine or coarse sea salt
- 1 tablespoon black peppercorns, dry-roasted (see page xx), half of them coarsely crushed

OPTIONAL ADD-INS

- 1 jalapeño or another hot chile (be judicious)
- 6 to 8 whole star anise
- 4 bay leaves, preferably fresh
- 3 to 4 sprigs fresh rosemary (do not use dried)
- 3 to 4 sprigs fresh thyme, or 1 teaspoon dried thyme
- ½ teaspoon coriander seeds, dry-roasted (see page xx)
- 2 to 3 black garlic cloves
- ½ bunch of fresh parsley with stems

1. In a large stockpot (I recommend 12 quarts or larger), place all the vegetables at the bottom. Set the chicken on top. Add 1 tablespoon sea salt, the peppercorns, and any of the optional add-ins. Cover with as much water as you can, leaving a few inches of room at the top so it doesn't boil over.
2. Bring to a boil over medium-high heat (this could take 30 minutes or more). Reduce the heat to medium-low, partially cover, and simmer, periodically skimming any scum off the surface, for 40 minutes. Taste a little broth. Is it salty? Add a little more water. Is it bland? Add a little more salt.
3. Reduce the heat to low and simmer for another 40 minutes. Taste it: Would it make a good base for chicken soup? If so, remove it from the heat.
4. Remove the chicken and place it in a large bowl. Let the vegetables stand in the pot for another 20 minutes to settle and cool slightly.
5. When the chicken has cooled down, remove the meat from the bones and save it for another use. Set a fine-mesh sieve over another large pot. Carefully pour (or ladle) the broth into the sieve. Go slowly. Discard the vegetables. Let the broth cool and settle for 1 hour.
6. Use a baster or large shallow spoon to skim the fat off the surface. Or chill it until the fat hardens and remove. I like a bit of fat, so I skip this step. For a clearer broth, strain again and again through a sieve lined with cheesecloth.

Vegetable Broth

Vegetarian soups should be just as flavorful as those made with meat. This is a very forgiving recipe: Evolve it as you wish. The amounts noted here are minimums, so feel free to add more carrots or red bell pepper if you prefer a sweeter broth, more ginger or peppercorns for a little more heat, or more dried mushrooms or black garlic for a stronger umami flavor.

MAKES 3 TO 4 QUARTS

3 carrots, trimmed and roughly chopped
4 celery stalks (with leaves), roughly chopped
1 fennel bulb, roughly chopped, plus the stalks and fronds
2 large yellow onions, quartered
1 red bell pepper, quartered and seeded
6 medium garlic cloves, halved
1/3 to 1/2 cup roughly chopped unpeeled fresh ginger, to taste
1/2 cup packed roughly chopped fresh dill with stems
1/2 cup packed roughly chopped fresh parsley leaves and stems
1/4 cup chopped fresh chives (optional)
1/4 cup dried mushrooms
1 sprig fresh rosemary
2 bay leaves, preferably fresh
5 whole star anise
2 to 4 large black garlic cloves
1 heaping teaspoon black peppercorns, dry-roasted (see page xx), half of them roughly crushed
Fine or coarse sea salt

1. In a large stockpot, combine all the vegetables, herbs, and spices, along with 1 tablespoon sea salt. Pour in 5 quarts water and bring to a boil over high heat. Reduce the heat to maintain a medium simmer, partially cover, and cook for 1 hour.
2. Let the vegetables stand in the pot for another 20 minutes to settle and cool slightly. Set a fine-mesh sieve over another large pot. Carefully pour (or ladle) the broth into the sieve. Go slowly. Press down on the vegetables and other solids with a ladle to squeeze out all the broth before discarding. Store in 1-pint containers so you only open and use what you need. It will last in the fridge for 1 week, in the freezer for a couple of months.

Tomato Rasam

SPICY TOMATO BROTH

Rasam is a classic homey broth that can be made in many ways, and South Indians all over the world love to disagree about what makes the ideal rasam. Every family has a slightly different recipe. Some will add a touch of jaggery, or palm sugar, to offset the sour notes; others would never think of such a thing. The rasam conundrum can even exist within a single family: You may have seen my mother and me bicker about this very topic on *Taste the Nation*. I prefer to use sambar powder, which is traditionally used in the classic lentil stew Sambar (page 59), but my mother uses rasam powder. Either is fine. You can make this soup with lemon, tamarind, pineapple, or tomato, or make one that includes all these ingredients. But the basic truth of rasam is that it should have some very expressive sour notes and some warm spicy notes. While many versions include boiled and mashed lentils, I've kept this one lentil-free. Other than being delicious, comforting, and restorative, the spices act as a curative for all sorts of aches and illnesses. You may want to double the batch and freeze half for a rainy day when you have a cold. If you do this, hold back the cilantro until just before serving.

SERVES 4

- 2 (1-ounce) chunks of tamarind pulp (about the size of golf balls)
- 1½ tablespoons neutral oil or ghee
- ¾ teaspoon black mustard seeds
- ½ teaspoon cumin seeds
- 24 fresh curry leaves, torn in pieces
- 1 to 2 serrano chiles, to taste, halved lengthwise
- 1 small garlic clove, minced (about 1 teaspoon)
- 1 teaspoon asafoetida powder
- 2 cups grape tomatoes, halved
- ¾ teaspoon sambar powder or rasam powder (I like Sri Ganeshram's 777 or MTR brands)
- 2 teaspoons jaggery, Thai palm sugar, or turbinado sugar, plus more to taste
- Kosher salt
- ¼ cup roughly chopped fresh cilantro
- Steamed basmati rice (optional), for serving
- Ghee (optional), for serving

1. In a medium bowl, pour 6 cups hot tap water over the tamarind and soak for 20 minutes.
2. Use your hand or the back of a spoon to knead the tamarind in the water to release the pulp. Strain through a fine-mesh sieve into a bowl, pressing out the liquid. Discard the solids and set the tamarind water aside.
3. In a deep pot, heat the oil over medium heat until shimmering. Add the mustard seeds and cumin seeds and cook until the mustard seeds begin to pop and crackle, about 2 minutes. Add the curry leaves, chiles, garlic, and asafoetida powder and stir until coated with oil, about 1 minute. Add the tomatoes and stir until they begin to soften, 2 to 4 minutes. Add the sambar or rasam powder, stir, and cook for about 3 minutes to combine the flavors.
4. Add the reserved tamarind water, jaggery, and 1 teaspoon kosher salt. Bring to a boil, stirring occasionally, then reduce the heat and simmer until the tomatoes break apart and the soup thickens slightly, about 10 minutes.
5. Remove from the heat and stir in the cilantro. Add salt to taste. Serve in cups, or in bowls over rice, with a dollop of ghee (if using).

Sambar

TAMARIND LENTIL STEW

This soupy lentil stew is a staple of the South Indian table. Growing up, our first course was always sambar and rice along with a vegetable curry. Sambar always accompanies a few other South Indian dishes, such as Dosas (page 155) and idlis (rice dumplings). It is a very specific sensory pleasure to enjoy a crisp dosa, alternately dunked in hot, savory sambar and cool Coconut Chutney (page 160). Sambar is usually made with toor dal, a brown lentil that is flat like a coin. I make mine with masoor dal (orange lentils) because I prefer the flavor. Either works. I also keep my stew on the thicker side so it's easy to scoop up with a piece of folded dosa. There are certainly simpler ways to make sambar, including with sambar powder. I don't use sambar powder here, because frying and grinding your own spices with fresh coconut imparts an unparalleled depth of flavor. You'll see the difference is worth it. The coconut ground with the spices adds a sweetness that contrasts the tamarind beautifully.

SERVES 4 TO 6

2 (1-ounce) chunks of tamarind pulp (the size of golf balls)
1 cup masoor (orange) lentils, washed until the water runs clear, drained
Kosher salt
6 large shallots, finely diced (about 1½ cups)
6 tablespoons neutral oil
1 teaspoon black mustard seeds
24 fresh curry leaves, torn into pieces
2 daikon radishes, chopped into large chunks (2 to 3 cups), or 8 to 12 red radishes, halved
2 to 4 serrano chiles, to taste, slit down the middle but left whole
½ teaspoon ground turmeric
1 tablespoon plus 1 teaspoon coriander seeds
1 tablespoon chana dal
½ teaspoon fenugreek seeds
4 dried red chiles
2 tablespoons unsweetened grated coconut, fresh or frozen
2 cups diced fresh tomatoes (do not substitute canned, which are more concentrated)
2 teaspoons jaggery, Thai palm sugar, or turbinado sugar, or more as needed
1 cup chopped fresh cilantro leaves, for garnish
Steamed jasmine white rice or Dosas (page 155), for serving
Ghee, if serving with rice

1. In a medium bowl, pour 4 cups hot tap water over the tamarind and soak for 20 minutes.
2. Use your hand or the back of a spoon to knead the tamarind in the water to release the pulp. Strain through a fine-mesh sieve into a bowl, pressing out the liquid. Discard the solids and set the tamarind water aside.
3. Meanwhile, in a medium pot, combine the lentils, 4 cups water, and ½ teaspoon salt. Bring to a boil over high heat. Reduce to a simmer and cook, stirring occasionally, until soft, 12 to 15 minutes. Skim off any foam from the top. Set aside.
4. Measure out 2 tablespoons of the diced shallots and set aside for later. In a large shallow pot, heat 2 tablespoons of the oil over medium-high heat until it shimmers. Add the black mustard seeds and heat until they begin to pop, about 1 minute. As soon as they start popping, add the rest of the shallots and half of the curry leaves (beware of splattering!). Sauté until the shallots start to turn glassy, reducing the heat to medium if the shallots brown too fast, about 2 minutes.

(Continued)

5. Add the tamarind water and bring to a simmer. Add the daikons, chiles, 1½ teaspoons kosher salt, and the turmeric. Cover and simmer until the liquid thickens and the daikon is soft, about 12 minutes.
6. Meanwhile, in a small nonstick skillet, heat the remaining ¼ cup oil over medium heat. Add the reserved 2 tablespoons shallots, the coriander seeds, chana dal, fenugreek seeds, and dried chiles and heat until the shallots soften, the chana dal becomes golden brown, and the coriander seeds darken, 1 to 2 minutes. Remove from the heat and stir in the coconut, the remaining curry leaves, and 2 cups water. Transfer the mixture to a blender and pulse until smooth. (You can also use a small blender or food processor and blend in batches.) Mix into the pot with the daikon and tamarind water.
7. Add the tomatoes to the pot and cook until they collapse, 5 to 7 minutes. Add the cooked lentils and 2 cups water and simmer until the daikon is very soft, about 3 minutes. Add the jaggery and ½ teaspoon salt and stir well to combine. Add more salt to taste. (At this point, if you're serving the sambar with dosas, let it sit uncovered for at least 30 minutes so that it's thick enough to scoop up with the dosas. Warm through before serving.)
8. Garnish with cilantro. Serve over rice, with a dollop of ghee, or alongside dosas fresh from the griddle.

My mom, Krishna (age 9), and me

Tomato Egg Drop Soup

I have had many versions of egg drop soup, but never one with tomato until I found this soup listed on a take-out menu. I was initially surprised at the combination of eggs and tomatoes, but friends of Chinese descent, such as *Top Chef* winner Melissa King, later told me it was a popular combination in Chinese home cooking. Tomatoes are indigenous to Mesoamerica, but dishes such as this soup and others with tomatoes stem from the comingling of Chinese and Western cuisines. You can whip up this soup with ingredients you probably already have on hand, and the technique for egg drop is easy. This soup is so pure and comforting, not to mention nourishing and protein packed. It's a humble dish, perfect for a winter's brunch with dumplings (see page 46). A warm hug in a deep bowl.

SERVES 4 AS A STARTER

- 2 tablespoons neutral oil
- 1 tablespoon minced fresh ginger
- 6 scallions, white and green parts, chopped (about 1 cup), 2 tablespoons of greens reserved for garnish, if desired
- 1 (14.5-ounce) can diced tomatoes, undrained, or 14.5 ounces canned whole peeled tomatoes, chopped or roughly crushed with your hands
- 4 cups Essential Chicken Broth (page 54) or store-bought chicken broth or stock
- 1/4 teaspoon ground white pepper
- Kosher salt
- 4 large eggs
- Soy sauce, for garnish
- Toasted sesame oil, for garnish
- 1 to 2 tablespoons toasted sesame seeds, for garnish

1. In a large pot, heat the neutral oil over medium heat. Add the ginger and sauté just until it starts to turn golden, about 1 minute. Add the scallions and sauté until softened, about 2 minutes. Add the tomatoes, stirring and smashing to break the tomatoes down with the end of your spoon, until the tomatoes resemble a pulpy sauce, 5 to 6 minutes.
2. Add the broth, white pepper, and ¼ teaspoon salt. Increase the heat to medium-high and bring the mixture to a boil. Reduce the heat to medium-low, cover, and simmer, stirring occasionally, to allow the flavors to blend, until the oil pools on the top and the tomatoes have broken down and become a little lighter in color, 15 to 20 minutes. Add salt to taste.
3. In a small bowl, beat the eggs with 2 tablespoons water. Stir the soup with a wooden spoon as you slowly stream the egg mixture into the pot with your other hand. Stir continuously until the egg is cooked into wispy strands, 2 to 3 minutes.
4. Serve warm, garnished with scallion greens (if reserved), drizzles of soy sauce and sesame oil, and a sprinkle of toasted sesame seeds.

Note: This recipe makes a thick, filling soup. If you prefer something brothier, feel free to use just 2 or 3 eggs. If using store-bought broth, you may want to increase the amount of ginger.

All-Clad
All-Clad

Tomorrow's Borsch

BEET AND VEGETABLE SOUP

This beet-filled soup, popular throughout Eastern Europe, has the magenta hue you'll see in so many other versions but is made in a fraction of the time. Mine is inspired by Lyudmila Gladkovitser, a Ukrainian Jewish cook in Brighton Beach, New York, with whom I made borsch on the Ukrainian episode of *Taste the Nation*. Lyudmila was born and raised in Odessa, Ukraine. Her borsch contains veal, though mine is a vegetarian version. Its key spice is caraway, so don't skimp on that. Why Tomorrow's Borsch? Because its flavor deepens significantly a day or two after cooking, which makes it the perfect soup to make ahead.

SERVES 6 TO 8

1/4 cup extra-virgin olive oil
1 medium yellow onion, chopped (about 1 1/2 cups)
2 small garlic cloves, chopped (about 2 teaspoons)
1 tablespoon dried thyme
2 teaspoons caraway seeds
1 bay leaf, preferably fresh
Kosher salt
1/4 cup tomato paste
1 pound Yukon Gold potatoes, peeled and diced (about 2 1/2 cups)
1/4 large head green cabbage, shredded (about 2 cups)
4 celery stalks, diced (about 1 cup)
6 cups Vegetable Broth (page 56) or store-bought vegetable broth or stock
4 tablespoons unsalted butter
3 large carrots, peeled and shredded on the large holes of a box grater (about 1 1/2 cups)
Freshly ground black pepper
3/4 pound beets (about 3 medium), peeled and shredded on the large holes of a box grater (about 2 cups)
1 (15.5-ounce) can red kidney beans, drained and rinsed
1/4 cup distilled white vinegar
1/4 cup chopped fresh dill, a bit reserved for garnish
Handful of chopped fresh parsley
Sour cream, for serving

1. In a large pot, heat the olive oil over medium heat. Add the onion, garlic, thyme, caraway seeds, and bay leaf and sauté for 1 minute. Add 1 teaspoon kosher salt, cover the pan after the first few minutes, and cook until the onions are softened, about 5 minutes. Add the tomato paste and sauté, stirring constantly, until the paste darkens in color and coats the aromatics evenly, about 1 minute. Add the potatoes, cabbage, celery, and 2 teaspoons kosher salt. Sauté until the cabbage has collapsed and the celery has softened, 2 to 3 minutes. Pour in the broth and bring to a boil. Reduce the heat to low, cover, and simmer until the potatoes are tender, 15 to 20 minutes.

2. Meanwhile, in a large skillet, melt 2 tablespoons of the butter over medium heat. Add the carrots, a pinch of salt, and a few grinds of black pepper and sauté just until the carrots soften, 1 to 2 minutes. Transfer to a bowl.

3. Return the skillet to medium heat and melt the remaining 2 tablespoons butter. Add the beets, a healthy pinch of salt, and a few grinds of black pepper and sauté until the beets slightly soften, 1 to 2 minutes. Transfer to a separate bowl until the soup is ready: Do not add to the carrots.

4. When the potatoes are tender, add the carrots, beets, kidney beans, vinegar, dill, parsley, and 1 teaspoon kosher salt to the soup. Bring to a simmer, cover, and cook until combined, about 10 minutes, or up to 20 minutes, if you want softer vegetables. Add salt and pepper to taste.

5. Serve with dollops of sour cream and a pinch of fresh dill.

No, I didn't misspell borsch! Ukrainians are proud of their culinary identity. They say this beet soup is a specifically Ukrainian borsch. All those I spoke to say "borsch" (without the "t"), not "borscht," which is why I've spelled it this way.

Tom Yum Goong

HOT AND SOUR SOUP WITH SHRIMP

At Thai Village, a hole-in-the-wall restaurant in a strip mall in West Covina, California, my heart was stolen by the tom kha. The soup was comforting and spicy, with a clean grassy bite from a profusion of fresh green chiles sliced down the middle. That was the first place I encountered a savory, brothy coconut milk dish outside my own South Indian cuisine. This soup, tom yum goong, contains no coconut milk, but over the years I've actually come to prefer it to tom kha. Without the creaminess to tamp down the flavors, the bright, floral lemongrass, sharp citrus makrut lime leaves, and piney galangal really stand out. Fragrant and aromatic, it's tom yum goong that has my heart now. I'm honored to have adapted my recipe from Tina Sangthongkum, mother of Mark Padoongpatt, a Thai American professor at the University of Nevada, Las Vegas. For more on the fascinating story of Thais in America, and the part food played in shaping their identity and community here, read Mark's excellent book *Flavors of Empire*.

SERVES 4 TO 6

- 3 (10-gram) chicken flavor bouillon cubes (I like Knorr)
- 2 stalks fresh lemongrass, woody green top and roots trimmed, leaves and hard outer layer removed, cut into 2-inch pieces
- 5 tablespoons jarred nam prik pao (sometimes labeled Thai chili paste with soya bean oil; Tina uses Pantai's medium-spicy version)
- 2 to 4 fresh Thai chiles, to taste
- 1½-inch knob fresh galangal, peeled and thinly sliced
- 5 fresh makrut lime leaves (to release more of the flavor, make two small tears on each side of the midrib)
- 5 tablespoons fresh lemon juice (about 2 lemons), plus more to taste
- ¼ cup fish sauce, plus more to taste
- 1 tablespoon sugar
- ½ teaspoon Thai chile powder, or to taste
- 1 cup fresh cremini mushrooms, sliced
- 2 pounds extra-large shrimp, peeled and deveined
- Kosher salt
- 1 cup chopped fresh cilantro
- 3 scallions, white and green parts, chopped (about ½ cup)
- Steamed jasmine or another long-grain white rice, for serving (optional)

1. In a large soup pot, bring 3 quarts water to a boil. Add the bouillon cubes, lemongrass, nam prik pao, fresh chiles, galangal, and lime leaves, stirring until the cubes and paste have dissolved. Reduce the heat to low and simmer for 10 minutes.
2. Add the lemon juice, fish sauce, sugar, and chile powder and bring back to a boil over medium-high heat. Add the mushrooms and cook until softened, 1 to 2 minutes. Add the shrimp and cook until just opaque, about 1 more minute. Remove from the heat. Taste and add salt or more fish sauce, if needed. If desired, discard the lemongrass, galangal, lime leaves, and chiles.
3. Garnish with the cilantro and scallions and serve with rice, if desired.

While traveling the country, I noticed there was a Thai restaurant in every town I passed through, no matter how small or far-flung. I wondered how that could be, given the relatively small size of the Thai community in the US overall. It was Mark Padoongpatt who explained to me that in 2001, the Thai government started a "culinary diplomacy" program, the Global Thai initiative, that trained chefs, taught standardized recipes, and offered loans to Thais setting up restaurants abroad, with the goal of increasing exports of Thai products and increasing tourism to Thailand. The initiative worked—the number of Thai restaurants in the US increased from two thousand at the time to more than five thousand today.

Tadka Dal

YELLOW LENTIL SOUP

During the twentieth season of *Top Chef: World All-Stars,* our contestants had to create Indian thalis: meals composed of six small dishes, which usually include rice and dal, that perfectly balance sour, salty, sweet, bitter, spicy, and astringent flavors. To my surprise, no contestant really got the dal right. Once the challenge was over, I made them a big pot of dal—the right way. Two-time winner Buddha Lo called it "the most delicious thing I've had all season." This type of dal is called "tadka dal" because it includes, well, a tadka—a mix of spices and aromatics fried in oil that are then added to the lentils. I include curry leaves in my dal, which is traditional in South India but isn't always the case in other parts of the country. I also add amchur (dried mango powder) to my dal because of my stepfather: He always includes a piece of dried green mango. While living in Italy, I discovered the fragrant beauty of fresh bay leaves. They are not traditional, but I like the woodsy note they add.

SERVES 4 TO 6

2 cups masoor (orange) lentils, washed until the water runs clear, drained
2 to 3 bay leaves, preferably fresh
Kosher salt
2 tablespoons neutral oil
1 teaspoon cumin seeds
4 large shallots, finely diced (about 1 cup) or substitute yellow onion
1 tablespoon minced fresh ginger
2 serrano chiles, slit lengthwise but left whole
12 fresh curry leaves, torn
2 cups grape tomatoes, quartered
½ teaspoon ground turmeric
½ teaspoon amchur (dried mango powder)
¼ teaspoon Kashmiri chile powder
½ cup chopped fresh cilantro, plus more for garnish
Fresh lemon or lime juice (optional)
Steamed basmati rice, for serving
Ghee, for serving

1. In a deep pot, stir together the lentils, bay leaves, 1 teaspoon kosher salt, and 7 cups water. Bring to a boil over high heat. Reduce the heat to medium and simmer until the lentils begin to break down and the mixture is pale yellow, 20 to 25 minutes. Use a shallow ladle to periodically skim off any foam that appears on the surface.

2. Meanwhile, in a large nonstick skillet, heat the oil over medium-high heat. Add the cumin seeds and fry until the seeds sizzle and begin to darken, 20 to 30 seconds. Add the shallots and sauté until they turn glassy, about 2 minutes. Add the ginger, chiles, and curry leaves and sauté until the shallots begin to brown at the edges, about 2 minutes. Add the tomatoes, ½ teaspoon salt, the turmeric, amchur, and chile powder. Stir constantly until the tomatoes collapse and become pulpy, 10 to 12 minutes. Remove from the heat and set aside the tadka until the lentils are done.

3. Ladle 1 to 2 cups of lentils into the skillet with the tadka. Stir to incorporate, then pour all of it back into the pot with the rest of the lentils. Return the pot to medium heat and simmer, stirring occasionally for the flavors to meld, about 5 minutes. The dal should be soupy and loose. If the dal is too thick, add a bit of water.

4. Taste and add more salt if needed. Remove from the heat and stir in the ½ cup cilantro. If you'd like to brighten the flavor, add a squirt of lemon or lime juice. Garnish with the remaining handful of cilantro on top. Serve over rice with a small dollop of ghee.

Level Up: Top the dal with fragrant black pepper brown butter instead of ghee. In a small dry pan, dry-roast ½ teaspoon black peppercorns (see page xx). Once the peppercorns become fragrant and just start to smoke, after about a minute, transfer the peppercorns to a mortar and coarsely grind with a pestle. In the same small pan, melt 3 tablespoons butter. As soon as the butter melts, add the ground pepper and stir just until the butter browns and smells nutty, about 30 seconds. Be careful not to burn the butter. Immediately drizzle over the dal.

Frying spices and leaves in oil—called "tempering" in English—is widely known as tadka in many parts of India. In my native Tamil, it is known as thalippu or poorichakottal (and yes, all Tamil words and names have lots of syllables). It's a quick pyrotechnic way to extract a ton of flavor from a few seeds and leaves, as well as a good example of how Indian cooking can be a contact sport. When using mustard seeds in a tadka, for example, make sure you're not standing too close to the frying pan as the seeds will pop like popcorn when they are ready (that's because the tiny bit of moisture inside the seed expands when heated, causing the seed to explode). Use a towel or pot holder to hold the pan and keep a lid handy to shield yourself from the splattering!

I highly recommend measuring out all the ingredients for the tadka before you begin and having them ready, right by the stove, to make your life easier. Just remember: Tadkas cook very quickly. If your spices burn, better to toss them and start fresh. A bad tadka can ruin a good dish, which is much more wasteful.

Ribollita

WHITE BEAN AND VEGETABLE STEW

This classic Tuscan stew began life as "poverty food," a peasant dish that stretched leftover minestrone by adding beans and day-old bread (*ribollita* literally translates as "reboiled"). Today, though most recipes still include bread, I prefer to skip it, because I find that it dulls the flavor of the stew. My ideal ribollita always starts with dried cannellini beans, but if you're in a hurry, feel free to use two 15-ounce cans of cannellini beans, drained and rinsed well, instead—and skip the bean-cooking step. I do this when I don't have the time or forethought to make beans from scratch (which is more often than I'd like to admit). This reheats beautifully—freeze leftovers and keep them on hand for busy nights. Served with crusty bread (even better if it's grilled), you've got a complete and hearty meal.

SERVES 6

1½ cups dried cannellini beans, soaked in hot tap water for 2 hours and rinsed
3 bay leaves, preferably fresh
Kosher salt
½ cup extra-virgin olive oil, plus a few tablespoons for serving
2 small yellow onions, diced (about 2 cups)
2 large garlic cloves, minced (about 1 tablespoon)
1 teaspoon red chile flakes
2 carrots, peeled and diced (about 1 cup)
1 large fennel bulb (white part only), diced (about 1¾ cups)
2 stalks celery, diced (1 cup)
Freshly ground black pepper
2 tablespoons tomato paste
1 bunch of Swiss chard (about 12 ounces), leaves stripped from stalks and cut into ½-inch-wide ribbons, stalks cut into ½-inch pieces
½ cup packed chopped fresh parsley leaves
3 cups Essential Chicken Broth (page 54)
5 ounces fresh spinach, coarsely chopped
2 tablespoons fresh lemon juice, plus more for serving

1. In a medium pot, combine the beans, bay leaves, 1 tablespoon kosher salt, and 6 cups cold water and bring to a boil. Reduce to a simmer and cook until the beans are tender, adding additional splashes of water as needed, 1 to 1½ hours. (Or, cook in a pressure cooker on high until the beans are tender, about 20 minutes. Let the pressure release naturally.)
2. Remove 1 cup of the beans, coarsely mash them with a spoon or fork, and set aside. Drain the remaining beans and set aside.
3. In a large Dutch oven, heat the olive oil over medium heat. Add the onions and after a minute, add a pinch of salt. Stir frequently until softened, about 3 minutes. Add the garlic and stir frequently until the onions are glassy, about 2 minutes. Add the chile flakes and stir just to combine.
4. Add the carrots and stir for 30 seconds. Add the fennel and stir for 1 minute. Add the celery and 1 teaspoon black pepper and stir well to combine, about 1 minute. Add the tomato paste and stir well until all the vegetables are evenly coated, about 1 minute. Add the Swiss chard stems and stir well to combine, about 1 minute. Add ¼ cup of the parsley and 1 tablespoon kosher salt and stir frequently until the stems begin to soften, about 3 minutes.
5. Pour in the chicken broth and bring to a simmer. Then add the whole beans and the mashed beans and stir well for about 2 minutes. Stir in the Swiss chard leaves and spinach, bring back to a simmer, and cook until the spinach has wilted, 3 to 5 minutes. Remove from the heat. Stir in the lemon juice.
6. Cover and let sit for about 30 minutes: This will improve the flavor.
7. Garnish with the remaining ¼ cup parsley, a drizzle of olive oil, and a squirt of fresh lemon juice. Serve warm.

Level Up: I like some of the vegetables in this stew to have a little more crunch for texture. In that case, before sautéing the carrots, fennel, and celery in the pan, set aside 2 tablespoons of each. Continue with the recipe as written, and add the reserved raw vegetables when you add the beans and before you add the Swiss chard leaves and spinach.

Pork and Kimchi Soondubu

SOFT TOFU AND PORK STEW

Chef Yoonjin Hwang rose to fame after David Chang crowned her Los Angeles K-Town café his "Restaurant of the Year." Cooking with her on *Taste the Nation,* I could see why. She approaches food with the meticulousness and gracefulness of a concert pianist, which she is. Watching her lay out dried fish, long branches of seaweed, aged kimchi, and roasted vegetables for her kimchi jjim (braised kimchi and pork belly) was like watching performance art. I loved the flavors and textures of the long-simmered dish (fifteen hours!) but wondered if I could replicate them on a weeknight. My mind went immediately to soondubu jjigae, the classic Korean stew of tofu and vegetables, which often includes meat. My riff on it, inspired by Yoonjin's kimchi jjim, is perfect for a cold winter evening. I love the flavor added by the pork, but you can omit it altogether and still arrive at something delicious. The egg, added at the very end, lends a silky richness to the spicy broth.

SERVES 4

1 tablespoon neutral oil
2 teaspoons toasted sesame oil
4 large shallots, finely chopped (about 1 cup)
1 tablespoon plus 1½ teaspoons minced fresh ginger
1 large garlic clove, minced (about 1½ teaspoons)
Kosher salt
¼ pound ground pork
1½ cups finely chopped napa cabbage
4 tablespoons chopped scallions, white and green parts (1 to 2 scallions)
2 tablespoons gochujang
4 tablespoons soy sauce
½ cup napa cabbage kimchi, chopped
1 large celery stalk, finely sliced on the bias (about ½ cup)
½ teaspoon gochugaru chile flakes or Aleppo chile flakes
2 cups Essential Chicken Broth (page 54) or store-bought chicken broth or stock
1 (16-ounce) package silken tofu
4 large eggs
Steamed rice, for serving

1. In a large pot, heat the neutral oil and sesame oil over medium heat. Add the shallots and sauté until glassy, about 3 minutes. Add the ginger, garlic, and a pinch of kosher salt and sauté for 1 minute. Add the pork, breaking it up with a spoon, and sauté until no longer pink, 3 to 4 minutes.

2. Add the cabbage, 2 tablespoons of the scallions, the gochujang, and 2 tablespoons of the soy sauce and sauté until the cabbage wilts, about 4 minutes. Add the kimchi, celery, and gochugaru and sauté for just 3 minutes. Add the chicken broth, bring to a simmer, and cook for 10 minutes, stirring occasionally, to allow the flavors to marry.

3. Stir in the remaining 2 tablespoons soy sauce and simmer for another 2 minutes. Add the whole block of silken tofu, submerging it in the liquid. Warm through for about 2 minutes, then, using the edge of a spoon, divide the block into 4 pieces.

4. Increase the heat to medium-high and bring the soup to a boil. Reduce the heat to medium-low and crack the eggs into the pot, leaving space in between them. Cover and poach over medium-low heat until the whites are set, 4 to 5 minutes.

5. Divide the soup among four large serving bowls, giving each one a piece of tofu and an egg. Serve immediately with rice, and garnish with the remaining 2 tablespoons scallions.

Aash

HEARTY NOODLE SOUP

On a bitter cold day in Washington, DC, Homayon Karimy, an Afghan American chef, taught me how to make this filling noodle soup, topped with both a rich meat sauce and a tart yogurt sauce. Homayon has lived in many parts of the world since leaving Afghanistan in the '90s, and his family's aash recipe, which I've adapted here, reflects that. Don't be intimidated by the length of this recipe. While it does have three major components, none of them are hard to make. Just save it for a Saturday and take your time. I promise you will be as captivated as I am. The spinach and herbs give the soup a green freshness, which lightens the richness of the lamb, while the tart lemony garlic yogurt sauce brightens everything. This is a meal in a bowl, hearty enough for goat herding or Afghan mountain climbing—or just going about your day in suburban America.

SERVES 8

¼ cup extra-virgin olive oil or ghee
1 medium yellow onion, chopped (about 1½ cups)
Kosher salt
1 to 2 jalapeño chiles, to taste, sliced
4 large garlic cloves, minced (about 2 tablespoons)
2 tablespoons minced fresh ginger
2 tablespoons tomato paste
6 celery stalks, chopped (about 3 cups)
2 carrots, peeled and finely diced (about 1½ cups)
1 turnip (optional), peeled and finely diced (about 1 cup)
1 tablespoon ground turmeric
1 tablespoon ground coriander
2 teaspoons Kashmiri chile powder
1 teaspoon sumac
1 (14.5-ounce) can diced tomatoes, undrained, or 2 cups diced fresh tomatoes
8 cups boiling water, plus more if necessary
1 (12-ounce) package enriched flour noodles (see Notes), broken in three
1 cup whole-milk yogurt
¼ cup fresh lemon juice (1 to 2 lemons)
1 cup packed baby spinach leaves or chopped fresh spinach
½ cup chopped fresh cilantro
¼ cup chopped fresh dill
¼ cup torn fresh mint leaves
Freshly ground black pepper
2½ cups Savory Minced Meat Sauce (recipe follows), plus more for serving
1½ cups Garlic Yogurt Sauce (page 78), plus more for serving

1. In a large pot, heat the olive oil over medium-high heat. Add the onion and a pinch of kosher salt and sauté until softened, about 5 minutes. Reduce the heat to medium and add the jalapeños and sauté for about 1 minute. Add the garlic, ginger, and a pinch of salt and sauté until softened, about 3 minutes. Add the tomato paste, stir, and mix vigorously until the paste darkens in color and coats the aromatics evenly, about 1 minute.

2. Add the celery, carrots, turnip (if using), turmeric, coriander, chile powder, sumac, and 2 teaspoons kosher salt and give it a good stir until nicely combined, about 1 minute. Stir in the tomatoes, add the boiling water, and bring the soup to a boil. Reduce the heat and simmer until the vegetables are tender but not mushy, about 10 minutes, or up to 20 minutes if you prefer your vegetables softer. Remove from the heat.

3. While the soup simmers, bring a large pot of salted water to a boil over high heat. Add the noodles and cook until a bit more tender than al dente, about 6 minutes. Drain.

4. Stir the noodles into the soup. Stir in the yogurt, lemon juice, spinach, cilantro, dill, and mint. Stir and add more salt and pepper to taste.

(Continued)

5. Pour the soup into a large serving bowl and spoon the meat sauce over the top, leaving some space in the center. Drizzle the yogurt sauce on top in the center. Serve the soup alongside bowls of extra meat sauce and yogurt sauce. Note that if the soup sits for a while, or if you have leftovers, the noodles will absorb the liquid, so add more water and season to taste while reheating.

Notes:

Look online or in a Middle Eastern grocery for Ash-Reshteh noodles, which are what Homayon uses. Japanese udon noodles or linguine are acceptable substitutes.

Homayon cooks the noodles right in the soup, which is the traditional way of preparing aash. I prefer to boil the noodles separately, so they don't overcook or release too much starch into the soup.

With Homayon Karimy at his home in Washington, DC

Savory Minced Meat Sauce

ACCOMPANIMENT

Rich and savory, this quick-simmered tomato meat sauce also comes from Homayon Karimy. Not only is it the perfect accompaniment to his noodle soup (Aash, page 74), but it's also delicious on dumplings, such as Aushak (page 20). The addition of Kashmiri chile powder gives it a mild heat; if you do have the optional sumac, I highly recommend adding it—the tartness offsets the richness of the meat. This recipe makes more than you'll need for the aash, which, trust me, is a good thing. I spoon it over pasta or even use it as a quick sloppy joe filling. If ground lamb is hard to find, use all beef.

MAKES 5 TO 6 CUPS

¼ cup ghee or extra-virgin olive oil
2 small yellow onions, chopped (about 2 cups)
Kosher salt and freshly ground black pepper
4 large garlic cloves, minced (about 2 tablespoons)
1 tablespoon minced fresh ginger
1 tablespoon tomato paste
1 pound ground lamb
1 pound ground beef (80/20)
1½ teaspoons sumac (optional)
1 teaspoon Kashmiri chile powder
1 teaspoon ground turmeric
1 (14.5-ounce) can diced tomatoes, undrained, or 2 cups diced fresh tomatoes
2 teaspoons ground coriander
¼ cup roughly chopped fresh cilantro

1. In a large pot, heat the ghee over medium-high heat. Add the onions, ¼ teaspoon salt, and a few grinds of black pepper and sauté until the onions are glassy, about 5 minutes. Reduce the heat to medium, add the garlic and ginger, and sauté for just a minute. Add the tomato paste and stir vigorously for about 1 minute until the aromatics are coated, taking care not to burn any of it.

2. Add the lamb and beef, breaking up the meat with a wooden spoon. Stir until the fat starts to release from the meat, about 1 minute. Then add the sumac (if using), chile powder, turmeric, 1 teaspoon kosher salt, and a few grinds of black pepper and sauté, stirring, until the meat goes from pink to just brown, about 5 minutes.

3. Add the diced tomatoes and ground coriander, bring to a simmer, and cook, stirring occasionally, until the tomatoes are well combined with the meat, about 8 minutes. Garnish with cilantro. The sauce will last in the fridge for 4 to 5 days; in the freezer it will last about a month.

(Continued)

Garlic Yogurt Sauce

ACCOMPANIMENT

In Afghanistan and neighboring countries, yogurt is traditionally made at home, and tends to be more sour than store-bought yogurt. That's why Homayon Karimy adds lemon to this yogurt sauce, which is excellent drizzled on Aash (page 74). It's also fantastic on Butternut Squash Bolani (page 23), as well as with Pakori (page 28). The addition of lemon zest is what makes this extra special. Letting the sauce chill for at least an hour is crucial so that the lemon juice and yogurt can fully marry, and so that the fragrant oils of the zest have a chance to really infuse the sauce. The flavor is even better on day two, so feel free to make this ahead of time.

MAKES 3 CUPS

- 3 cups whole-milk yogurt
- Grated zest of 1 lemon
- 1 tablespoon fresh lemon juice
- 2 large garlic cloves, finely grated or mashed well in a mortar with a pestle (about 1 tablespoon)
- 1 tablespoon dried mint, or ¼ cup chopped fresh mint leaves
- Kosher salt

In a medium bowl, mix the yogurt, lemon zest, lemon juice, garlic, mint, and 1½ teaspoons kosher salt. Taste and adjust the salt if needed. Refrigerate for at least 1 hour before serving. The sauce will keep in your fridge for 4 to 5 days.

Note: This sauce is very garlicky, so if you're sensitive to raw garlic, use just half the amount called for here. It'll still be delicious.

Avgolemono

CHICKEN LEMON SOUP

Over the course of my life, on actual Greek islands to the Greek-owned restaurants that checker New York City, I have gulped gallons of this iconic Greek soup. Thickened with eggs, brightened with lemon, and studded with bits of chewy orzo, it is utterly addictive: silky, creamy, and tangy all at once. Yet, despite my enduring infatuation with it, I had never made it at home. After filming an episode of *Taste the Nation* in Tarpon Springs—a Florida Gulf Coast town that may as well have been a Greek village—I felt emboldened to finally try my hand at it. There, Katerina Tsiliclis of Katerina's Taverna & Grill walked me through tempering the eggs to achieve the perfect creamy texture, without scrambling them in the hot liquid. As soon as I was back in New York City, I had a pot going. Excited, I called my dear friend of twenty years Christina Papadopoulos, who is very picky about her avgolemono, and begged her to come over for a bowl. Now, while most folks might not find a bowl of soup to be an urgent matter, she is a patient soul and indulged my request. After several spoonfuls, she announced, "Delicious. The real deal." I was pumped. "Almost as good as my mother's." High praise indeed.

SERVES 4

- 1 whole or cut-up chicken (4 pounds total), giblets removed
- 1 medium yellow onion, quartered, or 1½ cups chopped
- 1 russet potato, peeled and left whole
- ¼ cup packed fresh parsley leaves and stems, plus 2 tablespoons chopped fresh parsley leaves
- 1 teaspoon dried oregano
- 1 teaspoon dried dill
- 6 black peppercorns, smashed in a mortar with a pestle
- Sea salt
- ½ cup orzo
- 4 large eggs, at room temperature
- ½ cup fresh lemon juice (2 to 3 lemons), plus more to taste
- Grated zest of 1 lemon, plus more for garnish (optional)
- 2 tablespoons chopped fresh dill

1. In a large pot, combine the chicken, onion, potato, ¼ cup of the parsley leaves and stems, dried oregano, dried dill, peppercorns, and 1 tablespoon sea salt. Add 2½ quarts (10 cups) water and bring to a boil over medium-high heat. Reduce the heat to medium-low, cover, and simmer until the chicken is cooked through, 35 to 45 minutes. Carefully remove the chicken and place on a platter to cool.
2. Set a fine-mesh sieve over a large bowl. Strain the broth, spooning off the fat if you wish (I don't). Discard the solids.
3. Reserving 2 cups of the broth, pour the rest back into the pot and bring to a boil over medium-high heat. Add the orzo and cook until tender according to the package directions. Remove from the heat.
4. In a second large bowl, whisk the eggs and lemon juice until emulsified. By the time the orzo is cooked, the reserved 2 cups of broth should have cooled to lukewarm. Slowly stream that broth into the eggs and lemon juice, whisking constantly to avoid scrambling.
5. Remove the pot from the heat and slowly stream the egg-lemon mixture into the pot of soup and orzo, whisking constantly, until combined and slightly thickened. Stir in the remaining 2 tablespoons parsley leaves, the lemon zest (if using), and fresh dill.
6. When the chicken has cooled, remove the meat and chop into bite-size pieces. Discard the bones, fat, and skin. Stir the meat into the soup, set the pot over medium-low heat, and stir frequently until the soup is heated through. Taste and add more salt and lemon juice, if desired. Top each bowl with a pinch of lemon zest, if desired.

Level Up: It may sound odd, but trust me on this: A few drops of Salsa Macha (page 103) drizzled into a bowl of avgolemono adds such beautiful richness and earthy smokiness to it (don't tell Christina!), an unlikely discovery I made while testing recipes for this cookbook. That's what I love about cooking from various cultures at once—surprises at every turn.

VEGETABLES
AND
LEGUMES

Sabzi

SAUTÉED GREENS

Shamim Popal, the chef responsible for the showstopping lamb and rice pilaf Qabuli Pulao (page 253), also serves this beautiful side dish at her Afghan bistro, Lapis, in Washington, DC. Her sabzi is long-cooked, which is traditional: I've cut the cooking time, as I prefer tender greens like spinach sautéed only until just wilted. Doing so preserves their bright-green color and retains more of their nutrients. The leeks impart a layered allium goodness to these sautéed greens that sautéed onions alone can't match.

SERVES 4

¼ cup neutral oil
½ teaspoon cumin seeds
2 large leeks, white and light-green parts only, chopped (about 2 cups)
Kosher salt
2 medium yellow onions, chopped (about 3 cups)
1 tablespoon unsalted butter
2 large garlic cloves, minced (about 1 tablespoon)
1 tablespoon minced fresh ginger
1 tablespoon ground coriander
Freshly ground black pepper
10 ounces fresh baby spinach
2 cups chopped fresh cilantro

1. In a large skillet, heat the oil over medium-low heat. Add the cumin seeds and toast until darkened, 1 to 2 minutes. Add the leeks and a pinch of kosher salt and sauté until softened, 5 to 7 minutes. Add the onions, another pinch of salt, and the butter and sauté until the onions begin to collapse, another 5 to 7 minutes. Add the garlic, ginger, coriander, 1¾ teaspoons kosher salt, and 1½ teaspoons pepper and sauté for 2 minutes. Add ¼ cup water and scrape the bottom of the pan.
2. Add the spinach, a few handfuls at a time, and stir constantly until wilted, 2 to 3 minutes. Stir in the cilantro and remove from the heat. Add salt and pepper to taste.

Zucchini
with Sun-Dried Tomatoes

On a summer day when I had too many zucchini on my hands, I decided to experiment with a raw salad, shaving the squash into long ribbons and tossing them with a tangy dressing made with sun-dried tomatoes, fresh herbs, and dark Turkish Urfa chile, which lends a smoky flavor. The result was such a lovely dish, one that can go straight from the garden to the table. Gently frying the shallots, garlic, and sun-dried tomatoes creates a more mellow, well-rounded dressing. You can also use Aleppo chile if Urfa is unavailable. Keep the dish chilled in the fridge until ready to serve.

SERVES 4 TO 6

3 pounds zucchini (4 to 6 medium), trimmed and cut lengthwise into 1/8-inch-thick ribbons, preferably using a mandoline or strong and wide vegetable peeler
Kosher salt
3 tablespoons extra-virgin olive oil
3 small shallots, minced as finely as possible (1/4 cup plus 2 tablespoons)
1 garlic clove, minced (about 1 1/2 teaspoons)
1/4 cup plus 2 tablespoons oil-packed sun-dried tomatoes, drained and chopped
1/4 cup plus 2 tablespoons chopped fresh dill
3 tablespoons mayonnaise
3 tablespoons fresh lemon juice
1 tablespoon plus 1 1/2 teaspoons white wine vinegar
1 tablespoon plus 1 1/2 teaspoons dried mint
1 1/2 teaspoons Urfa chile flakes or Aleppo chiles flakes

1. Spread the zucchini in a large shallow pan, such as a baking dish. Sprinkle 1½ tablespoons kosher salt all over the zucchini, toss lightly to combine, and transfer to a colander to drain for about 1 hour.

2. In a medium skillet, heat the olive oil over medium-low heat. Add the shallots and garlic and sauté for 1 minute. Add a healthy pinch of kosher salt and continue to stir until the shallots are slightly glassy, about 1 minute. Add the sun-dried tomatoes and sauté for just 1 minute. Remove from the heat, transfer to a large bowl, and cool slightly, for about 3 minutes.

3. Mix in the dill, mayonnaise, lemon juice, vinegar, mint, and Urfa chile. Gently toss in the drained zucchini. Add salt to taste. Serve immediately or refrigerate for about 1 hour to deepen the flavors.

Blackened Corn
with Suya Spice

Nigerian American actress and comedian Yvonne Orji introduced me to suya one hot summer night on a Houston rooftop. An immensely popular street food in Nigeria, suya is typically grilled shaved beef, coated in the intensely savory spice mix that gives the snack its name. And there's always a little extra suya spice on the side, for dipping—my kind of snack. I knew my family back in India would love suya; all of us enjoy making our own spice mixes. Just one problem: My relatives are all vegetarians. Enter bhutta, an Indian street food I gobbled up as a kid: blackened corn charred over a fire, then coated with masala, salt, and lemon. What if I took the masala in a nuttier, more peppery direction? Smoky, fire-licked corn sprinkled with my interpretation of suya spice? Could this Indian-Nigerian mash-up work? The rooftop chef told me he'd only give up his suya blend for one billion dollars. I didn't have that, but I do have the nose of a bloodhound, and my taste buds are telling me that this is close to what was probably in it. You may end up with a little left over: It would also be great on other grilled vegetables, roasted potatoes, or eggs, or mixed into a yogurt dip.

SERVES 4

2 tablespoons raw red-skinned peanuts
1/2 teaspoon cumin seeds
1/2 teaspoon ground ginger
1/2 teaspoon garlic powder
1/2 teaspoon Spanish smoked paprika
1/2 teaspoon cayenne pepper
1/2 teaspoon ground white pepper
Kosher salt
4 fresh ears of corn, husks and silk removed
1 stick (4 ounces) unsalted butter (you need the stick for leverage; you may have some left over)

1. Warm a dry medium skillet over medium heat. Add the peanuts and roast, stirring or shaking the skillet constantly, until darkened, about 5 minutes. Transfer to a plate and cool. In the same pan, dry-roast (see page xx) the cumin seeds over medium heat for just a minute until fragrant.
2. In a small blender or spice grinder, combine the peanuts, cumin, ground ginger, garlic powder, smoked paprika, cayenne, white pepper, and ½ teaspoon kosher salt and blend into a powder.
3. Turn a stove burner to high. Using metal tongs, hold the ears of corn over the flame so that the fire laps up the sides of the corn, and rotate every 15 seconds, until the corn is charred all over, 6 to 8 minutes. (Alternatively, do this on a grill: Preheat the grill to high and place the ears of corn on the grates as close to the open flame as possible, rotating regularly until charred.)
4. Rub the end of a stick of unsalted butter all over the corn. Move the corn to a dish. Sprinkle 1 to 2 teaspoons of spice on each cob, rubbing to evenly coat all sides of the corn (this amount will vary depending on the size of each ear). Serve immediately.

With Yvonne Orji in Houston, Texas

Peppery Sweet and Sour Red Cabbage

This is an updated version of a traditional German recipe that calls for braising red cabbage for an hour or more. I prefer to stop well before that because I like some crunch in my cabbage. I've also added a healthy dose of black pepper, definitely *not* traditional, to accentuate the sweet and sour notes that are a hallmark of this classic dish. The pepper makes this easy veggie side just a little sassier than usual.

SERVES 4 TO 6

- 3 tablespoons unsalted butter
- 1 medium yellow onion, sliced (about $1\frac{1}{2}$ cups)
- Kosher salt and freshly ground black pepper
- 2 Granny Smith apples, peeled and shredded (about 2 cups)
- 1 head red cabbage (2 to 3 pounds), cored and shredded or thinly sliced (about 10 cups)
- $\frac{3}{4}$ cup apple cider vinegar
- 1 to 2 teaspoons honey, sugar, or jam, such as red currant (optional, to balance any acidity)

1. In a large deep pot, melt the butter over medium-low heat until frothy. Add the onion, 1 teaspoon kosher salt, and several generous grinds of black pepper and sauté until softened, about 3 minutes. Add the apples and stir frequently until the apples begin to release water, about 2 minutes. Add the cabbage and stir until evenly coated.
2. Pour in the vinegar, add a pinch of kosher salt, and mix to combine. Cover the pot and cook, stirring occasionally, until the cabbage is somewhat tender but maintains its crunch, and its purple color has turned to dark pink, about 20 minutes. (If you prefer a softer cabbage, continue to cook until the cabbage reaches your desired texture.)
3. Taste and add the honey, sugar, or jam (if using) and season with more salt and pepper to taste. Serve warm.

Julian Kegel at Kegel's Inn, Milwaukee, Wisconsin

Cabbage Poriyal

STIR-FRIED CABBAGE

The warm, nutty scent of curry leaves, mustard seeds, and ginger frying in oil: This is the telltale aroma of South Indian cuisine, the food of my childhood. They serve as the backbone of this stir-fried dish, which is on heavy rotation at our house, especially during winter when little else but cabbage looks good at the greenmarket. The coconut here is optional, though it is common in Tamilian versions of these quickly cooked vegetable dishes known as poriyal in South India. Substitute the cabbage with green beans or other vegetables—just vary the cooking time accordingly.

SERVES 4

- 1 tablespoon neutral oil
- 1/2 teaspoon black mustard seeds
- 1 tablespoon chana dal
- 1 1/2 teaspoons split skinless urad dal
- 10 curry leaves, torn, plus 2 whole leaves
- 1 serrano chile, quartered lengthwise
- 1 tablespoon minced fresh ginger
- 1/2 head green cabbage (about 1 pound), shredded
- Kosher salt
- 3/4 cup shredded unsweetened coconut (optional), fresh or frozen

1. In a large nonstick skillet, heat the oil over medium heat. Add the mustard seeds. As soon as they begin to sizzle and pop, add the chana and urad dals and stir until the smaller urad dal starts to turn golden, about 1 minute. Add the curry leaves (be careful because they will splatter), chile, and ginger and stir until the chana dal darkens, about 1 minute.
2. Add the cabbage and 1 teaspoon kosher salt, and sauté, stirring constantly, just until the cabbage softens and shrinks in size by half, about 5 minutes. Add the coconut (if using), and stir until heated through and well combined, another 5 minutes. Add salt to taste, if needed. Serve warm.

Braised Leeks

There's something so humble yet elegant about a leek. Like onions and shallots, leeks become soft and sweet when slowly braised. However, leeks are much more delicate in flavor, so they lend themselves to being served as a side dish on their own. I first ate leeks solo when I was in France—a lovely dish of tender leeks braised in butter, thyme, and white wine. You'll want to use leeks that are all the same size for even cooking. The leeks pair well with soy, ginger, and vinegar for a tangy, wonderfully rustic dish. Marrying the French technique that leads to oh-so-tender and caramelized goodness with the umami addictiveness of a glossy dumpling sauce, these leeks are pure bliss.

SERVES 4

SAUCE

- 1/4 cup soy sauce
- 2 tablespoons fresh lime juice
- 4 teaspoons finely minced fresh ginger
- 2 1/2 teaspoons rice vinegar
- About 2 teaspoons finely minced fresh green chiles (about 2 Indian or Serrano, depending on your heat preference)
- 1 teaspoon toasted sesame oil

LEEKS

- 1 tablespoon neutral oil, preferably untoasted sesame oil, plus more as needed
- 8 leeks (about 2 pounds total), white and light-green parts only, halved (or quartered if very big), washed, and patted dry
- 6 tablespoons (3 ounces) unsalted butter
- 4 large shallots, diced (about 1 cup)
- Kosher salt and freshly ground black pepper
- 4 garlic cloves, sliced
- 2 teaspoons finely minced fresh ginger

1. **Make the sauce:** In a small bowl, stir together 6 tablespoons water, the soy sauce, lime juice, ginger, rice vinegar, chiles, and toasted sesame oil. Set aside.
2. **Cook the leeks:** In a large nonstick skillet over medium-high heat, swirl the neutral oil over the surface to coat. Add the leeks in a single layer, in batches if necessary, cut-side down, and sear (both cut sides, if quartered) until deep brown, adding more oil if necessary, 4 to 6 minutes. Transfer to a plate.
3. Reduce the heat to medium-low and melt 4 tablespoons of the butter, swirling to coat the pan. Add the shallots, a pinch of kosher salt, and a healthy pinch of black pepper and sauté until glassy, about 1 minute. Add the garlic and ginger, reduce the heat to low, and sauté for just 15 seconds.
4. Scrape the bottom of the pan, then move the shallots, garlic, and ginger to the edges. Place the leeks cut-side down in the pan. Spoon some of the shallots, garlic, and ginger on top of the leeks. Pour in the sauce, cover the skillet, keeping the heat on low, and cook undisturbed until the leeks are tender and their bottoms are brown and caramelized, about 20 minutes.
5. Transfer the leeks to a serving platter. Add ½ cup water to the pan to deglaze. Add the remaining 2 tablespoons butter and stir until reduced and syrupy, 2 to 3 minutes. Pour as much of the sauce as you like over the leeks.

Calabaza con Mojo

ROASTED SQUASH IN A CITRUS-GARLIC SAUCE

This gorgeous squash with citrusy mojo sauce is deceptively simple to put together. Writer and historian of Cuban food Ana Sofia Pelaez taught me how to make this when we filmed our Noche Buena episode of *Taste the Nation* in Miami—and it would indeed be perfect on a holiday table. Noche Buena is typically a Catholic holiday celebrated in many countries on Christmas Eve. The mojo sauce makes everything better: A smidge of Spanish smoked paprika adds a scintilla of heat and an unmistakable smoky flavor, both of which are great counterpoints to the sweet squash; fresh oregano imparts a pepperiness and bright green color that enlivens the mojo in a way dried oregano just doesn't. Of course, if dried is all you have, go ahead and use it: Sometimes what's important is just to make the dish, rather than worry about whether it will be "perfect."

SERVES 6

1 calabaza (2 pounds), also known as West Indian pumpkin, unpeeled, seeded, and cut into 1-inch-thick wedges (see Notes)
3/4 cup extra-virgin olive oil
Kosher salt and freshly ground black pepper
6 large garlic cloves, thinly sliced (about 3 tablespoons)
1 large yellow onion, thinly sliced into crescents
Grated zest of 1/2 lime
Grated zest of 1/2 orange
1/4 cup fresh lime juice (about 2 limes)
1/4 cup fresh orange juice (about 1 orange)
2 tablespoons fresh oregano leaves, coarsely chopped, plus a few more whole leaves for garnish
1/2 teaspoon Spanish smoked paprika

1. Preheat the oven to 425°F.
2. On a large baking sheet, drizzle the squash wedges with ¼ cup of the olive oil, and season with pinches of kosher salt and black pepper on both sides. Roast until caramelized and fork-tender, 20 to 30 minutes. Transfer to a serving platter.
3. Using a mortar and pestle, mash the garlic, ¾ teaspoon kosher salt, and about ¼ teaspoon black pepper to form a paste.
4. In a large skillet, heat ¼ cup of the olive oil over medium heat. Add the onion and cook for 1 minute, then add a pinch of kosher salt and cook until the onions soften and become glassy, about 3 minutes. Add the garlic paste and mix well, mashing the garlic into the onions and stirring constantly for 1 minute.
5. Remove from the heat and stir in the remaining ¼ cup olive oil, the lime zest, orange zest, lime juice, orange juice, oregano, and smoked paprika. Taste and add kosher salt, if desired. Drizzle as much sauce as you like over the squash and serve the rest in a bowl at the table.

Notes:

If you can't find calabaza, substitute kabocha, acorn squash, or butternut squash. Note that the cooking times may vary.

If you happen to live near a Latin market and can find sour oranges, or naranja agria, do use them in place of the limes and oranges listed here.

For her cookbook, *The Cuban Table*, Ana Sofia Pelaez traveled throughout Cuba, Miami, and New York to document traditional Cuban cooking from across the Cuban and Cuban expat community—a combination of recipes and storytelling, it is a fabulous addition to any cookbook collection.

Saag and Grits

GREENS AND GRITS

At the Pakalachian food truck in southwest Virginia, Katlin and Mohsin Kazmi beautifully marry the foodways of Appalachia with Mohsin's Pakistani heritage. Saag and grits is emblematic of this culinary mash-up. Saag—a classic Indian curry of leafy greens—is one of the most beloved South Asian vegetable dishes, while grits are a staple of the Southern table. Katlin and Mohsin take it a sustainable step further by using the invasive weed kudzu—known as "the vine that ate the South"—in the saag. While my version forgoes the kudzu, it does include three different greens: Swiss chard, mustard greens, and baby spinach. I add each at different times to build flavor and preserve the texture of the greens. Garam masala gives the dish warmth, cream tempers the bitterness of the greens, and amchur (dried mango powder) rounds it all out. This is your antidote to boring sautéed greens.

SERVES 4 TO 6

- 1/2 teaspoon black peppercorns
- 2 whole cloves
- 3 dried red chiles
- 2 tablespoons neutral oil, plus more as needed
- 1 teaspoon cumin seeds
- 2 medium red onions, diced (about 2 1/2 cups)
- Kosher salt
- 2 large garlic cloves, minced (about 1 tablespoon)
- 1 tablespoon minced fresh ginger
- 1 to 2 fresh green chiles, such as jalapeños or serranos, to taste, quartered lengthwise
- 2 medium tomatoes, diced (about 2 cups)
- 1 teaspoon amchur (dried mango powder)
- 1/2 teaspoon ground turmeric
- 1 bunch of Swiss chard (about 12 ounces), leaves stripped from stalks and cut into 1/2-inch-wide ribbons, stalks cut into 1/2-inch pieces
- 1 bunch of mustard greens (about 9 ounces), stems and midribs removed, leaves cut into 1/2-inch-wide ribbons
- 2 tablespoons dried fenugreek leaves (also known as kasoori methi), crushed into a rough powder with your hands
- 5 ounces baby spinach
- 3 tablespoons unsalted butter
- 1 teaspoon garam masala
- 3/4 cup heavy cream, plus more to taste
- Grits (recipe follows)
- Chile Vinegar (page 99), for serving

1. In a small dry sauté pan, stir the peppercorns and cloves over medium-high heat until fragrant and smoking, about 1 minute. Transfer to a mortar and pestle or spice grinder. Add the dried chiles to the hot pan and sauté until darkened slightly, about 30 seconds. Add to the same mortar and pestle or spice grinder and grind into a fine powder. Set aside the spice mixture.

2. In a large pot, heat the oil over medium-high heat. Add the cumin seeds and stir until they darken slightly and become fragrant, about 30 seconds. Add the onions and sauté for a minute, then add a pinch of kosher salt, stirring frequently until the onions are glassy, about 5 minutes. Cover the pan in between stirring so the onions do not stick. If they do, add up to a tablespoon more oil.

3. Add the garlic, ginger, and green chiles and sauté just for a minute. Add the tomatoes and 1 teaspoon kosher salt. Cover, reduce the heat to medium, and cook, stirring occasionally, until the tomatoes have collapsed, 4 to 5 minutes.

4. Add the amchur and turmeric and stir for 2 minutes. Add the chard stems and 1 cup water, stir, cover, and simmer until the stems lose a bit of their color, 4 to 5 minutes. Add the mustard leaves and fenugreek leaves, cover, and cook until the mustard leaves wilt, about 3 minutes. Add the chard leaves, 1 cup water, and a pinch of salt and cook uncovered until wilted, about 10 minutes.

From left to right: Tray Wellington, Travis Milton, Ashleigh Shanti, me, Chi Shipman, Dr. Cynthia Greenlee, Mohsin Kazmi, and Kaitlin Kazmi, sharing a meal in Appalachia

5. Stir in the spinach and cook until wilted, about 2 minutes. The greens should be thick and moist; if they're watery, let them cook for a few more minutes. Add the butter, garam masala, 1 teaspoon of the spice mixture, and a pinch of kosher salt. Stir occasionally, covering the pan in between, and adding a little water if needed, until the greens cook down into a sludgy consistency, 8 to 12 minutes.

6. Stir in the cream, reduce the heat to low, cook for 2 to 3 minutes, then taste. The cream will have tamped down the heat level: Add more of the spice mixture if needed. Serve hot over the grits. Pass the chile vinegar at the table.

(Continued)

Grits

ACCOMPANIMENT

These all-purpose grits are perfect for both Saag and Grits (page 96) and Shrimp and Grits (page 186), or just to enjoy as a side. The recipe comes to me from the great Charleston chef BJ Dennis, who has taught me more than a thing or two about Gullah Geechee culture and cooking. Before tasting BJ's grits, I never put cheese in my grits, preferring just butter, but the sharp Cheddar here brings a tang and richness I can't deny. BJ prefers you make this dish with stone-ground grits: They are coarser and have a richer, heartier corn flavor than quick-cooking or instant grits. I could not find them easily in New York, so I ordered them online, and I'll never go back to regular grits again.

SERVES 4

- 1½ cups Essential Chicken Broth (page 54), Vegetable Broth (page 56), or store-bought broth
- Kosher salt
- 1 cup stone-ground grits, rinsed well in a fine-mesh sieve
- ⅓ cup shredded sharp Cheddar cheese
- ⅓ cup heavy cream
- 1 tablespoon unsalted butter
- ½ teaspoon ground white pepper or black pepper

1. In a large saucepan, stir together the chicken broth, ½ teaspoon kosher salt, and 3 cups water and bring to a boil over high heat. Slowly whisk in the grits, sprinkling with one hand and stirring with the other, until well combined (this will avoid clumping). Return to a boil, then reduce the heat to medium-low, cover, and simmer, whisking frequently to avoid sticking to the bottom of the pot, until the liquid is absorbed and the grits are tender (adding more water if the grits start to look dry), about 40 minutes. (Err on the side of adding more liquid: The grits will thicken as they stand.)
2. Remove the grits from the heat. Stir in the Cheddar, cream, butter, white pepper, and ½ teaspoon kosher salt. Taste and adjust the seasoning as needed. Cover to keep warm until ready to serve.

Chile Vinegar

ACCOMPANIMENT

Every fall I go to the Union Square greenmarket and buy a bag of mixed hot chiles. I wash them well, cover them with seasoned vinegar, and let them sit. Then, every 2 to 4 weeks, I drain off the vinegar and save it, then cover the chiles again with more seasoned vinegar—that way I always have a bottle of this flavor-boosting elixir on hand. Just a few drops instantly deliver pure heat and acidity. I add it to salad dressings, soups, stews, and cocktails—the uses are endless. I especially love drizzling a bit on a bowl of Aash (page 74) or Shrimp and Grits (page 186).

MAKES ABOUT 2 CUPS

12 whole chiles, the hottest you can find, ideally a mix of bird's eye, jalapeño, serrano, Scotch bonnet, and/or habanero (about 2 heaping cups)

2 cups distilled white vinegar

Kosher salt

2 teaspoons sugar

1 teaspoon dried oregano

1. Wearing surgical gloves and taking care to not touch your eyes, poke a small slit through each chile with a paring knife. Add the chiles to a clean mason jar and tamp down so that 1 inch of space is left at the top.
2. In a medium bowl, mix the vinegar, 2 teaspoons kosher salt, sugar, and oregano. Pour over the chiles. Place a small glass weight, bowl, or other nonmetal heavy object on top of the mixture to make sure the chiles are entirely submerged in the liquid. Cover tightly.
3. Let the chiles steep in the vinegar at room temperature, shaking the jar occasionally, for at least 2 weeks. Drain the vinegar into a squeeze bottle and drizzle on foods that need a little bit more punch. Feel free to add more seasoned vinegar to the same jar and the same chiles to make a second, third, or fourth batch. (After 6 months, the chiles will mellow enough to use as a condiment on their own; see Note.)

Note: Once you've made a few batches of the chile vinegar, the chiles will mellow. Chop one and add it to a sandwich or quesadilla or try as a garnish for Avgolemono (page 79), Ribollita (page 71), or Nam Banh Chuk (page 181).

1

2

3

4

Podimas

POTATOES WITH TURMERIC AND FRIED LENTILS

This classic South Indian potato side dish is also the traditional filling for dosas—indeed, it's what I use for Dosas (page 155). They're not quite mashed potatoes, not quite chopped potatoes, but something in between, with a sunny yellow hue from the turmeric. I especially love the textural contrast created by the crunchy, fried urad dal dotting the soft, pillowy potatoes. This dish is perfect to serve at a summer barbecue or as part of a buffet, because it's great at room temperature.

MAKES ABOUT 2 CUPS
(enough to fill four 8-inch dosas)

2 pounds Yukon Gold potatoes, unpeeled (to expedite cooking, buy smaller potatoes that are roughly the same size)
2 tablespoons neutral oil
1 teaspoon black mustard seeds
1 tablespoon split skinless urad dal
1/2 teaspoon cumin seeds
12 curry leaves, torn into pieces
1/2 small yellow onion, finely chopped (about 1/2 cup)
1 serrano chile or 2 green Indian chiles, minced
1/2 teaspoon ground turmeric
Kosher salt
1 tablespoon fresh lemon juice, plus more to taste
1/2 cup chopped fresh cilantro

1. Bring a large pot of water to a boil over high heat. Add the potatoes and boil until soft, 25 to 35 minutes, depending on their size. Remove the potatoes and set aside until they are cool enough to handle, about 15 minutes. Peel off the skins. Cool completely.
2. In a large skillet, heat the oil over medium-high heat until shimmering. Add the mustard seeds and reduce the heat to medium as soon as they start sizzling. Add the urad dal, cumin seeds, and curry leaves (be careful, they will splatter) and stir until the urad dal darkens slightly, about 1 minute. Add the onion and sauté until softened, about 2 minutes. Add the chiles and turmeric and sauté for just 1 minute.
3. Add the potatoes to the skillet, using your hands to crush them roughly as you do so. Add 2 teaspoons kosher salt and stir to incorporate the ingredients well. Sauté until the potatoes are yellow, about 5 minutes.
4. Add ¼ cup water and stir until incorporated, about 3 minutes. Add more kosher salt to taste. Stir in the lemon juice and cilantro. Serve warm.

H&H-Style Breakfast Burritos
with Homemade Pinto Beans

After high school football games back in La Puente, California, my friends and I would often hit up the Green Burrito on Hacienda Boulevard. The best thing about their burritos (which *never* included rice, the norm in Southern California back then) were the smoky, charred poblanos they grilled on the flattop along with the meat. Burritos have always been nostalgic for me, but after I visited El Paso for *Taste the Nation,* they took on new meaning. At H&H Car Wash and Coffee Shop, revered for its breakfast burritos, I met the women who crossed the border from Juárez to El Paso every morning at dawn to make them. I was moved not only by the hours they spent waiting in checkpoint lines every day just to work, but by their take on burritos: a nourishing, comforting care package that's portable and easy to eat for schoolchildren or laborers in factories and fields. This recipe is inspired by the amazing beans at H&H—always made from scratch. Any leftover beans you have after making the burritos can be served alongside a plate of Mushroom Tacos Campesinos (page 35) or another meal.

MAKES 6 BREAKFAST BURRITOS
(and about 3 cups beans)

PINTOS

8 ounces dried pinto beans, covered with cold water and soaked overnight, then drained
1 yellow onion, peeled and quartered
3 garlic cloves, peeled but whole
4 bay leaves, preferably fresh
1 teaspoon red chile flakes
Kosher salt
½ teaspoon dried oregano, preferably Mexican
2 slices bacon (optional), chopped

BREAKFAST BURRITOS

2 tablespoons neutral oil
3 jalapeño chiles, sliced into rounds
6 large eggs, beaten
6 (10-inch) flour tortillas
Salsa Macha (recipe follows), Salsa Verde (page 230), or your hot sauce of choice

1. **Make the pintos:** In a large pot, combine the beans, onion quarters, garlic, bay leaves, chile flakes, 1½ teaspoons kosher salt, the oregano, and bacon (if using). Add 6 cups water and bring to a boil over high heat. Reduce the heat to medium-low, partially cover, and simmer, stirring occasionally, and adding water, if necessary, until the beans are tender, about 2 hours.
2. Remove the bay leaves. Use an immersion blender to blend until smooth.
3. **Make the breakfast burritos:** In a large skillet, heat the oil over medium heat. Add the chiles and fry until browned at the edges, about 1 minute. Flip and cook until the seeds begin to brown, another minute. Transfer to a bowl.
4. Set the skillet back over medium heat and heat the oil remaining in the pan. Stir in the eggs and scramble until set, about 1 minute. Remove from the heat.
5. Over a medium flame on a gas stove, use tongs to char one tortilla at a time on both sides. (If you have an electric stove, heat a second large skillet over medium heat and warm the tortillas one at a time on both sides, about 1 minute per side.)
6. Place a tortilla on a plate. Add about ⅓ cup beans in a line in the middle of the tortilla. Place a few fried chile slices on top of the beans, followed by about 3 tablespoons of scrambled egg. Drizzle on a teaspoon or so of salsa to taste.
7. Tuck the sides and end of the burrito in, then roll it up. Fill and roll the remaining tortillas. Serve immediately.

Salsa Macha

ACCOMPANIMENT

CHILE OIL WITH NUTS AND SEEDS

Emiliano Marantes in El Paso

Salsa macha derives its deeply nutty, smoky spiciness from a combination of dried chiles, almonds, and sesame seeds. Somewhat akin in texture to Chinese chili crisp, every version has its own twist. I adapted this one from that of Emiliano Marantes of Elémi Restaurant in El Paso, Texas. When freshly made, salsa macha has a slightly bitter edge that will mellow over time; this is part of its character. Frying each type of chile separately, as well as the almonds and garlic, is crucial to prevent burning any of the ingredients. Stay vigilant and keep an eye on your pan. Drizzle salsa macha on tacos, burritos, or a bowl of Chile Verde (page 230). Know that if you have a jar of this on hand, you can make a supremely flavorful, heat-filled meal out of very little.

MAKES ABOUT 3 CUPS

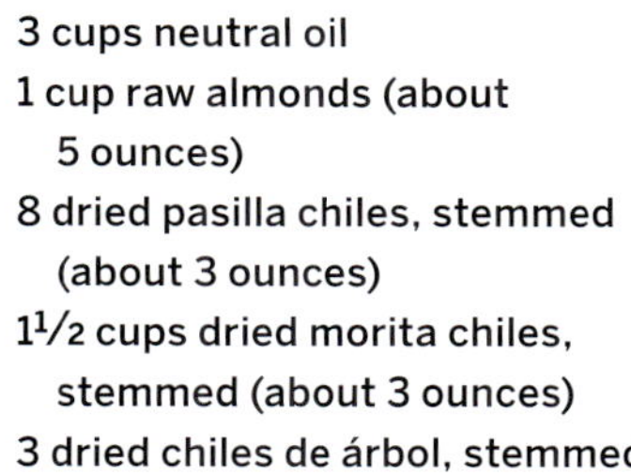

3 cups neutral oil
1 cup raw almonds (about 5 ounces)
8 dried pasilla chiles, stemmed (about 3 ounces)
1½ cups dried morita chiles, stemmed (about 3 ounces)
3 dried chiles de árbol, stemmed
12 medium garlic cloves, smashed and peeled
3 tablespoons sesame seeds
¼ cup red wine vinegar
1 teaspoon dried oregano, preferably Mexican
1 teaspoon kosher salt

1. In a large wide pot, heat the oil over medium-low heat. Set a plate nearby. Add the almonds to the pot and fry, stirring occasionally and reducing the heat if the oil bubbles up past a gentle simmer, until the almonds are just barely darkened and fragrant, about 8 minutes. Use a slotted spoon to remove the almonds from the oil and spread out on the plate to cool.

2. Return the pot to medium-low heat and set a sheet pan or tray nearby. Add the pasilla chiles to the pot, fry for just 1 minute, and remove with a slotted spoon to cool on the sheet pan. Add the morita chiles and árbol chiles, fry for just 1 minute, and remove with the slotted spoon to cool on the sheet pan. Cool the chiles completely.

3. Meanwhile, remove the pot from the heat. Add the garlic and let it sit in the warm oil, stirring occasionally, until barely golden, 8 to 10 minutes. Remove the garlic with a slotted spoon and set aside to cool. Strain out any burned seeds that may be remaining in the oil. Cool the oil to room temperature, about 30 minutes.

4. In a medium skillet over medium-low heat, toast the sesame seeds, stirring constantly, just until slightly golden, 1 to 2 minutes. Set aside to cool.

5. Pour the cooled oil into a food processor. Add the almonds, chiles, garlic, sesame seeds, vinegar, oregano, and salt. Process until the chiles are crushed, stopping short of a paste. Store at room temperature for up to 1 month.

Holishkes

SWEET AND SOUR STUFFED CABBAGE

I grew up knowing many Jewish people, but I came late to Ashkenazi food. Filming the Hannukah episode of *Taste the Nation* gave me a much-needed education on this vital part of New York cuisine. A highlight was the vegetarian stuffed cabbage I made with the energetic Liz Alpern and Jeffrey Yoskowitz of the Gefilteria, whose mission is to reimagine and share the joys of Eastern European Jewish foods. I immediately connected with these cabbage rolls, stuffed with mushrooms and lentils instead of the more traditional ground beef, because we always have lentils around, and they allow Krishna to share a dish from her Ashkenazi heritage with all the vegetarians in her Hindu family. Holishkes are sometimes called prakes—both are Yiddish words for this dish of humble ingredients that yield decadent results. Liz and Jeffrey's recipe from their cookbook, *The Gefilte Manifesto: New Recipes for Old World Jewish Foods*, inspired my own version. This is project cooking, best made with loved ones on the weekend, when things are more relaxed.

SERVES 4 TO 6

½ cup neutral oil
3 large yellow onions, chopped (about 6 cups)
1 teaspoon dried thyme
Kosher salt
¼ cup tomato paste
1 (28-ounce) can crushed tomatoes
2 tablespoons packed dark brown sugar
3 tablespoons red wine vinegar
1 teaspoon Kashmiri chile powder
Freshly ground black pepper
15 ounces sauerkraut (about 2 cups), drained and finely chopped
¼ cup fresh lemon juice (1 to 2 lemons)
1 pound portobello mushrooms, cleaned and chopped (about 6 cups)
1 medium head green cabbage (about 3 pounds), core removed with a sharp knife
2½ cups cooked French green lentils (see Note), at room temperature
¾ cup cooked basmati or jasmine rice, at room temperature
2 large eggs
2 tablespoons fine dried bread crumbs or matzo meal
¼ cup chopped fresh dill
¼ cup chopped fresh parsley
Lemon wedges, for serving

1. In a medium pot or Dutch oven, heat ¼ cup of the oil over medium heat. Add 3 cups of the onions, sauté for 1 minute, then add the thyme and 1 teaspoon kosher salt and sauté until glassy, about 5 minutes. Stir in the tomato paste and cook, stirring frequently, until the onions are evenly coated and the tomato paste has darkened, 2 to 3 minutes. Add the crushed tomatoes, brown sugar, 1 tablespoon of the vinegar, the chile powder, and ½ teaspoon black pepper. Bring to a simmer, then reduce the heat to medium-low and simmer gently with the lid ajar, stirring occasionally, to allow the flavors to marry and the sauce to thicken, about 30 minutes. Remove from the heat and stir in the sauerkraut, lemon juice, and salt to taste. Cover and set the tomato sauce aside.

2. In a large skillet, heat the remaining ¼ cup oil over medium heat. Add the remaining 3 cups onions and sauté for 1 minute. Add 1 teaspoon kosher salt and sauté, stirring often so the onions do not stick, until just starting to brown, about 10 minutes. Stir in the mushrooms, ½ teaspoon kosher salt, and ½ teaspoon black pepper and sauté, stirring often, until the mushrooms are shrunken and browned, 8 to 10 minutes. Remove from the heat, add the remaining 2 tablespoons vinegar, stir to loosen any browned bits, and spread on the bottom of a large bowl to cool at room temperature.

(Continued)

1
2
3
4
5
6
7
8
9
10
11
12
13
14
15
16

3. Bring a large pot of water to a boil. Line a large tray with paper towels. After the water boils, add 2 tablespoons kosher salt. Place the cabbage in the boiling water. Cover the pot and boil until the outer leaves begin to soften and release from the head, 15 to 20 minutes. Use tongs to grab the translucent outer leaves, trying not to rip them, and transfer to the prepared tray in a single layer. Repeat again and again, continually peeling off the outer leaves. When the tray is filled with a single layer, pat the leaves dry, place another layer of paper towels on top, and place another layer of cabbage in a single layer. Repeat with the rest of the cabbage.
4. To the large bowl with the cooled onions and mushrooms, add the lentils, rice, eggs, bread crumbs, 2 tablespoons of the dill, 2 tablespoons of the parsley, 1½ teaspoons kosher salt, and a few grinds of black pepper. Stir to combine, taste, and adjust the seasoning, if desired.
5. Preheat the oven to 300°F.
6. In a large Dutch oven, or another large, deep baking dish (use one with a lid, if possible), pour a layer of tomato sauce over the bottom.
7. On a cutting board, lay out the biggest cabbage leaf. Pat dry with a paper towel. Use a paring knife to trim off the tough center rib. Scoop about ⅓ cup of the filling into the center (adjust based on the size of your leaf). Fold the two outer sides of the leaf in over the filling, then roll it up away from you like a burrito, folding as tightly as you can. If you rip a leaf while rolling, just layer another leaf on top. Repeat until you have used all of the filling. If you run low on large leaves, overlap leaves to create a patchwork. Place each roll in the baking dish seam-side down and packed tightly in a single layer. Pour the remaining tomato sauce over the top, spreading evenly to cover the rolls completely.
8. Cover the dish with a lid or a tight layer of aluminum foil and bake until the rolls feel completely soft when pressed with a finger, about 2½ hours. Check occasionally that the rolls stay moist, and add a little water, ¼ cup at a time, if necessary.
9. Uncover and let sit at room temperature for at least 15 minutes. Serve hot, garnished with the remaining parsley and dill, and a squeeze of fresh lemon.

Note: Precooked green lentils can be purchased in cans and in vacuum-sealed bags. If using canned lentils, drain them and rinse well. Or purchase dry green lentils and boil with a bit of salt per package directions and drain before using.

KAMAL

I immediately took a liking to my sweet, sensitive friend Kamal the moment I met him, when he came into my life as the partner of our family friend Tucker. His gentle nature, guilelessness, and quirky sense of humor won me over right away. Though he works in the corporate trenches by day, like many millennials he has a side hustle: cooking and delivering homemade Lebanese meals for a roster of clients who, like him, are far from home. An excellent cook, Kamal always volunteers to help when he comes to dinner. We have an easy rapport—have had one since the beginning. But though he is warm and loving, there's something vulnerable, almost skittish, about Kamal. I'd never quite been able to put my finger on it: Was he nervous around me or was that just his nature?

When we took *Taste the Nation* to Dearborn, Michigan, I invited Kamal and his partner, Tucker, to join me. My crew and I would be there for Ramadan, and we were planning on filming at a large Suhoor festival. I thought Kamal might be excited to share in the festivities. Suhoor is the meal eaten just before sunrise, before fasting for the day begins. Like Iftar, the light meal that breaks your fast after sunset, suhoor is a way families come together. It's a chance to celebrate Ramadan by gathering to eat with your loved ones. I thought it might be nice for Kamal to be among chosen family when his own family was a world away. But he demurred, an uneasy expression on his face.

Kamal learned to cook from his mother, with whom he was exceptionally close. She had given birth to him at just fifteen, and in essence they had grown up together. They used to sit together at the kitchen table, drinking coffee and poring over cookbooks, planning meals and debating the merits of various recipes—did that dish really need a tablespoon of sumac? Food was the way he bonded with her most. Theirs was a close family: a younger brother, two younger sisters, countless cousins, aunts, and uncles. Life in the small village outside of Beirut could be both cozy and claustrophobic, dominated by traditional, more conservative cultural and religious values and the fact that everybody knew your business.

By eighteen, Kamal knew he was gay. He'd begun to suspect as much around age eight, when his first schoolyard crushes didn't quite match up with those of his friends. The intervening decade was a mixture of doubt, confusion, and fear. All throughout his childhood, Kamal had heard his mother and aunties speak negatively about men they identified as gay, as sinners who were immoral and would burn in hell. He once heard his mother tell a relative, "If I had a gay son, I would kill him." Kamal was conflicted. He was religiously observant, but could he really fathom, based on his growing certainty about his attraction to men, that his family would think he deserved to be condemned? Was he really a bad person?

After college in Beirut, Kamal returned home to his village, determined to pray and atone, to straighten out, so to speak. He was still a practicing Muslim, but no matter how much he prayed, he remained attracted to men. His first romantic encounter made him realize both that he could not be anyone but who he was and that he could not be that person in any kind of proximity to his family. Not only would it be dangerous for him, not only would it mean cutting ties with his family, but it would also bring shame on his parents, sisters, and brother. Through a friend, he secured a job in Miami and moved to the United States. He texted or spoke with his mom, his dad, his sisters, and brother regularly. He came to believe that they all knew he was gay but had reached an unspoken "don't ask, don't tell" policy. That if he was discreet, there was no impediment to loving him. With his mom, there was always the topic of food, of family recipes remembered and misremembered.

Returning from filming in Dearborn, I asked Kamal about the dishes I had tasted. When Ramadan circled back the next year, I asked him if we could make one of his family's recipes together. We made plans to cook fatteh batinjan, an elaborate and layered eggplant casserole—a mix of smoky, silky, and crunchy—perfect for a feast.

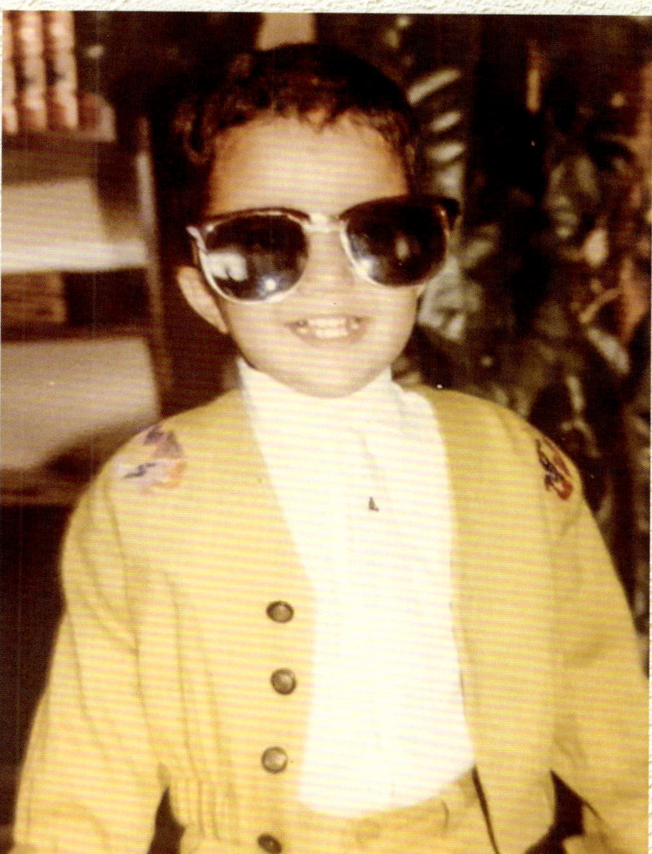

The day of our dinner, Kamal arrived with an armful of groceries, setting out the tahini, chickpeas, pomegranate molasses, and parsley haphazardly on the counter. Preparing the components of the dish, he seemed uncharacteristically befuddled. "Are you okay?" I asked him. In a shaky voice, he answered, "My mother called."

On social media, a cousin had found pictures of him and Tucker holding hands and shared the images with the larger group of cousins, who in turn posted screenshots to the family WhatsApp chat. When Kamal's phone rang at 3:00 a.m. the previous night, he had assumed the worst: Someone back home had died. Instead, his mother announced it was he who was dead to her. Then he started to receive threats from family members in Beirut suggesting he would be killed if he ever returned to Lebanon.

As an immigrant, it can feel like holding on to our roots, honoring our elders, and keeping up the traditions of our heritage are a sacred duty. Most of us want to stay true to the values we were raised with and do well by our parents. Yet sometimes the cost of embracing your truest identity comes at the expense of letting go of those you love most. Often, it can be more brutal than that. Living as who you are can mean being cast out of your own family, threatened even by those who claim to have loved you.

For Kamal, he hopes to one day sit down with his mother again, at a kitchen table laden with cookbooks and coffee. Though devastated by his mother's vitriol, he holds empathy for her. Married at fourteen and a mother at fifteen, she didn't have many options. Not long after Kamal came to the US, his parents divorced, leaving his mother largely dependent on her brothers. Kamal had sensed his uncles in the room when she called, a certain performative aspect to her rage.

Kamal and his mother no longer speak, though he still sends money home for her and his sisters. And he still cooks the beautiful, delicious foods of Lebanon he learned from her. When I ask Kamal if it hurts him at all to cook the dishes his mother taught him, he surprises me by saying no. It's through cooking that he feels closer to his family, even in exile. "It's a way to still spend time with them," he tells me. There are certain dishes he won't make, however—his mother's specialties. Those are too painful. But in general, he loves to cook the foods of his childhood, of his home, of his motherland, and share them with his found family, among whom Krishna and I are lucky to be counted. I am five years older than Kamal's mom, and happy to stand in for her in his life. But what I really want is for her to claim her elder son again, to realize that he is still the boy she raised, just grown now into the man he was always destined to be.

It's through cooking that he feels closer to his family, even in exile.

Fatteh Batinjan

ROASTED EGGPLANT LAYERED WITH CHICKPEAS, YOGURT, AND PITA

This is a grand-slam vegetable dish worthy of Ramadan or any occasion when you want to impress your guests. Smoky, sweet-tart, and tangy, the filling dish is also a riot of textures: silky, unctuous, crisp, and crunchy all at once. Fatteh batinjan should be served immediately—if you are including it as part of a large meal, add the butter-toasted pine nuts and garnishes just before everyone sits down to eat.

SERVES 12

3 large eggplants (about 1½ pounds each)
2 large red bell peppers
1 (15-ounce) can chickpeas, drained and rinsed
Kosher salt
½ teaspoon Spanish smoked paprika
Neutral oil, for frying
6 (6-inch) pitas, cut into 1-inch square pieces
2 tablespoons za'atar
2 teaspoons Lebanese 7-spice mixture (see Note)
1 cup plus 1 tablespoon well-mixed tahini (Kamal likes al Kanater brand)
4 tablespoons pomegranate molasses (I like Cortas brand)
½ teaspoon Aleppo chile flakes
3 cups whole-milk Greek yogurt
¼ cup fresh lemon juice (1 to 2 lemons)
1 garlic clove, mashed into a paste (about ½ teaspoon)
8 tablespoons (1 stick/ 4 ounces) unsalted butter
½ cup pine nuts
½ cup finely minced fresh flat-leaf parsley, for garnish
½ cup pomegranate seeds, for garnish

1. Preheat the oven to 450°F. Line a large sheet pan with parchment paper.
2. Use a sharp knife to poke holes all over 2 of the eggplants and both of the bell peppers and place on the lined pan. Roast until dark and wrinkled, 35 to 45 minutes.
3. In a wide pot, combine the chickpeas with water to cover by 1 inch and bring to a boil over medium heat. Boil until very soft and splitting, about 45 minutes. Drain, transfer to a large bowl, and mix with 1 teaspoon kosher salt and the smoked paprika.
4. Meanwhile, pour 1 to 2 inches of oil into another large wide pot and warm over medium heat to 290°F on a deep-fry thermometer; the oil should fizz when the end of a wooden spoon is dipped into it. Line a sheet pan with paper towels and set it near the stove. Working in batches to avoid crowding, fry the pita pieces until golden brown, stirring occasionally, 5 to 7 minutes. Transfer the pitas to the paper towels in a single layer. Immediately sprinkle the za'atar over the hot chips and toss gently to coat. Let the fried pita cool. Reserve the pot of oil.
5. Trim and peel the remaining raw eggplant and cut into 1-inch cubes. Spread the cubes out onto a large sheet pan and sprinkle with pinches of kosher salt. Use paper towels to dab excess moisture off the eggplant.
6. Set a rack over a sheet pan and keep it near the stove. Return the pot of oil to medium heat. Working in about 3 batches, add the eggplant cubes, stirring occasionally, until deep golden brown, 8 to 12 minutes. Transfer the fried eggplant cubes to the prepared rack and sprinkle with 1 teaspooon of the 7-spice mixture.
7. When the eggplant and red peppers are finished roasting, remove from the oven and cover with a dish towel for about 5 minutes to steam them. Remove the dish towel and cool until they can be handled, 5 to 10 minutes. Peel the skin off the eggplant and transfer the eggplant to a large bowl. (Or try this trick: Wrap plastic wrap around the eggplant, leaving an inch on the bottom exposed. Cut off the bottom and, holding the top, squeeze the soft eggplant out into the large bowl.) Rub the skins off the bell peppers, tear the peppers apart, discard the seeds and stem, and add to the bowl with the eggplant.

(Continued)

8. Use a potato masher to mash the eggplant and bell peppers together into a rough paste. Stir in ½ cup of the tahini, 2 tablespoons of the pomegranate molasses, the remaining 1 teaspoon 7-spice mixture, ¾ teaspoon kosher salt, and the Aleppo chile. Set aside.

9. In a medium bowl, mix the Greek yogurt and lemon juice. Then whisk in the remaining ½ cup plus 1 tablespoon tahini, ½ teaspoon kosher salt, and the garlic.

10. In a large (about 14-inch) round bowl (or 4-quart baking dish), spread the fried pita across the bottom. Top the pita with all of the fried eggplant, spreading evenly. Top with an even layer of the chickpeas. Use a spatula to gently spread the eggplant/pepper mixture on top. Carefully top the eggplant with the yogurt mixture. Do not mix it into the eggplant; you want the yogurt to remain white. Drizzle the remaining 2 tablespoons pomegranate molasses on top of the yogurt.

11. In a small skillet, melt the butter over medium-low heat. Add the pine nuts and cook, stirring constantly, until the pine nuts turn dark brown, about 2 minutes (the butter will also brown and foam). Immediately drizzle the pine nuts and butter on top of the dish. Garnish with the parsley and pomegranate seeds. Serve immediately.

Note: You can find Lebanese 7-spice mixture at Middle Eastern grocery stores or spice shops. You can also make it yourself: Mix together 1/4 teaspoon each of the following ground spices: black pepper, cumin, coriander, cinnamon, clove, nutmeg, and cardamom.

FEAST 3

Microplane

GRAINS

AND

NOODLES

Yogurt Tahdig

RICE WITH A CRISPY TOP

At first blush, this may seem like a simple pot of rice with some crunchy bits on the bottom. And yet I cannot overstate the amount of glee you will experience when successfully executing a showstopping tahdig. Flipping the pot and releasing the tahdig is a hold-your-breath moment. And, real talk, many times it sticks, even for those like Naz Deravian, who has made countless pots of this addictively crispy, saffron-hued Persian classic. I was lucky enough to learn how to make it at Naz's side when we filmed at her home in Los Angeles (see Maheecheh, page 235, for more on Naz). Persians are the only people I know who prize high-quality long-grained rice just as much as South Asians do and it was important to me to master this home-cooking benchmark. This recipe is adapted from Naz's excellent book, *Bottom of the Pot.*

SERVES 6

- **3 cups basmati rice, rinsed until the water runs clear**
- **Kosher salt**
- **½ teaspoon saffron threads, ground in a mortar with a pestle**
- **3 tablespoons whole-milk Greek yogurt**
- **4 tablespoons ghee or unsalted butter**
- **1 tablespoon extra-virgin olive oil**

Note: Make sure to set aside a platter that is wider than your pot. You will need this at the end to flip the tahdig.

1. In a bowl, combine the rinsed rice, cold water (2 to 3 cups, just covering the rice), and 2 tablespoons kosher salt and stir. Soak for a minimum of 30 minutes and up to 8 hours.
2. Fill a 5- or 6-quart nonstick pot with 12 cups water. Find a serving dish or plate that is just slightly wider than the pot and set it aside for now. Bring to a boil over high heat and add ¼ cup kosher salt. Drain the soaked rice (but do not rinse) and add it to the pot of boiling water. Stir once gently. Stand at the stove, watching for any boiling over. Skim any foam that rises to the top. As soon as you see the first grains float up, set a timer for 4 minutes. (I know this seems weird, but you'll get the best result.) Start testing the rice as soon as the time is up: You want a grain that's tender on the outside but a little hard in the center, which usually takes 5 to 7 minutes. As soon as the rice is ready, drain and give it one quick rinse with lukewarm water: A spray nozzle is great for this. Taste the rice. If it's too salty, give it another quick rinse. Drain completely. While the rice is draining, wash and dry the pot (remember, it's hot; be careful not to burn yourself).
3. Meanwhile, in a small bowl, steep the saffron in ¼ cup hot water.
4. Add 3 cups of the parboiled rice to a medium bowl. Add the Greek yogurt and 2 teaspoons of the saffron water and gently mix.
5. Heat the pot over medium heat. Add 2 tablespoons of the ghee and the olive oil and swirl together to melt the ghee. Gently ladle and spread the yogurt-rice mixture on the bottom of the pot, patting it lightly into an even layer, and taking care not to break the rice. Note how high this layer rises in the pot; this will become important later.
6. Gently pour in the rest of the rice in a pyramid-shaped mound. Make sure that the tahdig layer below is covered completely; use your ladle to mound from the outer edges to center, creating a mountain. Gently make 6 or 7 evenly spaced holes with a wooden spoon handle, being careful to push just to where the tahdig layer starts, not to the very bottom of the pot. This allows steam to escape, but don't poke through to the bottom because you want the tahdig layer to be solid and crispy.

(Continued)

7. Increase the heat to medium-high, cover the pot, and cook until the pot is hot enough so that a few drops of water splashed on the outside produce an instant sizzle and evaporate. This may take an additional 3 to 10 minutes.

8. While the tahdig sets, in a small saucepan on the stovetop or a microwave-safe bowl in the microwave, melt the remaining 2 tablespoons butter and add it to the remaining saffron water.

9. Reduce the heat under the pot of rice to medium-low. Lift the lid (without dripping the condensation trapped under the lid back into the pot) and drizzle the butter-saffron mixture over the rice. Wrap the lid in a kitchen towel or a couple of layers of paper towel to catch the condensation. Make sure the kitchen towel or paper towels are secured on top so that they don't catch fire. Place the lid firmly back on the pot. Increase the heat to medium and cook until steam begins to escape from the sides of the pot, about 10 minutes. Then reduce the heat to medium-low or low (depending on your burner) and place a heat diffuser under the pot, if you have one. Cook until the rice is tender and fluffy, 20 to 30 minutes.

10. To help release the tahdig, fill the sink with about 1 inch cold water and quickly set the rice pot in the water. Leave it in the water until the side of the pot is cool enough to handle, at least 10 minutes. (Alternatively, you can soak a couple of kitchen towels with cold water, set some ice cubes on top, and set the pot on top for a few seconds. The ice will melt, and the pot will cool.) At this point, you can release the rice (next step) or leave the pot at room temperature for 1 hour or so, though this may mean a less crunchy top.

11. To serve, top the pot with a serving platter that is just slightly wider than the pot. Grip the handles with your fingers while placing your thumbs tightly over the platter. Make sure they are pressed together to make a seal. Quickly and carefully flip the pot over, place the platter on the counter. Let it sit there for a second: you should hear a shuffling noise when the tahdig falls from the bottom of the pot. (If you don't hear this, tap the bottom of the pot with a heavy ladle to loosen the crust.) Gently lift the pot. You should see a crust of crispy golden charred rice. It may be broken, or it may be whole. Either way, if you've achieved this, congratulations. If you haven't, don't sweat it. Serve warm.

Note: Some tips that will boost your chances of tahdig success. First, it is imperative to use a nonstick pot. Yes, yes, we know that in the old country they did it beautifully without one, but why make this harder on yourself? Second, consider enlisting a friend to read the recipe out loud as you make it. Tahdig is one of those recipes that depends on timing. You do not want to be distracted or leave the side of the stove at the wrong time. And remember, if it doesn't work out, you still have an exceptional pot of rice.

Congri / Moros y Cristianos

RICE AND BLACK BEANS

I got to hang with the fabulous Cuban family of chef Monica "Mika" Leon for Noche Buena (Christmas Eve) while filming *Taste the Nation* in Miami. Mika's cousins are great dancers, and her uncle makes a killer rum cocktail (Emergency Mojito, page 298). But my favorite family member was Mika's mother, Lupita Estupiñan, mostly because she reminded me of my own mother. Mika and I have both built successful careers in food, and yet when we cook with our mothers, they insist on treating us as if we were still learning to walk. When Mika and her mother quarreled over when to add the rice in this dish, I was instantly reminded of my mother and me bickering over whether or not to add jaggery to rasam. Then Lupita really stole my heart by saving for me the ear of the roasted pig, a special treat reserved for an honored guest. Here I've adapted Mika's recipe for Cuban rice and black beans, which her family (and many others) call congri. It's also referred to as Moros y Cristianos.

SERVES 4 TO 6

4 ounces dried black beans, rinsed well
3 bay leaves
Kosher salt
4 ounces bacon, chopped
6 garlic cloves, finely chopped (2 to 3 tablespoons)
2 small white onions, finely chopped (about 2 cups)
1 teaspoon ground cumin
1 teaspoon dried thyme
1 teaspoon dried oregano, preferably Mexican or Dominican
½ teaspoon red chile flakes
1 small green bell pepper, finely chopped (about 1 cup)
2 cups parboiled rice (Mika likes Iberia brand), rinsed well
1 tablespoon extra-virgin olive oil, if desired

1. In a large pot, combine the beans, 1 of the bay leaves, 1 teaspoon kosher salt, and 5 cups water. Bring to a boil over high heat. Reduce the heat to medium-low, partially cover, and simmer until the beans are tender, about 1 hour. Add ¼ cup water at a time if necessary to keep the beans submerged. Remove from the heat. Do not drain.

2. Line a plate with paper towels and set near the stove. Warm a large Dutch oven over medium-low heat. Add the bacon and cook until crisp, stirring frequently and covering with the lid ajar to prevent sticking, 12 to 17 minutes. Remove the bacon with a slotted spoon and transfer it to the paper towels. Reserve the bacon fat in the pot.

3. Reduce the heat to low, add the garlic, and sauté for 30 seconds. Add the onion and the remaining 2 bay leaves, increase the heat to medium, and stir for just 1 minute. Add the cumin, thyme, oregano, and chile flakes and sauté until the onions are glassy, about 4 minutes. Stir in the bell pepper and ½ teaspoon salt, cover, and cook, stirring occasionally, until the pepper is soft, about 5 minutes.

4. Stir in the cooked beans and all their cooking liquid, the rice, cooked bacon, and ½ teaspoon salt. Add a splash of water to submerge the rice, if necessary. Increase the heat to medium-high and bring to a boil. Reduce the heat to low, cover, and simmer until the rice is cooked, stirring occasionally, 20 to 25 minutes. If desired, drizzle with the olive oil before serving.

Coconut Rice

This dish is one of the big reasons I always keep a bag of shredded coconut in the freezer. When I was young, and if there was little in the house except for leftover rice, my mom would throw this together in the time it took me to shower after playing outside. All it takes are a few handfuls of nuts, lentils, and aromatics, plus some fresh or frozen coconut, and you have a rice dish worthy of a dinner party. This goes fast, so it is imperative to measure out *all* your ingredients before cooking and have them at the ready next to the stove. Coconut rice tastes great at room temperature, so consider packing it for a picnic, adding it to a buffet, or bringing it to a potluck.

SERVES 4 TO 6

3 tablespoons neutral oil
1/2 teaspoon black mustard seeds
1/4 cup raw or roasted whole cashews
2 serrano chiles, halved lengthwise
12 fresh curry leaves, torn into pieces
4 dried red chiles, broken into small pieces
1 tablespoon chana dal
1 1/2 teaspoons split skinless urad dal
1/2 teaspoon asafoetida powder
2 cups shredded unsweetened coconut (about 1 pound), fresh or thawed frozen
1 teaspoon minced fresh ginger
4 cups day-old cooked basmati or other long-grain rice (see Note), at room temperature or cold
Kosher salt

1. In a large nonstick skillet, heat the oil over medium-high heat. Add the mustard seeds and fry until they start popping, about 30 seconds. Add the cashews and serrano chiles and stir until the cashews darken slightly and the skin of the chiles begins to loosen, 1 to 2 minutes. Add half of the curry leaves, the dried chiles, chana dal, urad dal, and asafoetida and stir until the lentils color slightly, about 20 seconds.

2. Add the shredded coconut, the remaining curry leaves, and the ginger. Stir to combine and sauté until the coconut is dry and golden and the lentils are golden brown, 2 to 3 minutes.

3. Reduce the heat to low, add the rice, and stir, gently breaking up any clumps, until the rice is heated through and lightly toasted, 2 to 3 minutes. Remove from the heat and add 1 teaspoon kosher salt, or to taste. Serve warm or at room temperature.

Note: If you want to make this but don't have leftover rice, go ahead and make fresh rice, then spread it out on a tray or baking sheet and use your fingers to gently break up any clumps. Let it sit uncovered for an hour or two so that the rice dehydrates slightly. This will help the grains stay intact when the rice is stirred into the coconut mixture.

Level Up: Sure, you can buy bags of frozen shredded coconut from Asian markets, but why not try cracking your own coconut? It's easier than you think, and so satisfying. Buy a mature brown coconut and find a super-sturdy, solid surface. Have a bowl ready to catch the coconut water that will leak out. Grip the coconut across its side, between the two ends, and smash it forcefully onto the surface, taking care not to smash your fingers in the process. Reserve as much coconut water as you can in the bowl. Separate the coconut halves, use a sharp paring knife to pry the meat off the hard shell, and toss the coconut meat into a high-powered blender to shred. Store extra coconut in the freezer.

Southeast Asian–Inspired Risotto

RICE PORRIDGE WITH SHRIMP AND COCONUT MILK

Living in Italy during my twenties, I ate many comforting, warming bowls of risotto. Years later, while enjoying a bowl of lemongrass-scented coconut curry with rice, it occurred to me that it was comforting in the same way that risotto always was. How great would it be to make a dairy-free risotto with all the Asian flavors that I loved? Two ingredients I knew would make the dish pop: fresh makrut lime leaves and fish sauce. The culinary boundary-crossing result has proved a major crowd-pleaser among my family and friends. As a bonus, making the dish leaves you with shrimp shells and tails, as well as mushroom stems, that you can save for a later batch of broth. Bay scallops would be a lovely swap for shrimp; just adjust the cooking time as needed.

SERVES 4

- 1 pound medium shrimp, peeled and deveined, tails removed
- 4 tablespoons fresh lemon juice (1 to 2 lemons), plus more to taste
- 4 tablespoons fish sauce (I like Red Boat 40°N brand)
- 1 medium yellow onion, roughly chopped (about 1 1/2 cups)
- 2 heaping tablespoons roughly chopped fresh lemongrass (cut from the tender bottom half of the stalk, outer layers removed)
- 2 tablespoons roughly chopped peeled fresh ginger
- 2 large garlic cloves, peeled but whole
- 6 fresh makrut lime leaves, stem and midrib removed
- 2 teaspoons coriander seeds, dry-roasted (see page xx)
- 1/2 teaspoon Thai chile powder
- 1/2 teaspoon ground turmeric
- 4 cups Essential Chicken Broth (page 54), Vegetable Broth (page 56), or store-bought chicken or vegetable broth or stock
- 1/4 cup neutral oil
- 1 1/2 cups sushi rice, rinsed until the water runs clear
- 10 ounces shiitake mushrooms, stems removed, caps thinly sliced (about 5 1/2 cups)
- 1 (13.5-ounce) can unsweetened coconut milk, preferably full-fat
- Kosher salt
- 1 cup roughly chopped fresh cilantro leaves
- 4 fresh green chiles, sliced (optional)

(Continued)

1. In a medium bowl, toss the shrimp with 1 tablespoon of the lemon juice and 1 tablespoon of the fish sauce. Cover and set aside to marinate at room temperature.
2. In a small food processor or blender, blend the remaining 3 tablespoons fish sauce, the onion, lemongrass, ginger, garlic, lime leaves, coriander seeds, chile powder, turmeric, and 1 cup of the broth. Blend until smooth and set aside.
3. In a large deep skillet, heat the oil over medium heat. When the oil starts to shimmer, add the rice and toast until golden brown, about 2 minutes. Add the mushrooms and cook, stirring constantly, for 2 minutes. Pour in the onion mixture. Add 1 cup of broth to the blender, swish around to capture all the leftover aromatics, and pour that into the skillet.
4. Reduce the heat to medium-low, cover, and cook until the water reduces and becomes a little cloudy, 5 to 6 minutes. Stir, add 1 cup of the broth, cover, and cook for 5 minutes. Add the remaining 1 cup broth and cook, stirring frequently, for 5 minutes.
5. Add the coconut milk and 1 teaspoon kosher salt, stir well, cover, and cook until the rice is al dente and the risotto is thick but still spreads out when spooned into a shallow dish, about 5 minutes.
6. Add the shrimp and stir until just cooked through, 2 to 3 minutes. Stir in ¾ cup of the cilantro and the remaining 2 tablespoons lemon juice, adding more to taste.
7. Garnish with the remaining ¼ cup cilantro and the chiles (if using) and serve immediately.

Jollof Rice

RICE WITH ROASTED TOMATOES AND PEPPERS

My friend Precious Okoyomon, an artist and poet, grew up in Ohio and is the child of Nigerian immigrants. Precious taught me how to make this unorthodox version of jollof rice—while it's safe to say that Nigerians do *not* normally add sun-dried tomatoes or dashi to their rice, Precious says that in their neck of the woods in Ohio, "this is how we do it now." I can see why: Both give this rice dish a deep umami flavor. Jollof is popular in various West African countries. Traditionally, Nigerian jollof rice is cooked in large batches over an open fire, which gives it its characteristic smoky element. Precious and I found a way to impart this smoky flavor in a home kitchen: Carefully singe a few sprigs of fresh rosemary over a flame and then use them to infuse the oil in which you toast the parboiled rice.

West African jollof rice is the ancestor to Gullah Geechee red rice, and it's easy to see the similarities once you've tried them both side by side, as food historian Michael Twitty demonstrated for me in the Gullah Geechee episode of *Taste the Nation*. Serve this with Maheecheh (page 235) or Desert Chicken (page 200), with Cabbage Poriyal (page 91) or Spicy Coleslaw (page 36) on the side.

SERVES 4 TO 6

4 plum tomatoes, halved
2 bell peppers, red and green, quartered and seeded
1 large red onion, quartered, layers separated, plus 1 small red onion chopped (about 1 cup)
½ cup neutral oil (see Notes)
Kosher salt and freshly ground black pepper
4 medium garlic cloves, peeled but whole
1-inch knob peeled fresh ginger, or 1 tablespoon chopped fresh ginger
1 to 2 fresh small habanero chiles, to taste, stemmed
2 (4- to 5-inch) sprigs fresh rosemary
4 (6-inch) sprigs fresh thyme
2 cups parboiled rice, rinsed well (I used Ben's Original brand)
2 tablespoons tomato paste
1½ cups dashi (see Notes), chicken stock, or vegetable stock
4 oil-packed sun-dried tomatoes, finely chopped (about 2 tablespoons)
2 tablespoons chopped fresh parsley leaves

1. Preheat the oven to 450°F. Line a large sheet pan with parchment paper.
2. Spread the tomatoes, bell peppers, and quartered onion on the lined pan. Toss with 2 tablespoons of the oil and sprinkle with kosher salt and pepper. Roast until the edges of the onions are charred, about 25 minutes. Remove the onions and continue to roast until the rest of the vegetables have charred edges, about another 10 minutes. Let cool.
3. Transfer the cooled vegetables to a high-powered blender and add the garlic, ginger, habanero, and 2 teaspoons kosher salt. Puree until smooth.
4. If you have a gas stove, turn one burner on low. Pick up one sprig of rosemary, carefully hold it about 6 inches over the flame, rotate constantly to char over the flame until lightly singed and smoky, 15 to 45 seconds. Transfer to a plate and repeat with the second sprig of rosemary, then each sprig of thyme, which will take less time. Be careful not to completely burn the herbs. (If you have an electric stove, use a lighter to do this.)
5. In a large skillet, heat 2 tablespoons of the oil over medium-high heat. Add the rosemary and thyme, then stir in the rice. Sauté the rice, stirring constantly for 2 minutes to toast. Remove from the heat and discard the rosemary and thyme stems.
6. In a large pot, warm 2 tablespoons of the oil over medium heat. Add the chopped onions and sauté for 1 minute. Add a pinch of salt and sauté until glassy, about 5 minutes. Add the tomato paste and stir constantly until darkened, about 1 minute. Add the dashi, stir to combine, scraping the bottom of the pan. Simmer stirring occasionally to reduce slightly, about 2 minutes.

7. Pour the vegetable puree out of the blender into the pot. It may look like a lot of liquid, but don't worry. Add ½ cup water to the blender, swirl to wash out the excess puree, stir that into the pot, and simmer for 3 minutes. Stir in the rice, increase the heat to medium-high, and bring to a gentle boil. Reduce the heat to low, cover the pot, and cook undisturbed for 25 minutes.

8. Uncover, and without disturbing the crust on bottom, stir in the sun-dried tomatoes gently. Cover, increase the heat to medium-low, and cook until the rice is tender, 5 to 15 minutes. Remove from the heat, uncover, and let sit for at least 10 minutes to continue to absorb the liquid. Garnish with the parsley.

Notes:

This dish is traditionally made with palm oil, which gives it an unmistakable flavor, but we use neutral oil in this version instead. Palm oil is a controversial ingredient for many reasons, including its role in deforestation and other environmental concerns, but it is also deeply rooted in West African culture. It's not my place to weigh in on that, other than to say that if you have palm oil in your larder already, better to use it than waste it.

You can make the dashi from 1½ cups warm water and 1½ teaspoons HonDashi, which is a brand of instant dashi.

BJ

I use everything I have to pull that crab trap out of the reedy marsh off Wadmalaw Island. It's a steamy August day in South Carolina. The air feels heavy and thick. When the trap surfaces, it's squirming with crabs. I feel a strange elation. This is like nothing I've ever done before. Gullah crabber Keith Smiley and I unlatch the trap door and dump the crabs into a crate. Then it's time to set the trap again. "Grab your fish," Keith tells me. I reach for a few shad to use as bait and lower the trap back into the water, my gloves covered in fish guts and blood. Keith encourages me the way you would a child learning to ride a bike for the first time: "We got a real crabber," he yells to his son, Jerrel Brown, as the trap sinks slowly back into the marsh.

For generations, crabbing has helped sustain families living in these parts. But now real estate development, offshore oil prospecting, and climate change have affected the marine ecosystem drastically. Each of Keith's fifty traps used to yield a bushel a day—today, he's lucky if he catches half that.

Back at Keith's property, we meet my old friend chef BJ Dennis. He greets me with open arms and a bag of my favorite boiled peanuts. It's like no time has passed since I last saw him in 2016. He and Jerrel haul the crabs to a long rickety table. Vegetables, a cutting board, and a portable camp stove rest on its surface. A large crab pot filled with water boils violently over the burner. BJ adds some crabs to the pot, then carefully pours in his secret "hot blend." I can smell the fumes of the Scotch bonnets, garlic, and parsley as the pot swallows the puree in its bubbles. Today, we are making crab rice.

We catch up under the lacy trees, and chop vegetables as I sneak handfuls of peanuts. BJ teaches me how to crack a hot crab claw by biting down on a specific spot on the shell. I am sure I crack a tooth in the process. We gather the crabmeat, toast it in a hot frying pan, then set that aside while we sauté the vegetables and aromatics. Then we toss in the Carolina Gold rice. My back is soaked with sweat and my fingers throb from the heat of the crabs and Scotch bonnets. Reunited with my friend, I am completely happy.

BJ and I met some years ago when I came to Charleston to film a season of *Top Chef.* We became fast friends during a biscuit challenge. I instantly fell in love with his Geechee accent, gentle manner, and shy smile. We would spend the filming breaks together, trading childhood stories and comparing notes on food. Later that season, I hired his team to cater lunch for all our *Top Chef* crew. Every season I hosted a lunch on set for everyone, usually bringing in a local specialty. I always felt bad that our camera operators and grips had to watch me, Tom, and Gail eat luxurious food all day while the catering they got was so basic and often bland. It was the meal the crew looked forward to most. BJ did not disappoint. At lunch, he explained how Gullah Geechee cuisine was based off the land. BJ said that most Gullah families fished and crabbed and had kitchen gardens where they grew all their own produce. BJ spoke lovingly of his grandmother's garden, where she grew okra and other seasonal vegetables. He was a compelling ambassador for Gullah cuisine, stoking my curiosity enough to bring me back here for *Taste the Nation*.

As the sun dips, we set the table, laying newspaper down first. Keith's wife, Mona Lisa, joins us, along with BJ's cousin Dr. Jessica Berry, an educator who works to preserve and protect Gullah Geechee heritage and culture, especially the Gullah language. The culture, which spans Georgia and both North and South Carolina, is understood to be a direct link to the West African cuisine and culture brought here by generations of enslaved Africans. This part of the Carolinas was quite rural until about seventy years ago. Many of the sea islands off South Carolina did not have bridges to connect them to the mainland until the 1950s. This is one of the reasons the culture has remained uniquely preserved. It's a deep, fascinating part of American history, especially when you consider that up to 65 percent of enslaved people came through Charleston and

were sold at what was called Ryan's Mart, now called the Old Slave Mart. I'm astonished that I didn't learn any of this in high school. We should have all learned about it.

The fireflies come out and the sun is only a memory. Burnt orange streaks the sky. We are drenched to the elbows with crab and pepper juice as the din of crickets and marsh frogs drowns out almost all conversation. Mona Lisa's smile can still be seen in the dimming light. Dr. Berry explains how Gullah children were discriminated against for speaking the Gullah language, which White teachers wrongly perceived as "broken English" rather than the distinct creole language it is, one that includes over three hundred loanwords from different African languages. This land contains so much important history; it tells us who we, as a country, are and perhaps can be, if only we would contend with it wholly and with humility. We cannot heal what we won't truly acknowledge.

I am full of crab and rice and heat. I make myself a promise to come back here without a camera crew and wander some more. The next morning as I'm packing the last bits into my suitcase, BJ arrives at my hotel with a care package: a hot breakfast of cheesy grits and shrimp for the road. A parcel of Gullah history and friendship that warms my lap as I ride to the airport.

This land contains so much important history; it tells us who we, as a country, are and perhaps can be, if only we would contend with it wholly and with humility.

From left to right: Dr. Jessica Berry, Keith Smiley, Mona Lisa Smiley, Jerrel Brown, me, and BJ Dennis

Crab Fried Rice

This dish is inspired by the crab fried rice my friend chef BJ Dennis and I made under the August sun after crabbing with Keith Smiley in South Carolina. It's a great way to feed a lot of people during crabbing season, but it's also wonderful year-round when made with high-quality jumbo lump crabmeat from a can. Bottom line: Use the best crab you can. And don't skip the caramelization; that helps keep the crabmeat distinct from the grains of rice. If you're a vegetarian, or don't have crab, this is still an excellent fried rice recipe without it. You could top the rice with a fried egg, or not. Traditionally, this dish is made with Carolina Gold rice, but I prefer basmati, because of its longer grain and firmer texture.

SERVES 4 TO 6

- ½ cup neutral oil
- 1 pound jumbo lump crabmeat, canned and drained, or fresh
- 2 small yellow onions, diced (about 2 cups)
- Kosher salt
- 4 small garlic cloves, minced (about 4 teaspoons)
- 2 tablespoons minced fresh ginger
- 1 red bell pepper, seeded and diced (about 1½ cups)
- 2 teaspoons smoked paprika
- 1 to 2 teaspoons cayenne pepper, to taste
- 2 tablespoons unsalted butter
- 6 cups day-old cooked basmati (or Carolina Gold) rice, at room temperature
- Freshly ground black pepper
- ½ cup chopped fresh parsley
- 4 to 5 scallions, white and green parts, chopped (about ¾ cup)
- 2 tablespoons fresh lemon juice (optional)

1. In a large skillet, heat ¼ cup of the oil over high heat. Add the crabmeat and sauté, gently stirring to preserve the lumps, until the crab is warmed through and slightly caramelized on the edges, 2 to 3 minutes. Transfer the crab to a bowl and set aside.
2. Reduce the heat under the skillet to medium. Add the remaining ¼ cup oil, scraping any bits of crab off the bottom of the pan, and add the onions and 2 teaspoons kosher salt. Sauté, stirring frequently, until the onions are softened, about 8 minutes. Add the garlic and ginger and stir until combined, about 1 minute. Add the bell pepper and sauté, stirring frequently, until just softened, 3 to 4 minutes. Add the smoked paprika and cayenne and stir until combined, 1 to 2 minutes.
3. Add the butter and stir until melted, a few seconds. Add the rice, 2 teaspoons kosher salt, and ½ teaspoon black pepper, reduce the heat to low, and gently mix, breaking up any clumps in the rice, until everything is combined and warmed through, 2 to 3 minutes.
4. Add the reserved crabmeat to the pan and stir to combine. Add the parsley and scallions, toss, and serve. Add the lemon juice (if using).

Rice "Stuffing"
with Chinese Sausage and Shiitake Mushrooms

Every year, my family changes up the flavors of our Thanksgiving. One year, our whole spread was inspired by Mexican flavors; the next year, we did Moroccan. One year, I really wanted to do a Chinese-influenced Thanksgiving, but I was struggling with how to do that beyond brushing soy sauce and five-spice powder on my turkey. This delicious old-school stuffing, adapted from my friend Meeling Wong's, became the shining star of our feast. Meeling makes it for Thanksgiving every year, and I now make it all the time as a main course, especially on those cold days when I just want a one-pot meal. Sometimes I serve it with steamed green beans with a little black bean sauce on top. It would also make a great second course after the Tomato Egg Drop Soup (page 62) or Tuna Larb (page 166). I recommend cooking this in a nonstick skillet, but if you can't, don't be upset by any char that develops on the bottom of your skillet; it just adds to the stuffing's flavor and texture.

SERVES 4 TO 6

1 cup dried sliced shiitake mushrooms (about 1 ounce)
4 ounces lap cheong (Chinese sausage), cut on the bias into slices 1/4 inch thick (about 1 cup)
2 large garlic cloves, minced (about 1 tablespoon)
1 tablespoon minced fresh ginger
2 tablespoons neutral oil
2 cups sushi rice, rinsed until the water runs clear
1/2 cup (about 3 ounces) roasted peeled chestnuts, quartered
2 tablespoons soy sauce, plus more to taste
1 teaspoon ground white pepper, plus more to taste
4 cups Essential Chicken Broth (page 54) or store-bought chicken broth or stock
Toasted sesame oil, for drizzling
Fried Shallots (optional; page 204), for garnish

1. In a small bowl, combine the dried shiitakes with room-temperature water and set aside to rehydrate for at least 15 minutes. Drain.
2. Heat a lidded large deep nonstick sauté pan or Dutch oven over medium heat. Add the sausage and sauté until the fat renders and the sausage is crisp and browned, 3 to 5 minutes. Use a slotted spoon to transfer the sausage to a medium bowl, reserving the fat in the skillet.
3. Add the shiitakes, garlic, and ginger and sauté until the mushrooms are lightly browned, 4 to 5 minutes. Transfer to the bowl with the sausage.
4. Add the neutral oil and rice to the skillet and stir frequently to coat the rice with oil, about 2 minutes. Add the sausage and mushroom mixture, chestnuts, soy sauce, and white pepper and stir frequently until the rice is uniformly brown and the ingredients are well mixed, 3 to 4 minutes.
5. Pour in the chicken broth, cover the pan, and bring to a boil. Reduce the heat to low to maintain a gentle simmer and cook undisturbed until the rice is tender and the liquid is absorbed, about 25 minutes. Taste and add more soy sauce or pepper to taste.
6. Serve drizzled with the sesame oil and garnished with fried shallots (if using). Serve warm.

Krishna's Upma-Style Sriracha Butter Couscous

In the mid-1970s, I came from India to live with my mother in New York City. "All I wanted was a job, an apartment, and Padma," she remembers. She achieved that, but our family and close friends all remained in India. Except for my mom, I was suddenly alone in a new country. To help me feel at home in this strange new place, she made familiar Indian comfort foods, adapting her recipes based on the ingredients she could find. One of my favorites was upma, a savory South Indian dish eaten for breakfast or afternoon tea. At the time, my mother couldn't find the rava or sooji (semolina) flour she needed to make upma, so she improvised with, well, Cream of Wheat. She would add the fried dals and seeds that are traditional in upma, as well as vegetables to make the dish more nutritious. The ingredients may have been different, but the scents, flavors, and textures seemed just right to me. When my daughter, Krishna, was little, I began making a version of upma for her, using couscous. This evolved into Krishna's making her own version with the sriracha she loves, its heat tempered by butter and milk. I've adapted it here and found that cooking couscous in milk (her idea) is a game changer as it gives the couscous an incomparable richness. I recommend topping it with a fried egg to turn it into a full meal. My daughter may see this just as delicious couscous, but I see it as a link in an enduring chain, the most recent translation of a dish that generations of my family have known and loved.

SERVES 4 TO 6

1 cup whole milk
8 tablespoons (1 stick/4 ounces) unsalted butter, cut into 1-tablespoon pieces
Kosher salt
2 cups couscous
1 small yellow onion, finely diced (about 1 cup)
2 large carrots, peeled and finely diced (about 1 cup)
3 to 4 small celery stalks, finely diced (about 1 cup)
6 tablespoons sriracha, plus more to taste

1. In a medium pot, combine 2 cups water, the milk, 1 tablespoon of the butter, and a pinch of kosher salt. Cover and bring to a rapid simmer over medium-high heat. Mix in the couscous, cover the pot, remove from the heat, and let stand for 5 minutes. Remove the cover and fluff the couscous quickly with a fork. Bury 3 tablespoons of the butter under the couscous and let it melt. Set aside uncovered.
2. In a large skillet, melt the remaining 4 tablespoons butter over medium heat. Add the onion and sauté for 1 minute. Add ½ teaspoon salt and sauté until glassy and slightly browned at the edges, 4 to 5 minutes. Add the carrots and sauté until slightly softened, about 3 minutes. Add the celery and ¼ teaspoon salt and sauté until softened, 3 to 4 minutes. Add 2 tablespoons of the sriracha and stir until the vegetables are coated, about 1 minute. Remove from the heat.
3. Stir the remaining 4 tablespoons sriracha into the couscous. Gently mix in the vegetables. Add more sriracha to taste. Serve warm.

Uova in Trippa

EGG "NOODLES" IN TOMATO-BASIL SAUCE

Eating this magical Roman dish of delicate ribbons of egg tossed in a fresh tomato and basil sauce feels like eating a plate of pasta. But there are no noodles here, just tender strands of pan-cooked eggs. If you overhear me ordering "the usual" for brunch on weekends at Il Posto Accanto in the East Village, you'll know this is coming to the table. Il Posto's owner (and my dear friend), Beatrice Tosti di Valminuta, grew up eating *uova in trippa,* which literally translates to "eggs in tripe" (probably because of its appearance, because despite its name there is no tripe in the dish). Marinating the tomatoes starts the cooking process: It releases their juices and deepens their flavor. Bea's favorite way to eat this dish is to refrigerate it overnight, then warm it in the oven the next morning; the eggs hold up surprisingly well and the flavors deepen. The uncooked sauce is also excellent on toasted or grilled crusty bread for a pitch-perfect bruschetta.

SERVES 4

SAUCE

1 pound Campari or Roma tomatoes, quartered, or 1 (14.5-ounce) can whole peeled tomatoes with juices, quartered
2 cups grape tomatoes, halved
1/4 cup extra-virgin olive oil
About 10 fresh basil leaves, torn or roughly chopped
2 small garlic cloves, coarsely chopped (about 2 teaspoons)
1/2 teaspoon red chile flakes
Fine sea salt

EGGS

8 large eggs
2 tablespoons grated Parmigiano-Reggiano cheese, plus more for serving
2 tablespoons grated Pecorino Romano cheese
2 tablespoons chopped fresh parsley
Fine sea salt and freshly ground black pepper
1 stick (4 ounces) unsalted butter, for the pan (you need the whole stick for ease; you will have some left)
Extra-virgin olive oil, for the pan

1. **Prepare the sauce:** In a large bowl, combine the Campari or canned tomatoes, the grape tomatoes, olive oil, basil, garlic, chile flakes, and ½ teaspoon sea salt. Stir and adjust the seasoning to taste, until it smells "interesting," as Beatrice says. Cover and let rest.

2. **Prepare the eggs:** In a medium bowl, combine the eggs, Parmigiano, pecorino, parsley, ½ teaspoon sea salt, and a few grinds of black pepper. Whisk or use an immersion blender to combine well.

3. Warm a 10-inch nonstick skillet over medium heat. Have a wide spatula ready, and place a flat plate or platter next to the stove. Use the end of the stick of butter to coat the pan, followed by a few drops of olive oil. When the fat is bubbling slightly, ladle ¼ cup of the egg mixture into the hot pan, swirling the pan right away to spread the egg over the whole surface of the pan like a crepe. Cook until the edges are lacy and the egg sheet loses its gloss, about 45 seconds. Gently loosen the edges of the sheet, then push the spatula under and flip over. Cook until solid and opaque, about 20 seconds. Transfer the egg sheet to the flat plate or platter.

4. Repeat with the remaining egg mixture, each time adding more butter and oil to the pan and whisking the eggs before ladling another ¼ cup onto the skillet. Expect that at least one "sheet" of eggs will break. This is fine and happens. Expect that one might get too brown. Ideally, you want no brown. After you make two or three, the pan may get scalding hot; don't be afraid to cool it off with a quick rinse, wipe dry, and resume. Stack the cooked egg sheets on top of one another on the plate. You should have about 8 sheets. Cool to room temperature, about 5 minutes.

5. Stack 2 egg sheets at a time on a cutting board. Roll them up into a cylinder and cut each roll crosswise into ½-inch ribbons. Do this with the remaining sheets. Transfer to a plate and set aside while you cook the sauce.

(Continued)

1
2
3
4
5
6
7
8
9

6. Reheat the skillet over medium heat. Carefully ladle the tomato mixture into the pan. Increase the heat to high and mix the tomatoes until they begin to bubble. Reduce the heat and let the sauce simmer, stirring occasionally, until the tomatoes collapse and the liquid reduces, about 10 minutes. Add salt and pepper to taste.

7. Separate the egg ribbons and add to the skillet. Gently stir and simmer until the flavors marry, 3 to 4 minutes. If you'd like, you can serve immediately, topped with some grated Parmigiano. Or you can transfer to a baking dish, cover, and refrigerate overnight. The next day, preheat the oven to 400°F, shower with extra Parmigiano, and bake for 20 minutes to warm through.

Pasta all'Amatriciana

RIGATONI AND PORK CHEEK PASTA

For years, Krishna had a play kitchen; she loved making pretend versions of dishes I made. There were Velcro veggies cut with a play knife, then a tiny salad with real cottage cheese and pomegranate seeds—the first recipe she made up herself and insisted I write down. I still eat it today. She would often pull up a stool at the stove to watch me cook. She also had a tiny colander, pretending to strain pasta for Amatriciana. She loved the dish, in large part because it was a hard word to say. She felt grown up. We used rigatoni instead of bucatini because that's what fit in her strainer. It also catches the sauce better. Many traditional recipes use onion and/or garlic, but I keep it simple. The addition of white wine to the sauce gives it a complexity that goes beyond just fat and acid. But don't worry, the alcohol burns off before serving. For more on sharing cooking with kids, please read *Tomatoes for Neela,* a children's book based on our adventures in the kitchen.

SERVES 4

1 to 2 tablespoons extra-virgin olive oil
6 ounces guanciale, cut into 1/4 × 1/2-inch pieces (or substitute pancetta or thick-cut cured bacon)
3 tablespoons dry white wine
1 teaspoon red chile flakes
1 (28-ounce) can whole tomatoes and their juices, cut into quarters or broken up with your fingers
Fine sea salt
1 pound rigatoni pasta (I like De Cecco brand)
1/2 cup shredded Pecorino Romano cheese, plus more for serving

1. Bring about 4 quarts water to a roaring boil in a large covered pot over high heat.
2. Meanwhile, in a Dutch oven or large, deep sauté pan, heat the olive oil over medium heat. Add the guanciale and distribute evenly across the surface of the pan. Cover the pan to avoid sticking and cook until the fat becomes translucent, about 2 minutes. Uncover and cook, stirring constantly, until the guanciale is crisp, about 5 minutes. Add the white wine (beware of splattering!). Reduce for about 10 seconds, then use a slotted spoon to remove the guanciale and set aside on a plate.
3. Add the chile flakes to the pan and cook for a few seconds, then carefully add the tomatoes (again, beware of splattering). Bring to a simmer and cook, breaking up the tomatoes with the ladle, until the sauce begins to thicken and reduce, 8 to 10 minutes. Remove from the heat.
4. When the water comes to a boil, add 2 tablespoons salt and stir. Add the pasta and cook until almost al dente, about 2 minutes less than the package directions. Reserving 1 cup of the pasta cooking water, drain and add the pasta to the Dutch oven.
5. Add ¼ cup of the reserved pasta water, stir to combine, and place the pan over low heat. If you feel the sauce is too dry, stir in more pasta water, a little at a time. Mix in the pecorino until melted. Add the guanciale, stir to combine, and simmer for about a minute, reducing the liquid further, if you like. Remove from the heat and serve with additional pecorino.

Spaghetti alla Carbonara

PASTA WITH EGGS AND PANCETTA

Banish everyone from the kitchen when you make this unctuous Roman dish. It deserves your undivided attention. Timing and technique are critical and you don't want to miss a vital step because someone distracts you at the wrong moment. Many cooks, including the great Marcella Hazan, add garlic and parsley to carbonara or make it with guanciale instead of pancetta. My carbonara has only five ingredients: pancetta, eggs, noodles, salt, and black pepper. This simple version relies on the spiky heat from freshly cracked dry-roasted black peppercorns (see page xx). So don't skimp on dry-roasting and grinding the pepper fresh; it'll be worth it. I prefer cubed pancetta to sliced as it cooks up crisper, but either works. I somehow never realized that this dish usually includes cheese (I know, I know), but I don't feel like it needs it. There's a purity of flavor that comes just from the richness of eggs and pork contrasted by the pepper. If you'd like to include cheese, however, I recommend grating it fresh with a Microplane tableside.

SERVES 4

8 ounces pancetta (I like Citterio pre-cubed 4-ounce packs), guanciale, or applewood-smoked bacon, finely chopped or cubed
Fine sea salt
1 pound spaghetti (I like De Cecco brand)
1½ to 2 teaspoons black peppercorns, to taste
6 large eggs, at room temperature
Parmigiano-Reggiano or Pecorino Romano cheese (optional), for serving

Note: At first, the finished dish may look glossy, but the egg will soon be absorbed into the pasta.

1. Warm a large skillet over low heat. Add the pancetta, distributing it across the surface of the pan. Cover and cook slowly, uncovering and stirring occasionally, then redistributing in a single layer so that all sides render evenly into crunchy bitty bacon shards, 20 to 25 minutes. Covering keeps the pancetta from sticking. You may have to uncover the pan in the last few minutes to get the pancetta crispy. The slower you cook the pork, the more fat will render.
2. Remove the pan from the heat and set it aside. Make sure to do this before you add the pasta to the boiling water.
3. Bring a large pot of water to a boil over high heat. Stir in 2 tablespoons salt. Add the spaghetti and cook until al dente according to the package directions.
4. While the water is boiling, heat a small dry skillet over medium heat. Add the peppercorns and stir gently until they start to smoke, about 1 minute. Remove immediately, transfer to a mortar and pestle or spice grinder, and grind into a coarse powder. Set aside.
5. In a medium bowl, combine the eggs and a healthy pinch of salt. Use an immersion blender or a whisk to beat the hell out of the eggs until they are well combined and frothy. Transfer half of the eggs to a large serving bowl.
6. When the pasta is done, drain and add at least half of the pasta to the pan with the pancetta. Stir rapidly to sop up all the fat.
7. Transfer all the pasta and pancetta to the large bowl with half of the eggs and mix, mix, mix. Add the remaining egg mixture, stirring constantly. Stir in the black pepper and salt to taste.
8. If desired, use a Microplane grater to finely grate cheese over the top. Serve warm.

Spicy Noodles
with Sesame Chutney and Mint

I was at Minero, chef Sean Brock's Charleston, South Carolina, restaurant, digging into his sampler of salsas, when suddenly the aroma of toasted sesame seeds and chiles sent me back in time to my grandmother's kitchen. What was South Indian sesame chutney doing in a Mexican restaurant? Well, it wasn't really. The delicious and transporting aroma came from a sesame salsa. Both South India and Mexico have similar climates and grow many of the same ingredients. Sean kindly shared his sesame salsa recipe with me, and I made it as soon as I got home, adapting it for my home kitchen, inspired as well by the sesame chutney of my childhood. Because the nutty, fiery flavor of the salsa/chutney also called to mind Chinese-style sesame noodles, I decided to toss it with linguine and, voilà, Spicy Noodles with Sesame Chutney and Mint. The chutney recipe yields enough for you to both make chutney for the noodles and still have extra to keep in your fridge. Feel free to halve the recipe if you want only enough for the noodles. (But you might regret that decision.)

SERVES 4

- Sea salt
- 1 pound linguine
- 4 tablespoons toasted sesame oil
- 2 cups Sesame Chutney (recipe follows), at room temperature
- 1½ cups chopped fresh cilantro leaves (about 2 tablespoons reserved for garnish)
- ½ cup torn fresh mint leaves (about 2 tablespoons reserved for garnish)
- 2 tablespoons black sesame seeds (optional), for garnish

1. Bring a large pot of water to a boil over high heat. Add 2 tablespoons sea salt. Add the pasta and cook until al dente according to the package directions.
2. Reserving 2 cups of pasta cooking water, drain the pasta and transfer to a bowl. Toss with 2 tablespoons of the sesame oil.
3. Add the sesame chutney and 1 cup reserved pasta water and toss to evenly coat, adding additional pasta water, a few tablespoons at a time, if necessary. Toss with the cilantro and mint.
4. Serve warm, garnished with the reserved cilantro and mint, and black sesame seeds (if using). Any leftover sauce will keep in the fridge for seven days.

(Continued)

Sesame Chutney

ACCOMPANIMENT

My grandmother Raji

In addition to using this for the Spicy Noodles with Sesame Chutney and Mint (page 150), I also slather the chutney on toast with eggs or brush it over roasted chicken thighs, and it's *fantastic* as an accompaniment for Dosas (page 155). Some in my household even try to hide it in the back of the fridge so they can eat it all themselves.

MAKES 4 TO 5 CUPS

- 1½ cups sesame seeds
- 2 tablespoons plus 1½ cups neutral oil
- 2 large onions, chopped (about 3 cups)
- 16 large garlic cloves, chopped (about 1 cup)
- 1 tablespoon morita chile powder or chipotle powder
- 1 tablespoon chile de árbol powder
- 2 tablespoons dried oregano, preferably Mexican
- Kosher salt
- 1 tablespoon ground allspice
- 1 tablespoon ground cumin
- ¾ cup raw agave syrup
- ½ cup apple cider vinegar

1. In a large nonstick skillet, toast the sesame seeds over medium heat, stirring frequently, until browned, 3 to 5 minutes. Transfer to a plate and set aside. Wipe out the skillet to avoid residual seeds burning.
2. Return the skillet to medium heat and heat 2 tablespoons of the oil. Add the onions and sauté until softened, 6 to 8 minutes.
3. Add the garlic and sauté until softened, 1 to 2 minutes. Add the sesame seeds, morita chile powder, chile de árbol powder, oregano, 2 tablespoons kosher salt, the allspice, and cumin and sauté until the mixture is well-combined and spices have slightly toasted, 1 to 2 minutes.
4. In a blender (see Note), combine 1½ cups water, the remaining 1½ cups oil, the agave, vinegar, and the sesame mixture. Blend until completely smooth, about 2 minutes. Store in the refrigerator for about 1 week.

Note: The key to your success here is a high-powered blender, such as a Vitamix, which can fully emulsify the sesame seeds, pulverizing them until they are the texture of a loose peanut butter.

Opposite, clockwise, from top row: my uncle Ravi, my aunt Neela, my uncle Vichu, me, my mom, my grandmother Raji, and my grandfather K. C. Krishnamurti (circa 1972)

Dosas

SAVORY FERMENTED CREPES

There's nothing like a hot, crispy dosa, filled with potatoes and served alongside cool Coconut Chutney (page 160) and hot, savory Sambar (page 59). It's the combination that most sums up my South Indian childhood. Dosas are naturally gluten-free crepes made from a fermented batter that includes twice as much rice as lentils. They're commonly served at breakfast or teatime (called tiffin) as a snack. At the NY Dosas Cart (where you can get one of the best dosas in all of New York City), Thiru Kumar does things a little differently, though. While his dosas are still gluten-free, he uses twice as much lentils as rice. I was shocked when I learned this. Not only had I not noticed, but it also meant his dosas were protein-packed. This was a revelation: Was it possible to make dosas that were healthier but still preserved the flavor and texture of my beloved childhood favorite? Yes! These days, this is the only way I make dosas from scratch and I even prefer their nuttier flavor. While dosas are usually a savory dish, millions of children enjoy dosas with ghee and sugar. Feel free to stuff yours with anything you'd like.

MAKES ABOUT 6 CUPS BATTER
(hypothetically about 2 dozen dosas, but expect to lose a few in the cooking process)

Special equipment:
tava (flat dosa pan), crepe pan, or griddle

2 cups urad gota (skinless *whole* urad dal), rinsed until the water runs clear
1/4 teaspoon ground fenugreek (optional)
1 cup idli rice (see page xxx) or parboiled basmati rice (see Notes), rinsed until the water runs clear
Kosher salt
Neutral oil, for drizzling
Podimas (page 101)
Sambar (page 59)
Coconut Chutney (recipe follows)

1. In a large bowl, combine the urad gota, fenugreek (if using), and cold tap water to cover by an inch or two. In another large bowl, combine the rice with cold tap water to cover by an inch or two. Cover both bowls and soak at room temperature for about 12 hours.
2. Reserving the soaking liquid, drain the urad gota. In a high-powered blender, add 1 cup of the soaking liquid, then all the urad gota. Blend at high speed, adding up to ½ cup more soaking liquid if needed to blend the urad, until smooth, 2 to 3 minutes. (Rub a bit between your fingers: If you feel any grit, keep blending.) Pour the urad into a large bowl or soup pot, preferably metal. (Be sure to choose a vessel that leaves room—about 6 inches at the top—for the batter to rise so it doesn't overflow.) Discard the rest of the soaking liquid. Do not wash out the blender.
3. Reserving the soaking liquid, drain the rice. In the blender, combine ½ cup of the soaking liquid and about half of the rice. Blend at high speed, adding more water, if necessary (try to use as little as possible, but it may need ½ cup or more), until smooth and grit-free, 2 to 3 minutes. Pour into the bowl with the urad. Repeat with the remaining rice and more soaking liquid.
4. Add 2 tablespoons kosher salt and mix until well combined. Cover with a plate or lid and place in a cold oven. Turn on the oven light to slightly warm the oven (or use the Proof setting, if you have one) and let sit undisturbed until the batter has risen slightly, the texture is light and airy, and small bubbles have formed on the top. Depending on the climate, this could take 6 or more hours, or at least 12 for regular basmati rice.
5. At this point after fermentation, you can refrigerate the dosa batter for at least 1 week. Bring to room temperature before making dosa. Add water, a tablespoon at a time, until it reaches the consistency of melted ice cream; you should be able to pour it.

(Continued)

Krishna, age 7, with her great-grandmother and my aunt Neela in India

6. Set a small bowl of oil next to the stove with a teaspoon. Heat a nonstick skillet or crepe pan over medium-high heat.

7. Use a ladle to drop ¼ cup of batter in the center of the skillet. Starting from the center of the pan, quickly use the bottom of the ladle to glide the batter in concentric circles, spreading it over the surface of the pan into a thin pancake. (If it starts to pull and tear, you may need more fermentation time.)

8. Drizzle about ½ teaspoon oil around the perimeter of the dosa so the edges get crispy. Bubbles will start to form and the dosa will brown in the grooves of the concentric circles. When the edges of the dosa lift easily with a spatula and are golden brown on the underside, about 1 minute, loosen the dosa by running the spatula under the edges and quickly flip the dosa. Cook for about 30 seconds on the second side just to remove the moisture, then transfer to a plate.

9. Repeat with the remaining batter. Remember, this takes practice. Ideally, you want a uniform, golden brown color on one side. If the dosas start to stick, that means the pan is too hot: rinse it off quickly under cool running water, then dry and return to the stove.

10. To serve, scoop about ½ cup podimas into the center of each fresh dosa. Fold the sides of the dosa over the podimas so that they meet in the middle. Turn the dosa over and place on a plate. Serve immediately, with bowls of hot sambar and cool coconut chutney on the side.

Notes:

You can use regular basmati rice instead of parboiled; the batter will just take longer to ferment.

Dosa batter takes a lot of blending! A high powered blender is necessary. Even so, be patient with your blender; ours occasionally overheated and needed a few minutes to rest.

Dosas are all about the details—there will be a learning curve for beginners, especially those of you who didn't grow up helping your grandmothers grind lentils and rice in a gigantic mortar with a pestle. Fermenting times will depend on the climate you live in, and how warm you keep your kitchen. Be prepared for your first dosa to be ugly, malformed, and not very appetizing. This is okay and very common. I sometimes go for months without making a dosa and then am subsequently horrified by the first few that I spin on the stove. Failure is a beloved part of the dosa process. So is the extreme joy and gratification you will get when your fourth or fifth dosa turns out thin and crispy, with lovely concentric circles. And if all else fails? Many Indian markets now have premade dosa batter in the refrigerated section and it's pretty good. But do try this recipe for homemade batter, as it's healthier than those.

(Continued)

CBGB
&
OMFUG

CBGB
&
OMFUG

CBGB
&
OMFUG

1
2
3
4

5

6

7

8

Coconut Chutney

ACCOMPANIMENT

This mild chutney is milky from the shredded coconut, spicy from the chiles, and as integral to the experience of eating Dosas (page 155) as cream cheese is to a bagel. No self-respecting dosa joint would serve dosas without offering coconut chutney and Sambar (page 59), the trifecta of South Indian cuisine. The thick, cool chutney provides a contrast to the hot, sour notes of the sambar.

MAKES ABOUT 3 CUPS

6 cups grated or chopped unsweetened coconut, fresh or thawed from frozen
2 cups chopped fresh cilantro
1/4 cup whole-milk yogurt
2 serrano chiles, stemmed
Kosher salt
1/4 cup neutral oil
1 teaspoon black mustard seeds
1 tablespoon split skinless urad dal
1/2 teaspoon asafoetida powder
24 fresh curry leaves, torn into pieces

1. In a blender, combine ½ cup water, the coconut, cilantro, yogurt, chiles, and a pinch of kosher salt. Blend until smooth. Add more water, a tablespoon at a time, if needed to blend the ingredients. Transfer to a medium bowl, taste, and stir in salt to taste. Set aside.
2. To make the tadka, in a small skillet, heat the oil over medium heat. Add the mustard seeds. Have a lid at the ready. As soon as the seeds begin sizzling, turn the heat down to medium-low. About 30 seconds later, add the urad dal. About a minute later, when the urad dal colors slightly, and the mustard seeds start popping out at you, add the asafoetida powder and curry leaves, quickly covering the pan, as the oil will splatter. Remove from the heat and immediately pour the tadka into the chutney.
3. Stir, taste, and add more salt if needed. This chutney is best when freshly made, but you can store it in the refrigerator for two days.

Note: For a "white" version of this chutney (see opposite), omit the cilantro and green chiles. Add one small garlic clove to the blender and two small dried red chiles to the oil once the urad dal colors, when making the tadka.

SEAFOOD

Tuna Larb

TUNA WITH HERBS

Larb is a classic Lao and Northern Thai salad typically prepared with ground chicken or pork and lots of fresh herbs. Subbing out the ground meat for raw sushi-grade tuna makes for an opulent yet easy appetizer or entrée for any special occasion. The inspiration for this recipe came from the late Oywan Sawyer, a leader in Las Vegas's Thai community, with whom I prepared food for the Thai episode of *Taste the Nation*. Oywan's daughter, Dr. Christian Giovanni, told me her mother often made a weeknight version of larb with canned tuna. As an homage to how Oywan transcended her humble beginnings in this country, I've made a more luxurious version here. Placing the raw tuna in the freezer for just 20 minutes will make it firmer and easier to cut.

SERVES 6 AS AN APPETIZER, 4 AS A MAIN DISH OVER RICE

2 tablespoons Thai glutinous (sticky) rice
3 scallions, white and green parts, thinly sliced (about 1/2 cup)
1/4 cup fresh lime juice (about 2 limes), plus more to taste
1/4 cup fish sauce (I like Red Boat 40°N brand)
1 to 2 teaspoons Thai chile powder, to taste
2 fresh makrut lime leaves, stems and midribs removed, minced
1 1/2 pounds sushi-grade tuna (see Note)
1/2 cup chopped fresh cilantro leaves
1/2 cup torn fresh mint leaves
Kosher salt, if needed
Romaine lettuce, for serving
Cucumber slices, for serving
Steamed basmati or jasmine rice, if serving as an entrée

1. Warm a small nonstick skillet over medium-low heat for a few minutes. Add the glutinous rice and toast, stirring or swirling the pan constantly, until deep golden, 2 to 4 minutes. Be careful: Once the rice starts getting a light tan color, the toasting goes fast; you can slow it down by lifting the pan an inch off the heat. Pour the rice into a mortar and pestle or a spice grinder and grind into a powder. Set aside.
2. In a medium bowl, stir together the scallions, lime juice, fish sauce, chile powder, and lime leaves. Set aside while you slice the tuna.
3. Cut the tuna into ½-inch cubes. Work quickly: Tuna becomes harder to slice when it warms up. Add the tuna to the scallion mixture and toss gently to combine. Mix in the toasted rice powder.
4. Add the cilantro and mint and toss gently to combine. Taste and add salt, if needed.
5. Serve the larb alongside romaine lettuce and cucumber slices. If serving as a main course, add rice.

Note: If you're looking for a more budget-friendly option, take it back old-school to Oywan Sawyer's canned tuna version: There are excellent brands of tuna in oil available these days (I like Ortiz or Tonnino)—just remember to drain well!

Peruvian Ceviche

FISH MARINATED IN CITRUS AND ONION

Of the hundreds of ceviches I've tasted around the world, this bright, pungent version is the best I've ever had. I learned it from Michelin-starred chef Erik Ramirez while filming the Peruvian episode of *Taste the Nation*. With too many other ceviches I've tried, the sharp flavors of citrus, onion, and chile overwhelmed the delicate fish. Ceviche shouldn't be a vehicle just for heat and tartness. Ceviche should heighten the glory of the exquisite fish you are undoubtedly paying a lot of money for. The secret to Erik's ceviche is the from-scratch fish stock that fortifies his leche de tigre sauce. Layering both raw and cooked fish with both raw and cooked aromatics results in incredible nuance and depth.

The success of this dish is wholly dependent on the quality of the fish; go to a trusted fishmonger who will sell you the freshest sushi-grade firm white fish—and who will give you seafood scraps for the stock, as well. Both elements are critical: Do not make this dish without either. This is an appetizer for a beautiful summer meal, although I confess that when I made it with Erik at his Brooklyn restaurant, Llama Inn, I ate the whole large bowl—intended for four people—while sitting by myself.

SERVES 4 TO 6

STOCK

- 1/2 teaspoon extra-virgin olive oil
- 1/2 small red or yellow onion, roughly chopped (about 1/2 cup)
- 1/4 cup chopped fennel bulb, tops, or both
- 1 celery stalk, roughly chopped
- 1/2-inch slice unpeeled fresh ginger
- 1 garlic clove, peeled and whole
- 2 cilantro stems
- 2 parsley stems
- 2 black peppercorns
- 1 small bay leaf
- 5 to 6 ounces (about 1 cup) shrimp shells, heads, and/or tails (see Notes), well rinsed

CEVICHE AND LECHE DE TIGRE

- 2 1/2 pounds chilled sushi-grade firm-fleshed white fish, such as golden corvina, wild striped bass, halibut, fluke, snapper, or sea bream
- 1 sweet potato (4 to 5 ounces)
- 2 small red onions, quartered, then very thinly sliced into crescents (about 2 cups)
- 2 garlic cloves, peeled but whole
- 2 tablespoons finely chopped celery
- 1 teaspoon chopped fresh ginger
- 8 cilantro stems, plus 1/2 cup chopped cilantro leaves
- 1 1/2 to 2 teaspoons seeded minced habanero chiles, to taste
- Kosher salt
- 1/4 cup fresh lime juice (about 2 limes), plus more to taste
- 1/2 cup corn nuts (such as CornNuts brand)

1. **Make the stock:** In a medium pot, heat the olive oil over medium heat. Add the onion, fennel, celery, ginger, garlic, cilantro stems, parsley stems, peppercorns, and bay leaf. Sauté until softened and fragrant, about 5 minutes. Add the shrimp shells, heads, and tails and sauté for about 2 minutes. Pour in 2 cups water, partially cover, and bring to a simmer. Reduce the heat to medium-low and simmer gently for 10 minutes. Skim the scum off the top. Strain the stock through a fine-mesh sieve and cool completely. Measure out 1½ cups, and save any extra for another use.
2. **Make the ceviche and leche de tigre:** Place the fish in the freezer for 15 to 20 minutes to firm it up; this will make it easier to slice. Place 4 to 6 shallow bowls in the refrigerator to chill.
3. Preheat the oven to 350°F.

(Continued)

4. On a small baking pan, roast the sweet potato until just tender, not mushy, about 35 minutes. When cool enough to handle, peel and cut into ¼-inch dice. Transfer to a small bowl and refrigerate until ready to use.

5. Line a large sheet pan with paper towels. Pour ice water into a medium bowl. Submerge the red onions in the water, tossing them to break up the slices, 1 to 2 minutes (this step will temper the raw flavor of the onions). Drain, transfer to the prepared sheet pan, and pat dry with a paper towel. Chop some crescents finely to make 2 tablespoons and reserve separately.

6. Use a sharp knife to cut the fish into ½-inch cubes. Reserve about 8 cubes of fish (about 2 ounces). Transfer to the refrigerator.

7. To make the leche de tigre, in a small blender or food processor, combine the 1½ cups stock, the reserved 2 tablespoons red onion, the reserved 8 cubes of fish, the garlic, celery, ginger, cilantro stems, 2 tablespoons of the cilantro leaves, ½ teaspoon of the minced habanero, and ½ teaspoon kosher salt and puree. Add more kosher salt to taste. Pour into a large cup and immerse in an ice bath for about 30 minutes to chill, if serving immediately, or transfer to the refrigerator to chill.

8. In a large bowl, combine the remainder of the cubed fish, 1 cup of the sliced onion, the lime juice, 1 teaspoon of the minced habanero, 2 tablespoons of the chopped cilantro leaves, and ½ teaspoon kosher salt and gently mix. Add 1 cup of the leche de tigre, gently toss, and refrigerate for just 10 minutes to let the flavors marry. Add more leche de tigre, lime juice, habanero, and/or salt to taste.

9. Divide the ceviche and juices among the chilled bowls. Garnish with the diced sweet potato, corn nuts, the remainder of the red onion, and cilantro. Serve chilled.

Notes:

If you don't have shrimp shells, make the stock with fish bones, scraps, skin, or head, lobster shells, or crab bodies or claws.

You can make both the fish stock and the sweet potato up to a day in advance.

Level Up: To fancy up the presentation for a dinner party, place each guest's bowl of ceviche inside a larger bowl filled with ice. This not only looks beautiful but is also a practical way to keep the fish chilled while enjoying it on a hot day.

Shoyu Poke

RICE AND TUNA BOWL

Classic Hawaiian poke is a pretty simple, yet delicious, affair: diced raw fish—usually tuna—mixed with limu (seaweed), scallions, red or white onions, shoyu (soy sauce), and sesame oil. These days, poke has become wildly popular on the mainland, too—with poke spots offering up innumerable twists on the classic. In Hawaii itself, you'll find delis with long counters of scoop-your-own poke in countless combinations. When chef Mark "Gooch" Noguchi made me his version of poke on a Hawaiian beach, he encouraged me to freestyle a bit with my own bowl. Since then, I have been working on my poke skills; this combination is one of my favorites. Buy the most pristine fish you can, then top it with macadamia nuts for crunch, lemon juice for tartness, and a bit of avocado for rich creaminess.

SERVES 4

1 pound sushi-grade ahi tuna
1/4 cup soy sauce
1 tablespoon rice vinegar
1 tablespoon ginger paste
1 teaspoon toasted sesame oil
1/4 teaspoon grated lemon zest
1 teaspoon fresh lemon juice
3 cups steamed sushi rice
2 avocados, cut into 1/2-inch cubes
1 cup shelled edamame
1/4 cup salted roasted macadamia nuts, roughly chopped
1/4 cup (about 2 ounces) pickled ginger
1/4 cup Pickled Onions (recipe follows)
1/4 cup very thinly sliced scallions (1 to 2 scallions)
4 dried seaweed sheets, thinly sliced into shoestrings
2 teaspoons toasted sesame seeds

1. Place the tuna in the freezer for about 15 minutes while you assemble the rest of the ingredients; this will make it easier to cut.
2. In a small bowl, mix the soy sauce, rice vinegar, ginger paste, sesame oil, lemon zest, and lemon juice.
3. Remove the chilled fish from the freezer. Cut it into ½-inch cubes and place in a medium bowl. Pour the soy mixture over the fish and toss gently with a flat spatula.
4. Divide the rice among four serving bowls and gently smash it down on the bottom of each bowl, creating a bed. Divide the fish among the bowls. In mounds surrounding the fish, place in this order: the avocado, edamame, macadamia nuts, pickled ginger, pickled onions, scallions, and seaweed. Sprinkle each serving with ½ teaspoon sesame seeds. Drizzle any leftover sauce (from the bowl of fish) on the poke and serve immediately.

Pickled Onions

ACCOMPANIMENT

I'm very sensitive to eating raw onion, which is used as a garnish on top of many Asian and Latin dishes. This is my way of softening their sulfuric flavor while still enjoying their pungency. The oregano gives the pickle a spiky nuance that complements the onion and vinegar. The thinner you cut those crescents, the faster they'll pickle.

MAKES ABOUT 2 CUPS

1 1/2 cups apple cider vinegar
1 teaspoon dried oregano
1/2 teaspoon kosher salt
1/2 teaspoon sugar
1 medium red onion, thinly sliced into crescents (about 2 cups)

In a glass jar, mix the vinegar, oregano, salt, and sugar together. Add the onion, seal the jar, and shake to combine. Let sit at room temperature for at least 1 day before storing in the refrigerator.

Pad Thai Fish

TAMARIND STEAMED FISH WITH SPINACH

The ever-popular stir-fried noodle dish pad Thai is a surprisingly recent invention—it was created only in the 1930s, in an effort by the Thai prime minister to build national identity. Since then, many Thai chefs have made it their own. I made this popular noodle dish while filming in Las Vegas with chef Dan Coughlin. His mother, Nikki Bujadham, was one of the pioneers who first brought Thai food to America. I often find myself craving the flavors of pad Thai, but without the noodles—a desire that inspired this dish. Healthy and delicious, this is a great weeknight meal that comes together in minutes without much chopping or fuss. Tossing in baby spinach to steam at the end makes this, served alongside steamed rice, a complete meal.

SERVES 4

3/4 cup fresh lemon juice (3 to 4 lemons)
2/3 cup fish sauce (I like Red Boat 40°N brand)
2/3 cup sugar
1/4 cup tamarind concentrate (I like Swad or Laxmi brands)
6 scallions, white and green parts, chopped (about 1 cup)
4 cod fillets (8 ounces each)
5 ounces spinach leaves
Handful of chopped cilantro leaves (optional)
Steamed rice, for serving

1. In a medium bowl, whisk together the lemon juice, fish sauce, sugar, and tamarind.
2. Pour the sauce into a large skillet and heat over medium heat. Add ¾ cup of the scallions and stir until the sauce bubbles, about 1 minute. Gently place the cod in the sauce (be careful, as cod breaks easily) and spoon the sauce over the fish. Cover and steam until the fish is firm and opaque and flakes easily, 4 to 5 minutes, depending on the thickness of your fish.
3. Remove from the heat and immediately throw in the spinach leaves, the remaining ¼ cup scallions, and the cilantro. Spoon some sauce over the top and cover to let the greens wilt for a few minutes. Serve over steamed rice.

Amok Trei

COCONUT CURRY FISH

This Khmer curry is often described as the national dish of Cambodia, though many consider it "tourist food." I can see why tourists love it, though (and why many Cambodian home cooks reserve it for special occasions)—not only is it delectable, but it looks beautiful, too. Traditionally, the curry is steamed in banana leaves and served in banana leaf bowls, which imparts a subtle fragrance to the dish. It's not mandatory to serve my version of amok trei in a banana leaf bowl, but they are really fun and easy to make. You can also simply line a serving bowl with cut banana leaves, which will still slightly perfume the steaming curry with their aroma.

I became a big fan of this curry while shooting the Cambodian episode of *Taste the Nation* in Lowell, Massachusetts. I first made it with the chef and owners of the restaurant Simply Khmer, whose own love story and journey to this country moved me to tears. It's a dish that introduces all the flavors of Cambodian cuisine and features the aromatic paste kreung, a staple of Cambodian food. I add the chile powder to the coconut milk rather than to the hot oil to prevent it from turning dark and to preserve its beautiful orange color.

SERVES 4

1 cup chopped fresh lemongrass (about 6 stalks), cut from the tender bottom half of the stalk, outer layers removed
20 makrut lime leaves, stem and midrib removed, ripped into pieces
10 garlic cloves, peeled but whole
2 tablespoons chopped peeled fresh galangal
2 tablespoons chopped peeled fresh turmeric
1 shallot, quartered
2 pounds skinless tilapia fillets, rinsed and patted dry
¼ cup fresh lime juice (about 2 limes), plus lime wedges, for serving
Kosher salt
¼ cup neutral oil
½ teaspoon ground turmeric
1½ cups canned unsweetened coconut milk
2 teaspoons Kashmiri chile powder
1 tablespoon fish sauce (I like Red Boat 40°N brand)
Kosher salt
Banana leaves (optional), for serving
Slivered Thai basil, for garnish
Steamed jasmine rice, for serving

1. In a small blender or food processor, blend the lemongrass, lime leaves, garlic, galangal, fresh turmeric, shallot, and ½ cup water (add more water to help the mixture blend, if necessary). This is your kreung. Set aside.

2. Place the tilapia fillets on a platter. Coat both sides of the fish with the lime juice, then sprinkle lightly with kosher salt. Cover and marinate at room temperature for about 15 minutes.

3. In a large skillet or wok, heat the oil over medium heat until it shimmers. Add the ground turmeric and stir quickly, until it sizzles and darkens, only about 20 seconds. Add the coconut milk, reduce the heat to low, and swirl to gently heat the milk, about 30 seconds.

4. Add the chile powder and stir to dissolve, gently pressing down with the back of a ladle to remove all clumps, 2 to 3 minutes. Stir in the fish sauce and simmer until little bubbles begin to rise on the surface, 2 to 3 minutes.

5. Mix in the kreung, stirring constantly to blend. Increase the heat to medium-low, bring to a simmer, and cook, stirring frequently, for 3 to 5 minutes to blend the flavors. Add up to ½ teaspoon salt to taste.

6. Gently add the fish and any leftover lime juice from the platter, and ladle the sauce over the top of the fish to make sure the fillets are fully immersed. Increase the heat to medium, cover, and cook undisturbed for 4 minutes. Uncover and check to see if the fish flakes easily and is cooked through; if not, cover and continue to cook, 1 to 3 more minutes (the total time will depend on the thickness of the fish).
7. Serve warm, in banana leaves, if desired. Garnish with basil and serve with lime wedges and rice.

Level Up: This dish is traditionally made with prahok, a pungent Cambodian fermented fish paste. I've used fish sauce here for ease and availability, but feel free to use ½ teaspoon of prahok if you can find it.

Fish Simmered with Potatoes and Lemon

This beautiful simple soup evokes a day off the coast of a Greek island: sun sparkling on gentle waves, citrus scenting the air. In reality, I first tasted it on a fishing boat off the Gulf Coast of central Florida; the captain of the boat, Anastasios Karistinos, whom everyone calls Taso, made it for me. A handsome but curmudgeonly fisherman and sponge diver, Taso came to Tarpon Springs, Florida, from Greece as a teen—at the time, Tarpon Springs was the epicenter of the sponge industry, and Greeks were the best sponge divers in the world. That scorching hot day, it was just me, Taso, and a skeleton camera crew on deck. I don't swim well, so I'm not at ease on boats. Taso agreed to sponge dive for us, but he surfaced with more than we had bargained for: Along with the sponges, he brought up a fat, shiny fish. He made quick work of turning it into a pot of soup but refused to let me help with the food. He really didn't care for women on his boat at all! My first spoonful, brimming with pure, clean flavor, erased any of the discomfort that had been creeping in. This is a simple stew of fish, potatoes, and lemon. How delicious it turns out depends almost entirely on the quality and freshness of your fish. Otherwise, it's quite forgiving, and while Taso's rustic version contained bones and skin, I've opted to forgo them here for ease.

SERVES 4

2 pounds skinless white fish fillets, such as grouper, cod, sea bass, sole, or halibut
½ cup fresh lemon juice (2 to 3 lemons)
Kosher salt
⅓ cup plus 1 tablespoon extra-virgin olive oil
1 large yellow onion, diced (about 2 cups)
1 teaspoon dried oregano
2 carrots, peeled and cut on the bias into ½-inch slices (1 heaping cup)
2 large celery stalks, cut into ½-inch slices (about 1 cup)
1 pound baby Yukon Gold potatoes, peeled and halved or quartered (about 2 cups)
½ cup fresh flat-leaf parsley leaves
1 teaspoon grated lemon zest
1 teaspoon freshly ground black pepper

1. Rinse the fish and pat dry, then cut into 2- to 3-inch chunks. Sprinkle the fish with 1 tablespoon of the lemon juice and ¼ teaspoon kosher salt and let sit at room temperature while you cook the onion.
2. In a deep pot, heat ⅓ cup of the olive oil over medium heat. Add the onion, stir for about 1 minute, then stir in the oregano and ½ teaspoon salt and sauté until glassy, about 5 minutes.
3. Add the carrots and celery, cover the pot, and sauté, stirring occasionally, until softened, 3 to 5 minutes.
4. Stir in the potatoes, 4½ cups water, and 2 teaspoons kosher salt. Cover the pot, bring to a boil, reduce the heat to medium-low, and simmer until the potatoes are tender, 10 to 12 minutes. Add salt to taste if needed.
5. Carefully immerse the fish in the broth along with the parsley. Cover the pot and simmer gently, stirring occasionally, being careful to keep the fish intact, until the fish is cooked through, 3 to 6 minutes.
6. Gently stir in the remaining 7 tablespoons lemon juice. Serve drizzled with the remaining 1 tablespoon olive oil and sprinkled with the lemon zest and pepper.

Nam Banh Chuk

FISH AND NOODLE SOUP

Lemongrass, makrut lime leaf, garlic, galangal, turmeric, onion: These are the flavors and scents of Cambodian food. It takes some work to collect these ingredients, peel them, and puree them, but once you do, you'll understand why I'm so enamored of this flavorful soup. While it's traditionally made by boiling fish with bones and skin, I've simplified this dish in a way that I hope leads more people to try it, using fish fillets and shell-on shrimp to produce a broth that's just as flavorful as the old-school style. Cambodian food tends to be milder in heat than other Southeast Asian cuisines, so I like to serve this with some sliced chiles on the side.

SERVES 4

1/2 pound rice vermicelli
1 cup chopped fresh lemongrass (about 6 stalks), cut from the tender bottom half of the stalk, outer layers removed, plus 2 stalks lemongrass, smashed and cut in half
30 fresh makrut lime leaves, stems and midribs removed
12 garlic cloves, peeled but whole
2 tablespoons chopped peeled fresh galangal
2 tablespoons chopped peeled fresh turmeric
8 ounces large shrimp, peeled and deveined, tails removed (shells and tails reserved)
1 medium yellow onion or 2 large shallots, peeled and cut into quarters
Kosher salt
1 1/2 pounds skinless tilapia fillets (about 5)
1/4 cup fish sauce (I like Red Boat 40°N brand), plus more to taste

FOR SERVING

1 cup shredded green papaya or green apple, tossed with 2 tablespoons fresh lime juice
1 cup bean sprouts
1/2 cup cut green beans, sliced into 1/4 inch pieces
Lime wedges, for squeezing
Sliced bird's eye chiles (optional)
Soy sauce
Fish sauce

1. Cook the noodles according to the package directions. Drain and divide them into 4 bundles and place on a platter.

2. To make the kreung, in a small blender or food processor, combine the 1 cup chopped lemongrass, 20 of the lime leaves, 10 of the garlic cloves, the galangal, turmeric, and ½ cup water and blend (add more water to help the mixture blend, if needed). Pour into a large bowl and set aside.

3. In a large pot, combine 8 cups water, the onion, the remaining 2 stalks of halved lemongrass, the remaining 10 lime leaves, and 2 teaspoons kosher salt. Bring to a boil over high heat. Add the tilapia, shrimp, and the reserved shrimp shells and tails. Reduce the heat to medium, bring to a gentle simmer, and cook until the fish flakes easily and the shrimp is cooked through, 3 to 5 minutes.

4. Use a slotted spoon to remove the shrimp and transfer to a small bowl. Use the slotted spoon to remove the fish fillets and transfer to the bowl with the kreung. Mash the fish and kreung into a paste.

5. Strain the broth through a fine-mesh sieve into a bowl and discard the solids. Return the broth to the pot and bring to a simmer over medium heat. Gently stir the tilapia-kreung paste into the broth. Add the fish sauce and bring to a boil. Add more salt or fish sauce to taste.

6. **To serve:** Divide the shredded papaya, bean sprouts, and green beans among four medium individual serving bowls. Top each bowl with a bundle of noodles, then pour the hot soup over the top. Divide the shrimp among the bowls. Serve immediately, with lime wedges, sliced chiles (if desired), soy sauce, and fish sauce.

Mussels with a Rasam Vibe

MUSSELS SIMMERED WITH TOMATOES AND SPICES

During my time in France, I came to love mussels Provençal. The classic French dish showcases briny plump mussels steamed in a white wine and tomato bath. Though I loved the fragrant broth, especially soaking bites of crusty, toasted bread in it, part of me was always dying to sneak in a smidge of tamarind and toasted coriander seeds. What can I say? My first association with anything brothy and tomatoey is inevitably the South Indian soup Tomato Rasam (page 57). All of this lay dormant in my head, however, until a *Top Chef: All-Stars* challenge at Rao's, the Italian American institution in Harlem. Chef Antonia Lofaso won with a delectable bowl of mussels. The dollop of aioli on the toast served alongside it dissolved into little pools of fat in the broth, reminding me of the oil or ghee that pools in rasam. Setting out to create the mussels Provençal of my dreams, I ended up with this dish: It tastes an awful lot like rasam, and reminds me of the flavors of South Indian coastal cooking.

SERVES 4

- 2 tablespoons ghee or unsalted butter
- 1 teaspoon cumin seeds
- 1 teaspoon fennel seeds
- 1 teaspoon coriander seeds
- 4 large shallots, minced (about 1 cup)
- 2 tablespoons minced fresh ginger
- 1 tablespoon minced garlic (about 2 cloves)
- 1 to 2 serrano chiles, to taste, slit lengthwise but left whole
- 2 bay leaves, preferably fresh
- 1 medium fennel bulb, finely chopped (about 1½ cups), plus 2 tablespoons chopped fronds
- Kosher salt
- 1 (28-ounce) can whole tomatoes, cut into roughly 1-inch chunks, and their juices
- ½ teaspoon ground turmeric
- 1 teaspoon Kashmiri chile powder
- ½ teaspoon saffron threads, roughly crushed with your fingers
- ¼ cup tamarind concentrate (I like Swad; you may want to use less if it's very syrupy)
- ¼ cup minced fresh cilantro stems, plus ½ cup chopped cilantro leaves
- 1 tablespoon sugar, preferably turbinado
- 2 pounds mussels, debearded and rinsed
- Toasted crusty bread or steamed rice, for serving

1. In a large heavy pot or Dutch oven, melt the ghee over medium-high heat. Add the cumin seeds, fennel seeds, and coriander seeds and sauté until slightly darkened, about 30 seconds. Add the shallots and sauté until barely softened, about 2 minutes. Add the ginger, garlic, chiles, and bay leaves and sauté for just 1 minute. Add the fresh fennel and 1 teaspoon kosher salt and sauté for about 2 minutes. Add the tomatoes and turmeric and sauté, stirring constantly, for 2 minutes.

2. Stir in the chile powder, saffron, and 6 cups hot tap water. Cover and bring to a boil. Stir in the tamarind concentrate, cilantro stems, sugar, and 1 teaspoon kosher salt. Reduce the heat to medium to maintain a vigorous simmer, cover the pot, and cook, stirring occasionally, until the tomatoes have collapsed, the flavors have married, and oil pools on the top, about 20 minutes.

3. Stir in the mussels and the cilantro leaves. Cover the pot, increase the heat to medium-high, and cook until the mussels fully open, 5 to 7 minutes. Serve immediately, with toasted crusty bread or atop rice.

Sweet and Sour Shrimp

with Cherry Tomatoes

This recipe is based on a taste memory of a luxurious shrimp dish I had in Goa years ago: I still remember its intense sweet, spicy, and tart undertones. It had the telltale signs of other Indian curries but tasted more like a pickle, fermented even. My version is not traditional, as you'll see from the lack of many Indian spices, so I don't call it balchão, a traditional Portuguese Goan dish that also uses shrimp paste. The Portuguese colonized this part of India for five hundred years, and that influence can still be felt. This dish was developed with what I had on hand, to invoke those flavors, and I love the result. The sweetness of the shrimp is amplified by the dried apricots, and the preserved lemon and tomatoes give a nice tang. You can serve this with rice, but I usually just grab a tortilla out of the fridge, char it right on my stove's open flame for a minute, and stuff it with a heaping ladleful of the shrimp. I suppose the addition of preserved lemon could beg the question: Is it Indian or Moroccan? Or is it Indian only if we swap the preserved lemon for lemon pickle? Culinary borders can be more blurred than geographical ones.

SERVES 4

1 pound large shrimp, peeled, deveined, tails removed
Kosher salt
1 tablespoon fresh lemon juice
2 tablespoons neutral oil
½ teaspoon cumin seeds
½ teaspoon fennel seeds
4 large shallots, diced (about 1 cup)
1 small yellow bell pepper, diced (about 1 cup)
2 dried red chiles
2 tablespoons minced fresh ginger
1 small garlic clove, minced (about 1 teaspoon)
4 cups cherry tomatoes, quartered
2 tablespoons unsalted butter
⅓ cup dried apricots, diced
1 whole preserved lemon, seeded and diced, or 2 heaping tablespoons mild Indian lemon pickle
½ teaspoon ground turmeric
½ cup chopped fresh cilantro
Steamed rice or tortillas, for serving

1. In a medium bowl, toss the shrimp with ¼ teaspoon salt and the lemon juice. Cover and set aside to marinate at room temperature while you prepare the rest of the ingredients.
2. In a deep skillet or wok, heat the oil over medium heat. Add the cumin and fennel seeds and cook until fragrant, about 30 seconds. Add the shallots and sauté until softened, 2 to 3 minutes. Add the bell pepper and ½ teaspoon salt and sauté until softened, 5 to 7 minutes.
3. Add the dried chiles, ginger, and garlic and sauté until softened, 3 to 4 minutes. Add the tomatoes and butter, reduce the heat to low, and simmer uncovered until the tomatoes release their juices and the liquid reduces by half, about 15 minutes.
4. Add the apricots, preserved lemon, and turmeric. Stir and simmer until the apricots break down and become pulpy, 5 to 7 minutes. Add salt to taste.
5. Add the shrimp, submerging them in the tomatoes, and cover, cooking just until the shrimp become opaque, 3 to 4 minutes. Remove from the heat and toss in the cilantro. Serve immediately with rice or tortillas.

Shrimp and Grits

South Carolina chef BJ Dennis and I became fast friends shooting *Top Chef* in Charleston. When I went back to that city for *Taste the Nation*, I knew BJ would be my first stop. We spent a blazing hot day together cooking Crab Fried Rice (page 137) under the August sun, but what stands out most in my memory is the warm breakfast of shrimp and grits he brought me the morning after. Eating it, I felt so cared for—and so lucky to have a friend like BJ. Each bite evoked a whole world. BJ has spent most of his professional life immersed in Gullah foodways—educating, studying, cooking. But BJ's deep well of Gullah knowledge began forming long before he ever picked up a knife. At the side of his grandfather, a laborer who lived off the land in Clements Ferry, South Carolina, BJ learned how to bank sugarcane and how to dry shrimp and fish on the roof of his home. A whole value system of "being self-sustaining and taking care of family," as BJ described it, was woven into these lessons. Re-creating BJ's shrimp and grits from memory, I thought of his grandfather, shrimping in the swampland, and all the ways we transmit our cultures—and our love for them—"just" by feeding our families.

SERVES 4

1 pound medium shrimp, peeled, deveined, tails removed
1 tablespoon plus 1 teaspoon fresh lemon juice
1/2 teaspoon Spanish smoked paprika (optional)
Kosher salt
2 ounces bacon (2 to 3 slices), finely chopped
Neutral oil, if needed
1 tablespoon all-purpose flour
3 scallions, white and green parts, chopped (about 1/2 cup)
1 small garlic clove, minced (about 1 teaspoon)
1/4 to 1/2 teaspoon red chile flakes, to taste
1/2 cup Essential Chicken Broth (page 54) or store-bought chicken broth or stock
1 tablespoon minced fresh parsley leaves
Grits (page 98), warmed through

1. In a medium bowl, toss the shrimp with 1 teaspoon of the lemon juice, the smoked paprika (if using), and a pinch of kosher salt. Cover and set aside to marinate at room temperature while you prepare the rest of the ingredients.

2. Line a plate with paper towels and set near the stove. In a large skillet, cook the bacon over medium heat until crisp, about 10 minutes. Use a slotted spoon to remove the bacon and drain on the paper towels. Leave about 2 tablespoons of fat in the bottom of the pan, pouring out any excess carefully. (If you have less than 2 tablespoons, add a little neutral oil.)

3. Place the skillet over medium heat and heat the bacon fat. Stir in the flour until well incorporated, about 1 minute. Stir in the scallions, garlic, and chile flakes and sauté until the scallions are wilted and slightly darkened, 2 to 3 minutes.

4. Stir in the broth and a pinch of salt, scraping any bits from the bottom of the pan, and whisk constantly until the gravy is smooth and thick, about 1 minute. Add the shrimp, stir to coat, and heat until just cooked through, 2 to 3 minutes. Remove from the heat and stir in the remaining 1 tablespoon fresh lemon juice and the parsley. Add kosher salt to taste.

5. Divide the grits evenly among four shallow bowls. Ladle the shrimp and gravy over the grits. Crumble the bacon over the shrimp and serve immediately.

CHICKEN

Chicken Larb

GROUND CHICKEN WITH HERBS

This fragrant dish, inspired by Lotus of Siam, comes together quickly. It's also healthy and filled with protein. Its intense flavor comes from aromatic lemongrass and fresh makrut lime leaves, two ingredients worth going the extra mile to find and both of which freeze beautifully. A hearty appetizer when paired with lettuce cups, it becomes an entrée when accompanied by rice. I usually double the recipe so that I have leftovers for lunch the next day. If you do make double, reserve some of the rice powder and herbs and add just before serving the second batch.

SERVES 4

4 large shallots, coarsely chopped (about 1 cup)
1/4 cup fresh lime juice (about 2 limes)
4 tablespoons fish sauce (I like Red Boat 40°N brand)
1 (2-inch) length of lemongrass, cut from the tender bottom half of the stalk, outer layers removed, roughly chopped
1 to 2 teaspoons Thai red chile flakes, to taste
2 fresh makrut lime leaves, stems and midribs removed
3 tablespoons Thai glutinous (sticky) rice
2 tablespoons neutral oil
1 pound ground chicken or ground turkey (preferably dark meat with a higher fat content)
1/2 cup thinly sliced cipollini onions (about 3 small) or Maui or other sweet onion
1/2 cup torn fresh mint leaves
1/2 cup roughly chopped fresh cilantro
Bibb or butter lettuce leaves, for serving
Steamed basmati or jasmine rice (optional), for serving

1. In a small blender or food processor, combine the shallots, lime juice, 2 tablespoons of the fish sauce, the lemongrass, chile flakes, and lime leaves and puree until smooth. Transfer to a large bowl and set aside.

2. Warm a large nonstick skillet over medium-low heat. Add the glutinous rice and toast, stirring or swirling the pan constantly, until deep golden, 2 to 4 minutes. Be careful: Once the rice gets a bit of light tan color, the toasting goes fast; you can slow it down by lifting the pan an inch off the heat. Pour the rice into a mortar and pestle or spice grinder and grind into a powder. Set aside.

3. In the same skillet, heat the oil over medium-high heat for about a minute. Add the ground meat and the remaining 2 tablespoons fish sauce and stir, breaking up the meat, until just cooked through, 3 to 5 minutes. Drain off any excess liquid that pools in the bottom of the pan. Stir in the onions and cook until just warmed through, about 1 minute. Remove from the heat.

4. Add the chicken to the bowl of shallot puree and mix well to combine. Add the rice powder and most of the mint and cilantro and toss well.

5. Garnish the top with the remaining herbs and serve over lettuce leaves (or steamed rice, if desired).

Yogurt Chicken

As a nurse who worked long hours, my mom had very little time to cook dinner during my childhood. This dish was a staple she relied on to get a quick, flavorful meal on the table with little effort. In the morning before heading to work she'd combine the chicken, yogurt, and spices in a bowl, then let it marinate all day in the fridge, before popping it in the oven when she got home. Yogurt is a frequent tenderizing agent in Indian cuisine, enhancing everything from tandoori to biryani. Here, it also results in a delicious sauce to spoon over the chicken and rice, as well as balancing the heat in the spices. It's not the most attractive of dishes because the sauce may separate, so if you're serving a gathering of people who think stuff like that is important, make sure you garnish it with cilantro right before serving. You could even make it a day ahead: The flavor will only improve, even if its appearance does not.

SERVES 4 TO 6

2 pounds boneless, skinless chicken thighs (6 to 8)
Kosher salt
1/2 teaspoon black peppercorns
2 teaspoons cumin seeds
2 medium red onions, thinly sliced (2 to 2 1/2 cups)
1 1/2 cups whole-milk yogurt
1/2 cup fresh lemon juice (2 to 3 lemons)
4 large garlic cloves, minced (about 2 tablespoons)
2 tablespoons minced fresh ginger
2 teaspoons garam masala
1 teaspoon cayenne pepper
1 teaspoon amchur (dried mango powder)
1/2 teaspoon ground turmeric
1/4 cup neutral oil
Steamed basmati rice, for serving
Handful of chopped cilantro leaves (optional), for garnish

1. Place the chicken thighs on a cutting board and make 3 even slits ¼ inch deep across the top of each thigh. Sprinkle the thighs with 1½ teaspoons kosher salt and use your hands to rub it over the chicken. Transfer to a large bowl and let rest at room temperature.
2. Meanwhile, heat a small dry skillet over medium heat. Add the peppercorns and roast until fragrant, stirring for 1 to 2 minutes. Transfer to a mortar and pestle or spice grinder. Add the cumin seeds to the skillet and toast until fragrant, 1 to 2 minutes. Transfer the cumin seeds to the same mortar and pestle or spice grinder and grind both into a fine powder.
3. Transfer that pepper/cumin mixture to the bowl with the chicken. Add the onions, yogurt, lemon juice, garlic, ginger, garam masala, cayenne, amchur, turmeric, and 2 teaspoons kosher salt. Mix with your hands, rubbing everything into the chicken. Cover and let the chicken marinate for 30 minutes at room temperature. (You can also cover and refrigerate for up to 8 hours or overnight. Bring to room temperature for 30 minutes before baking.)
4. Preheat the oven to 450°F. Spread the oil over the bottom of a 9 × 13-inch baking dish.
5. Pour the chicken and yogurt mixture into the dish, arranging the chicken in a single layer. Bake uncovered until the chicken is cooked through, 20 to 30 minutes. Serve warm with rice. Garnish with cilantro (if using).

TWILA

Interstate 60—I drive ninety minutes out of Phoenix, past the town of Globe, and turn onto Highway 70, an endless two-lane road that splits the desert in half. Low-slung hills in the distance frame the Arizona desert. Miles of dry red earth. I pull over when I see her, a stark silhouette against the predawn light. Twila Cassadore. Two graying braids of hair snake down a strong, solid back.

The San Carlos Apache reservation spans 1.8 million acres—a patchwork of meadow, desert, and pine forest inhabited by elk, antelope, bighorn sheep, and javelina. Twila has spent her whole life here, on this very land, foraging and hunting.

She takes me to a spot between Natural Corral and Talkalai Lake. Here you can turn in a circle and see nothing but distant mesas and rolling grasses. There are four kinds of edible onions in this part of the desert, Twila tells me. We walk the scrub searching for the one she calls a gentle onion, mild and sweet. She shows me how to use a stick to dig into the hard-packed soil, how to extract the plant without breaking the stalk or bulb. We wrap this delicate bounty in a bit of muslin.

Next, we look for barrel cactus fruit, a small pineapple-like sphere. "You want the bright yellow ones, the green ones are still turning ripe," Twila tells me. She schools me on how to nudge them and gingerly extract the fruits. They have crunchy black seeds inside, like black sesame seeds.

Born in 1966, Twila grew up munching on barrel fruits and wild onions like other kids ate apples and grapes. Her parents, an electrician and a teacher, hunted deer, elk, rabbit, quail, turkey, and ducks and kept a thriving farm. They rarely had to go to the store.

But a way of life can disappear in a generation.

For nine years starting in the mid-sixties, airplanes would fly over the San Carlos reservation, releasing a thick shower of oily droplets onto the land near the river. Kids would stand under the mysterious showers, waiting for rainbows. And then entire families sickened with cancer, with other illnesses, too.

The oily substance was a dioxin-heavy herbicide. The federal government was conducting an experiment to kill the vegetation sucking up groundwater as part of an effort to protect resources for the city of Phoenix.

Concern about the dioxin contributed to a break with the land, Twila says. Parents wanted neat, processed, packaged food for their children—"safe" food. "When you foraged food, you were a poor person," she says. "People would laugh at you for bringing foraged items to school."

Slowly, her connection with her ancestral land was severed.

But Twila's break with the land began in her own body, she would come to realize. Before Twila was in kindergarten, she tells me, a man she knew took her down by the river and sexually assaulted her. She never went swimming again.

She grew up feeling a deep emptiness inside. By the time she was seventeen, she was trying any drug available—and on the reservation, *everything* was available. She spent more than twenty years as an addict. Then, one day in 2002, elders who loved her took her foraging. "Something in my senses woke up; I fell in love with the plants," she tells me. She began to join the foragers on regular excursions. She stopped using drugs and has not relapsed since. "Food is what healed me," she explains. "It made me feel alive, and loved, and like I belonged."

She began to understand her experience in a new way: She had to disconnect from her body, which was a part of Mother Earth, and therefore became disconnected from Mother Earth. Losing your connection to the land is a slow death for an Apache, she came to believe.

Today, Twila documents Apache food traditions that are in danger of being lost. She combs through interviews conducted in the 1990s by the Elders Cultural Advisory Council, recording any information related to traditional foodways. She has identified more than 240 traditional Apache foods and has located 200 of them in the wild.

The morning's chill evaporates with the blazing Arizona sun. I chop barrel fruit as Twila sets three gutted gloschos—commonly called desert pack

"Food is what healed me.
It made me feel alive, and loved,
and like I belonged."

rats in English—in a pot bubbling over an open fire. "Don't look in the pot!" Twila tells me. I abide her command with the meekness of a child. I am working up the courage to taste the pack rat—my first rodent. Twila says we'll know they're done when the tails fall off. I do not check to see if this has happened.

Once the animals are ready, we make a glaze with agave syrup and ground sumac. Twila applies the glaze to the legs with a kind of pastry brush fashioned out of soft twigs tied together, then roasts the meat over the fire. My first bite is tiny, a nibble really. *It's not bad.* Then I have another bite, a half bite. *Wait—it's delicious!* It has something of the flavor of squab or quail, with no gaminess at all. I eat more than I ever thought I would—and with much delight.

Twila bakes ash bread from blue corn and acorn flour on the ashes at the edge of the open fire. It is crusty, dense, warm, and delicious. I have never cooked in the open desert before. I have never truly foraged before. I have never eaten a meal where everything I put in my mouth comes from the very ground beneath my feet.

I feel a connection to the land on which I am standing—different than I have ever felt before—because of Twila. She has made me a part of this earth, by simply sharing so much of it, and herself, with me. Driving away at the end of the day, I feel a calm that both moves and perplexes me. I want to hold on to the feeling—that *grounding,* for as long as I can, knowing that it will inevitably evaporate.

Sometimes there is a crackle of energy between women who have suffered bodily trauma, usually at the hands of men. A two-way street of recognition that says, "I see you; I feel you. And I know you see me, too." A temporary unburdening of the hurt we have swallowed, a thing that eats us.

Twila walks that red earth with the weight of someone who has known enough pain to recognize it in others. In sharing her story, she has given me strength, possessing so much of it herself. In her eyes I see what is possible, to be saved and to help save others.

SHAPE

Desert Chicken

CHICKEN THIGHS WITH SUMAC AND AGAVE

The afternoon I spent in Arizona with Apache forager Twila Cassadore was the first and last time that I have ever eaten rodent. While the desert pack rat, known as gloscho, was surprisingly tasty, it's hard to source it in Manhattan. I'm assuming that like me, you're also not going to find desert pack rat at your local supermarket, so I've adapted the recipe for chicken thighs, which I simmer and then finish in the oven. I use indigenous ingredients such as sumac, chile tepín (the only existing indigenous North American chile today), sage, and juniper berries—a sublime combination of tangy, tart, hot, and sweet (a flavor combo that inspired another of my cookbooks).

SERVES 4

8 bone-in, skin-on chicken thighs (3 to 4 pounds), patted dry
Kosher salt
2 teaspoons plus a few pinches sumac
1/4 cup neutral oil
1 cup chopped scallions, white and green parts (5 to 6)
8 juniper berries (optional; for a woodsy note)
2 fresh sage leaves, torn
2 teaspoons roughly crushed dried chile tepín or other dried red chile

AGAVE GLAZE

1/4 cup raw agave syrup
1/4 cup sumac
2 tablespoons neutral oil
1 teaspoon roughly crushed dried chile tepín or other chile
1 teaspoon kosher salt

1. Sprinkle the chicken on both sides with generous pinches of kosher salt and sumac.
2. In a Dutch oven or large deep ovenproof sauté pan, heat the oil over medium-high heat. Add the chicken and brown on both sides, in batches, if necessary, until golden, about 5 minutes per side. Set the chicken aside on a platter.
3. Reduce the heat to medium and add the scallions, juniper berries (if using), sage leaves, the remaining 2 teaspoons sumac, the crushed chile, and 1 teaspoon kosher salt. Sauté until the scallions wilt, 3 to 4 minutes.
4. Gently add ½ cup water and bring to a simmer, scraping the bottom of the pan. Return the chicken to the pan in a single layer, skin-side up. Simmer uncovered until the chicken is cooked through, 18 to 20 minutes, adding additional water, ¼ cup at a time, to keep the bottom of the chicken saucy while keeping the skin dry.
5. Meanwhile, preheat the oven to 450°F.
6. **Make the agave glaze:** In a small bowl, mix the agave, sumac, oil, crushed chile, and salt.
7. Transfer the Dutch oven or skillet to the oven and roast until the skin starts to dry out, about 15 minutes. Brush the agave glaze on top of the chicken skin. Serve warm.

Note: If you end up with any leftover glaze, spread it over toast and top with Manchego cheese.

Arroz Caldo

CHICKEN AND RICE PORRIDGE

There's something so irresistible and comforting about a bowl of chicken and rice. Jeanie Syfu, my longtime hairdresser, was raised in Maryland by Filipino immigrant parents from Manila and Cavite. This hearty porridge, in which chicken and rice are slowly simmered until the rice breaks down, was in her mother's regular rotation (along with chicken adobo, pancit, and perhaps one of the most cherished Filipino home cooking dishes, spaghetti with hot dogs). Traditionally, Filipino food is not spicy, but Jeanie likes her arroz caldo with jalapeño, an addition that is downright magical: The pepper cuts through the fat of the chicken with a nice spike of heat. The scallions and cilantro stems also brighten the dish.

SERVES 4 TO 6

4 bone-in, skin-on chicken thighs (about 1½ lbs)
Kosher salt
¼ cup neutral oil
2 small yellow onions, chopped (about 2 cups)
½ teaspoon ground turmeric
¼ cup minced cilantro stems, plus ¼ to ½ cup chopped cilantro leaves
8 garlic cloves, minced (about ¼ cup)
2 tablespoons minced fresh ginger
1 jalapeño chile, minced
1 tablespoon fish sauce (I like Red Boat 40°N brand)
⅔ cup jasmine or short-grain rice, rinsed until the water runs clear
6 cups hot Essential Chicken Broth (page 54) or store-bought chicken broth or stock (see Note), plus more if necessary
4 hard-boiled eggs, quartered lengthwise
Fried Shallots (recipe follows) or 1 cup store-bought fried shallots
½ cup chopped scallion greens (from 4 to 6 scallions)
Lemon or lime wedges, for serving (or fresh calamansi citrus if you can find them)

1. Season the chicken with a few pinches of kosher salt.
2. In a wide 6-quart pot, heat the oil over high heat. Brown the chicken until the skin is crisp and golden and the fat is rendered, 3 to 5 minutes per side. Transfer to a plate.
3. Reduce the heat to medium, add the onions and ¼ teaspoon salt, and sauté for 4 minutes, frequently scraping the browned bits off the bottom of the pan. Add the turmeric, cilantro stems, garlic, ginger, and jalapeño and stir until softened, about 1 minute. Add the fish sauce and stir for about 45 seconds. Add the rice and stir to coat well, about 1 minute.
4. Make 4 divots in the rice and nestle a chicken thigh into each divot. Pour in 3 cups of the hot broth (do not stir), plus more if necessary to submerge the chicken. Bring to a boil. Reduce the heat to medium-low to maintain a gentle simmer, and cover. Simmer until the rice has dissolved into mush, the liquid around it is cloudy, and the rice is the texture of porridge, 1 hour to 1 hour 15 minutes. Occasionally scrape the bottom to reduce sticking while disturbing the chicken as little as possible. Gradually add the remaining 3 cups hot broth so that the chicken and rice stay submerged.
5. Use tongs to gently remove each chicken thigh, shaking off any extra porridge, and transfer to a bowl. Remove the bones and skin. Shred the chicken and stir into the porridge. Add kosher salt to taste, if needed.
6. Serve in bowls, topped with egg quarters, fried shallots, scallion greens, cilantro, and a squirt of lemon or calamansi juice.

Note: Instead of broth, you could use 6 cups water whisked with a chicken bouillon cube.

(Continued)

Fried Shallots

ACCOMPANIMENT

Fry up a batch of these and keep them on hand for when a dish needs a bit of savory crunch—be it noodles, an omelet, or fried rice. Try them sprinkled on Som Tum (page 5) or Braised Leeks (page 93). Note that I start by combining the shallots with cold oil to keep them from cooking too quickly and burning.

MAKES ABOUT 1 CUP

1 pound shallots (about 10 large), sliced into ⅛-inch-thick rings, rings broken up with your fingers (about 4 cups)

1 cup neutral oil

Kosher salt

1. Line a sheet pan with paper towels and set near the stove. In a large skillet, combine the shallots and oil and set over medium-high heat. Stir occasionally until the oil starts to bubble.
2. Stir often until the shallots begin to brown, about 10 minutes. Reduce the heat to medium and cook, stirring constantly, until all the shallots are browned, another 5 to 8 minutes (watch out; shallots may go from light to dark quickly).
3. Using a slotted spoon or spider, transfer the shallots to the paper towels and immediately sprinkle with a pinch of kosher salt. Let cool completely.
4. Carefully lift the edges of the paper towels and pour the shallots into an airtight container. Store at room temperature for up to 3 weeks. Reserve the oil for another use within a week.

Chicken Adobo

BRAISED CHICKEN IN COCONUT AND VINEGAR

This dish is an homage to the chicken adobos I ate growing up, at the tables of Filipino friends who, lucky me, would invite me to stay for dinner. While the adobos I grew up eating did not contain coconut milk, I think it mellows the acid of the vinegar nicely and results in a thick, velvety sauce. I roughly crush the peppercorns rather than grind them so that every other bite has a pop of their spiky flavor.

SERVES 4 TO 6

1 cup distilled white vinegar
2 medium garlic cloves, crushed, plus 1/3 cup sliced garlic (about 8 medium cloves)
Kosher salt
1 teaspoon black peppercorns, roughly crushed, plus more to taste
8 bone-in, skin-on chicken thighs (3 to 4 pounds)
3 tablespoons neutral oil, plus more if needed
6 bay leaves, preferably fresh
1 to 2 (2-inch) dried red chiles, to taste
1 (13.5-ounce) can unsweetened coconut milk, well stirred
1/4 cup soy sauce
Fried Shallots (recipe opposite), optional
Steamed jasmine rice, for serving

1. In a large bowl, stir together the vinegar, crushed garlic cloves, 1 teaspoon kosher salt, and half of the crushed black peppercorns. Add the chicken thighs, toss to coat, cover the bowl, and marinate at room temperature for 30 minutes to 1 hour.

2. In a large pot or Dutch oven, heat the oil over high heat until it shimmers. Working in batches, shake any moisture off the chicken (reserving the marinade) and sear until golden brown, 3 to 5 minutes per side. Add more oil as needed for the remaining batches. Remove the chicken and set aside.

3. Reduce the heat under the Dutch oven to medium and add the sliced garlic, bay leaves, red chiles, and the remainder of the crushed peppercorns and sauté until the garlic is toasted, about 1 minute. Pour in the reserved chicken marinade and loosen the bits off the bottom of the pan (feel free to skim out any burned bits). Stir in the coconut milk and soy sauce, bring to a boil, then reduce the heat to medium-low to maintain a simmer. Add salt to taste.

4. Carefully nestle the browned chicken in the pot (it will not be fully submerged in the liquid), cover, and simmer, checking occasionally for sticking, until the chicken is cooked through, the sauce turns brown, and the flavors have married, about 45 minutes. Feel free to skim off any excess fat, if desired.

5. Remove the chicken from the pot and place on a serving dish. Simmer the sauce until it thickens slightly, 5 to 10 minutes. Remove and discard the bay leaves. Pour the sauce over the chicken. Garnish with fried shallots (if using). Serve warm, with rice.

Jerk Chicken

SPICY MARINATED CHICKEN

When we were taping the proof of concept for *Taste the Nation* here in New York City, we met with a lovely Jamaican couple, Magnus and Anthyne McKellar. Their jerk chicken street cart, Jam Rock Jerk, was the first legally permitted food cart in NYC equipped with the smoker necessary to produce authentic Jamaican jerk chicken. I always loved the time I spent working in and visiting Jamaica over the years, but at that point hadn't been there in almost a decade. Not long after, I finally returned, to speak at the Calabash Literary Festival. I was quickly reminded of the many reasons to love Jamaica, including but in no way limited to its beauty, the cultural contributions of its deep-rooted Indian community (Indo-Jamaicans are the third largest ethnic group on the island), its people, and, of course, its food. Back in New York, I was inspired to develop a jerk chicken recipe for those, like me, who are craving its subtly sweet heat but don't have a smoker at home (traditionally, jerk chicken is smoked in a big drum—think Jamaican barbecue). I knew that I could combine Jamaican peppers and allspice for something that at least tasted legit. Serve it with Garlic Yogurt Sauce (page 78) if your jets need a little cooling. If you do have a home smoker or any kind of smoking element on your grill, this is an excellent use for it. And if you are out and about in New York at lunchtime, check out Jam Rock's website—they've enjoyed much deserved success in the years since I met Magnus and Anthyne and now run two carts serving up deliciousness all over the city.

SERVES 4

- ½ cup neutral oil, plus more for the baking sheet
- 6 scallions, white and green parts, roughly chopped (about 1 cup)
- 3 to 6 Scotch bonnet chiles, to taste, stemmed
- 4 medium garlic cloves, peeled but whole
- 3 tablespoons ground allspice
- 2 tablespoons dried thyme
- 2 tablespoons firmly packed light brown sugar
- 2 tablespoons dark rum
- 2 teaspoons ground or grated nutmeg
- ½ teaspoon distilled white vinegar
- Kosher salt and freshly ground black pepper
- 3 to 4 pounds chicken drumsticks, bone-in thighs, or a combination

1. In a blender, combine the oil, scallions, chiles, garlic, allspice, thyme, brown sugar, rum, nutmeg, vinegar, 2½ teaspoons kosher salt, and 1 teaspoon black pepper and puree until smooth.
2. Place the chicken in a large bowl or resealable bag and coat with the marinade. Refrigerate for at least 6 hours and up to overnight.
3. Remove the chicken from the fridge and let sit for about 30 minutes to bring to room temperature. Cook the chicken in the oven or on the grill.

   To roast: Position a rack in the middle of the oven and preheat the oven to 400°F. Oil a large baking sheet. Remove the chicken from the marinade, shaking off the excess, and place skin-side down on the baking sheet. Roast undisturbed for 20 minutes. Turn the pieces over and roast until just cooked through, 10 to 20 minutes.

   To grill: Preheat a gas grill to about 400°F. Clean and oil the grates. Remove the chicken from the marinade, shaking off the excess, and place on the grill. Grill over a medium flame, with the cover closed, for about 15 minutes. Flip the pieces over and grill, with the cover open, until just cooked through, another 15 to 20 minutes.

Chicken Tikka Masala

CHICKEN IN A CREAMY SPICED TOMATO SAUCE

For most of my life, I did not cook or eat chicken tikka masala. It's strictly restaurant food. And not just because I grew up vegetarian, but because this dish didn't really exist in India. Nope, chicken tikka masala is a purely third culture food, a dish that evolved out of *British* Indian cooks looking for a way to use leftover tandoori chicken they didn't sell. They began simmering it in a rich, creamy tomato sauce, and the national dish of England was born (that's one small way to get back at your colonial oppressors in their home country). I do understand the appeal of the warmth and heat from the spices, the creamy sauce, and the tender chicken with its slightly smoky edge from the tandoor. But it was only when the *Today* show asked me to develop a recipe to commemorate my last season of *Top Chef*—shot in London—that I decided to finally embrace the dish that, for so many people, embodies "Indian food." Here I marinate the chicken in yogurt and broil it to achieve a bit of smoky char. I also use yogurt—rather than cream—in the sauce, because it gives the dish a tang it would otherwise lack. To boost the richness of the sauce, I stir in ground cashews, which add a thick, buttery nuttiness. The deep woodsy flavor of black cardamom is integral to the sauce; green cardamom is not an adequate substitute. The result is a much livelier tikka masala than you'll find in most restaurants. Krishna took one bite and declared that we should eat it every week. Go figure.

SERVES 4 TO 6

2 cups whole-milk yogurt
4 tablespoons fresh lemon juice (1 to 2 lemons), plus more if needed
2 teaspoons garam masala
1 teaspoon ground turmeric
1 teaspoon amchur (dried mango powder)
Kosher salt
2 pounds boneless, skinless chicken thighs (6 to 8)
½ cup raw or roasted cashews
2 large dried Indian chiles
2½ teaspoons cumin seeds
2 teaspoons coriander seeds
2 black cardamom pods
3 whole cloves
2 tablespoons ghee or neutral oil, plus more if needed
2 small yellow or red onions, chopped (about 2 cups)
2 tablespoons chopped fresh ginger
2 large garlic cloves, chopped (about 1 tablespoon)
2 fresh serrano or bird's eye chiles, preferably red, slit lengthwise but left whole
2 cups canned tomato puree (I like San Merican Tomatoes brand)
2 tablespoons tomato paste
2 teaspoons Kashmiri chile powder
¼ to ½ teaspoon sugar (optional), preferably turbinado
1 cup chopped fresh cilantro leaves
Steamed basmati rice, for serving

1. In a large bowl, whisk together 1 cup of the yogurt, 2 tablespoons of the lemon juice, the garam masala, turmeric, amchur, and 2 teaspoons kosher salt. Submerge the chicken in the mixture, massaging it in with your hands, cover, and marinate for 30 minutes to 1 hour at room temperature. (Or marinate for longer in the refrigerator, but take out of the fridge 30 minutes before cooking the chicken.)
2. In a small blender or food processor, or a clean spice grinder, blend the cashews into a fine powder. Set aside.
3. In a small dry sauté pan, toast the following spices individually over medium heat, transferring each to the same spice grinder or mortar and pestle after they are done: dried chiles until fragrant, about 30 seconds; 1½ teaspoons of the cumin seeds until the color darkens, about 1 minute; coriander seeds until they turn a light brown, about 1 minute; black cardamom pods until they darken slightly, about 90 seconds; and cloves until fragrant, about 20 seconds. Grind all the spices together into a fine powder and set aside.

4. In a large sauté pan or Dutch oven, heat the ghee over medium heat. Add the remaining 1 teaspoon cumin seeds, stirring until dark brown, about 1 minute. Add the onions, stir for 1 minute, then add ½ teaspoon kosher salt. Cook, stirring frequently, until the onions are softened and glassy, 3 to 5 minutes.

5. Add the ginger, garlic, and fresh chiles and cook until the onions are slightly darker at the edges and the chiles begin to soften, 3 to 5 minutes. Add the ground toasted spice mixture and sauté for about 1 minute, adding up to 1 more tablespoon ghee if necessary to prevent sticking.

6. Add the pureed tomatoes, tomato paste, 2 cups water, and 1 teaspoon kosher salt. Mix well, cover the pan, reduce the heat to medium-low, and simmer, stirring occasionally to prevent sticking at the bottom, until the sauce thickens, about 25 minutes.

7. While the sauce is simmering, preheat the broiler to high. Line a large sheet pan with foil. Shake off excess marinade from the chicken thighs and place in a single layer on the sheet pan. Broil on both sides until the chicken is charred and browned but not necessarily cooked through, 3 to 5 minutes per side. Transfer to a plate and set aside to cool. Chop the chicken into bite-size pieces.

8. Stir the Kashmiri chile powder into the simmering sauce and simmer for 2 to 3 minutes to marry the flavors. Fold in the remaining 1 cup yogurt and the ground cashews and stir to warm through, 2 to 3 minutes. Add the sugar (if using) and more kosher salt to taste.

9. Stir the chicken into the sauce. Cover the pan, leaving the lid slightly ajar, and simmer until the chicken is cooked through, about 10 minutes.

10. Just before serving, stir in the remaining 2 tablespoons lemon juice. Garnish with the cilantro. Serve with the rice.

Tagine-Inspired Chicken

SPICED CHICKEN STEW WITH LEMON, APRICOTS, AND OLIVES

This may surprise you, but the best part of filming *The Ten Commandments* in 2005 was not the blunt bangs I rocked as Princess Bithia. Nope. It was shooting in Morocco. I loved wandering the souks in Marrakech, lined with pyramids of spices evocative of my grandmother's kitchen. I loved the food: the fish marinated in herbaceous chermoula, the tender lamb braised with prunes, the insanely fluffy couscous, gently mounded and topped with saffron-scented vegetables. My favorite, though, was the chicken tagine I ordered at my hotel every night, comforting and restorative after a long day of filming. I loved the briny green olives and the tart funk of the preserved lemons. Chicken with olives and preserved lemon is one of the classic tagine dishes of Morocco. Here, I leave tradition behind and add apricot, which some might find blasphemous. The sweetness of the apricots rounds out the lemon and olives, offering a complex and well-balanced dance of sweet and savory notes.

Because many of us do not own an authentic tagine—a kind of earthenware pot with a conical lid—this recipe is designed for a Dutch oven. If you're making this in a true North African tagine, you may need to reduce the amount of broth to fit, which is totally fine. It'll be beautifully steamed and tender. Just remember to brown the chicken in a separate pan first.

SERVES 4

- 8 bone-in, skin-on chicken thighs or 1 whole chicken cut into 8 pieces (3 to 4 pounds)
- Kosher salt and freshly ground black pepper
- 1/4 cup neutral oil
- 2 teaspoons cumin seeds
- 1 1/2 teaspoons fennel seeds
- 2 large red onions, thinly sliced (about 4 cups)
- 2 (3-inch) cinnamon sticks
- 3 dried red chiles
- 3 bay leaves, preferably fresh
- 1 teaspoon dried thyme
- 2 medium garlic cloves, minced (about 1 tablespoon)
- 1 tablespoon minced fresh ginger
- 1 large fennel bulb, halved, cored, and sliced 1/4 inch thick (about 2 cups)
- 2 large carrots, peeled and cut on the bias into 1/4-inch-thick slices (about 1 cup)
- 2 to 3 medium preserved lemons, seeded and chopped (about 1 1/4 cups), depending on size
- 1 medium red bell pepper, seeded and diced (about 1 cup)
- 1 cup picholine or Moroccan green olives
- 3 cups Essential Chicken Broth (page 54) or store-bought chicken broth or stock
- 1 tablespoon harissa paste, or 1 1/2 teaspoons red chile flakes
- 1/4 cup diced dried apricots
- 1/2 teaspoon saffron threads

(Continued)

1. Season the chicken on both sides with healthy pinches of kosher salt and pepper. In a large Dutch oven, heat the oil over high heat until smoking. Working in batches, add the chicken and sear on all sides until browned, 3 to 4 minutes per side. Place on a plate and set aside.
2. Reduce the heat to medium, add the cumin seeds and fennel seeds, and stir until darkened slightly, about 30 seconds. Add the onions, cinnamon sticks, dried chiles, and bay leaves and sauté for just 1 minute. Add the thyme and 1 teaspoon kosher salt and sauté until the onions are glassy, 6 to 8 minutes. If necessary to prevent burning, add a splash of water and scrape the bottom of the pot.
3. Add the garlic and ginger and sauté for just 30 seconds. Add the fresh fennel and carrots and sauté, stirring frequently, until the fennel loses its rawness, 4 to 5 minutes.
4. Stir in the preserved lemons, bell pepper, and olives. Add the chicken broth and harissa, stir to dissolve the harissa, cover, and bring to a gentle simmer. Nestle the chicken into the pot, skin-side up, and pour in any chicken juices that have collected on the plate. Cover the pot, reduce the heat to medium-low, and simmer until the chicken is cooked through, about 40 minutes, checking occasionally for sticking.
5. Use tongs to remove the chicken and place in a single layer on a baking sheet. Stir the liquid, scraping any bits off the bottom. Add the apricots and saffron to the pot and stir. Remove the bay leaves and cinnamon sticks, if desired. Nestle the chicken back into the pot. Serve warm.

Fesenjan

BRAISED CHICKEN WITH POMEGRANATE AND WALNUTS

When my family moved from New York City to Southern California in the '80s, I was less than thrilled. But one of the happy outcomes of my stint on the West Coast was my exposure to Persian food, still one of my all-time favorites. I moved back to New York as soon as I could, but the best Persian food is still in LA. When a trip to "Tehrangeles" isn't in the cards, I make this earthy, sweet-tart stew. Traditionally, fesenjan is long simmered; my simplified version offers the same tang and warmth but in a fraction of the time.

SERVES 4 TO 6

4 cups walnuts (1 pound)
2 pounds boneless, skinless chicken thighs (6 to 8), cut into thirds
Kosher salt and freshly ground black pepper
1 teaspoon ground turmeric
3 tablespoons extra-virgin olive oil
1 medium yellow onion, finely diced (about 1½ cups)
1 teaspoon ground cinnamon
1 cup pomegranate molasses (I like Cortas brand)
¼ teaspoon saffron threads, ground in a mortar with a pestle
2 cups ½-inch-diced butternut squash (optional)
½ teaspoon sugar, preferably turbinado, plus more to taste (optional)
Steamed basmati rice, for serving
¼ cup fresh pomegranate seeds, for garnish

1. Preheat the oven to 350°F.
2. Spread the walnuts evenly on a baking sheet and bake until lightly toasted, 10 to 12 minutes. Let cool to room temperature.
3. Generously season the chicken with several pinches of kosher salt, 1 teaspoon pepper, and the turmeric.
4. In a deep pot, heat 2 tablespoons of the olive oil over medium-high heat. Working in batches if necessary, sear the chicken until golden: 3 to 5 minutes per side. Transfer to a plate and set aside.
5. Pour 2½ cups hot water into a blender, then add the toasted walnuts and grind until smooth.
6. Return the pot to medium heat and add the remaining 1 tablespoon olive oil. Add the onions and sauté until glassy, 4 to 5 minutes. Add the cinnamon and a pinch of kosher salt and stir until fragrant and well combined, 1 to 2 minutes. Add the ground walnuts and the pomegranate molasses and stir to combine, about 2 minutes.
7. Cover the pot, turn the heat to low, and simmer until the sauce has a thick, gravy-like consistency, 30 to 40 minutes, stirring every 5 minutes to prevent sticking and adding ½ to 1 cup water if necessary. Add more kosher salt to taste.
8. Add the seared chicken, cover the pot, and simmer, stirring occasionally, until the chicken is cooked through and tender, about 20 minutes.
9. Meanwhile, steep the saffron in 2 tablespoons hot water and set aside.
10. Add the saffron water and squash (if using) and simmer, stirring occasionally, until the squash is tender and the sauce is slightly reduced, 15 to 25 minutes. Add more salt or sugar to taste to balance the flavors.
11. Serve hot over rice. Garnish with fresh pomegranate seeds.

Level Up: To achieve the rich chocolate-brown hue of other fesenjan recipes, feel free to take that first simmer of 30 to 40 minutes (where you are looking for the sauce to have a gravy-like consistency) a little longer. Just keep in mind that pomegranate molasses has a lot of sugar in it, so it's crucial to keep scraping the bottom of the pot and adding water so the sauce does not stick.

ROSA

For the Peruvian episode of *Taste the Nation,* I traveled to Paterson, New Jersey, home of the country's first planned industrial city, built by immigrants, and situated alongside the Great Falls, one of the largest waterfalls in the United States. Nothing about Paterson prepares you for how sudden and stunning the Great Falls are when you first see them. That's true of Rosa Carhuallanqui as well. She is small in stature but mighty in will. I visit her one summer day at her lovely and well cared for home in a middle-class neighborhood about twenty minutes outside downtown Paterson.

Rosa teaches me to make Amazonian tamales, the traditional way—with cassava and boiled rice kneaded together, instead of corn. With our hands, we scoop small fistfuls of dough and fill them with chicken stewed in a rich ají panca sauce, smoky and piquant. We wrap each in a banana leaf, then a layer of corn husk, then foil, and place each parcel in a huge pot lined with more leaves, arranging them like bricks as though we're building a chimney in a stockpot. As the tamales steam, a sweet humid funk escapes out the kitchen door. We follow it, seeking relief from the heat as we talk about her long journey to the United States.

We sit under the cool canopy of a spreading shade tree, light dappling the Peruvian blanket beneath us. Rosa has brought out a carafe of deep purple chicha morada, an icy cold, sweet, tart tea made from corn and fruit. I sip from a small cup, as Rosa describes her childhood in a valley tucked in Peru's Andean mountains. She would wake in the mornings to the sound of her father's harp and gather with her eight brothers and sisters at a big wooden table for a breakfast of potatoes, corn, and eggs from chickens they had raised on their farm. Her father often cooked a meat dish known as pachamanca, roasting the meat over hot stones in a hole dug underground. There was always singing and dancing. They were Indigenous Quechua people, her mother a traditional embroiderer and her father a musician who had also worked as a chef in the capital city of Lima. Their life was built around artistic creation—music, dance, embroidery, feasts. An idyllic upbringing for an idealist at heart.

Now a dance teacher, Rosa is a study in perseverance and fortitude. As a university student, she earned a degree in folkloric dances, conducting research on the traditions of the Quechua peoples. But during this time, Peru was being torn apart by the conflict between the Maoist Shining Path guerilla group and the government. "You couldn't have dreams because you didn't know if you were going to live," Rosa tells me. The Shining Path would kill you if you didn't join them and the government would arrest you if you did. Between 1980 and 2020, almost 70,000 people died or disappeared due to the conflict. Artistic expression—individual expression—was nearly impossible. "I think maybe if I had stayed in Peru, I would have lost my identity," she told me.

In 1999, Rosa was invited by Rutgers University to deliver a lecture on Peruvian dance. The freedom of expression she experienced in America was intoxicating, casting in sharper relief the limits of life back home. A year later, she came back with her daughter and stayed on. Leaving Peru was a matter of survival, but life in America was not easy. When she first arrived, her husband—who had gone ahead of her—was living in a basement apartment with one small window, through which only a sliver of grass was visible. Her young daughter cried. Peru had been dangerous, but there they had been middle class and Rosa had had work she cared about. "It's okay. I'll get a job and we will save money while we wait for our papers," she told her husband. Her husband protested, insisting that the jobs available to her were not worthy of her education or experience, and that people here would see her as "a different person." As "just" an immigrant. "I am the same person," she told him. She got a job first at Wendy's, then in a paper factory, never losing sight of her passion for dance and teaching. "If you think little, you will be little," she tells me. "If you think big, you will be big."

It is this bigness, this unshakable understanding of self-worth, that Rosa now instills in the children who study with her at the Peruincafolk Company, her dance school. Classes for first-, second-, and now third-generation Peruvian kids are free. Rosa affirms to these tiny dancers that their Peruvian identity is the key to their uniqueness and value in the great American experiment. She is the rare and gifted teacher who teaches you how to value yourself for who you *are*, rather than who you think you want to become.

When the tamales are ready, we tote them to Rosa's dance studio to feed her students. They wear flowers and colorful ribbons braided into their hair, full skirts, starched white ruffled blouses, and chandelier earrings dangling with freshwater pearls. I imagine Rosa as a child dressing up this way, in her former life. How pretty she must have looked. How elegant she looks even now, after cooking all day.

One of the girls says, "I don't like tamales."

"Why?" I ask.

"I don't know," the girl says. "Because I *have* to eat them."

I think of my own daughter, Krishna, who tells me she doesn't like lentils, which I ate for dinner, in varied colors and shapes, nearly every day of my childhood. *Isn't it genetically impossible for this child to dislike lentils?* I look at the kids around me, in their traditional clothes yet still very American, and laugh. I tell her to shush and try the tamal. "It's beautiful and we made it just for you."

She tastes it. "Pretty good," she sniffs.

Actually, it is ridiculously delicious.

"If you think little, you will be little.
If you think big, you will be big."

Amazonian Tamales

TAMALES STUFFED WITH CHICKEN

Before I met Rosa Carhuallanqui, the word "tamal" immediately suggested to me a Mexican-style tamal, made with corn masa. But Rosa's tamales are made with a mixture of rice and yuca (also known as cassava) seasoned with ají panca (a type of Peruvian chile), pan juices from the chicken filling, and olive oil—rendering them incomparably silky and flavorful. This style of tamal originates in her husband Luis Zelada's northern Peruvian hometown, Celandín, which is close to the Amazon River. Rosa learned to make them from her mother-in-law, Rosa Almira Zevallos. These are labor-intensive but special, and not something you're likely to find in a Peruvian restaurant in the United States. Make and assemble all the components and invite over a few friends for a tamal-making party. Packaged banana leaves (and dried corn husks) can be found at Latin markets and freeze well.

MAKES 12 TO 15 TAMALES

CHICKEN FILLING

- 2 tablespoons extra-virgin olive oil
- 1 small yellow onion, chopped (about 1 cup)
- Kosher salt
- 4 large frozen ají amarillo, seeded and finely chopped or pulsed in a blender or food processor (Rosa says do not substitute the paste)
- 1/4 cup minced garlic (about 8 cloves)
- 1 1/2 pounds boneless, skinless chicken thighs (about 6)
- 2 tablespoons jarred ají panca paste (Rosa uses Peru Food brand)
- Freshly ground black pepper

AJÍ PANCA OIL

- 1/2 cup neutral oil
- 6 tablespoons minced garlic (about 12 cloves)
- 2 tablespoons jarred ají panca paste (Rosa uses Peru Food brand)

DOUGH

- 2 pounds frozen grated yuca/cassava, thawed (about 4 cups), or 4 cups grated peeled fresh yuca, if available
- 6 cups warm freshly steamed jasmine rice
- 2 tablespoons extra-virgin olive oil
- Kosher salt and freshly ground black pepper

ASSEMBLY AND SERVING

- 1 (1-pound) package banana leaves, fresh or thawed frozen (Rosa uses La Fe brand)
- 12 to 15 dried corn husks, rinsed with hot water
- Rosa's Green Sauce (recipe follows), for serving

1. **Make the chicken filling:** In a large skillet, heat the olive oil over medium heat. Add the onion and a healthy pinch of kosher salt and sauté until glassy, 5 minutes. Add the ají amarillo and garlic and stir for just 2 minutes. Add the chicken, ají panca paste, 1 teaspoon kosher salt, and several grindings of black pepper. Increase the heat to medium-high until a bit of liquid is released and bubbles, then reduce to low, cover the pan, and cook until the chicken is cooked through and has released its juices, about 20 minutes. Reserve about ½ cup of the chicken juices for making the dough. Then, using a knife and fork, shred the chicken in the pot into bite-size pieces.
2. **Meanwhile, make the ají panca oil:** In a medium skillet, warm the neutral oil over low heat. Add the garlic and ají panca paste. Stir constantly until the oil starts to bubble and the garlic becomes fragrant, about 2 minutes. Remove from the heat and set the mixture aside.

(Continued)

3. **Make the dough:** In a large bowl, use your hands to mix the yuca and cooked rice, kneading well until you cannot distinguish between yuca and rice. Stir in the ají panca oil, the reserved chicken juices, the olive oil, 1 tablespoon kosher salt, and 1 teaspoon black pepper. Taste. The dough should be a bright orange, moist, and a little too salty. Keep in mind that the tamales will lose some of their salinity in the water.

4. **Prepare to assemble the tamales:** Cut aluminum foil, preferably heavy-duty, into twelve to fifteen 12-inch squares. Trim the banana leaves into 12 to 15 pieces, about 11 inches long and 6 to 7 inches wide. (Save the trimmings to line the pot.) Place a square of foil on a flat surface. Then place one corn husk on top: If it curls, position it so that the flattest and widest side is closest to you, and for some that are less wide, use 2 or 3 to overlap. Place a banana leaf on top with a short side closest to you.

5. **Fill the tamales:** Oil your hands, a ¼-cup dry measuring cup, and a 1-tablespoon measuring spoon, and keep a bowl of oil handy. Using the greased measuring cup, add ¼ cup of dough to the middle of the banana leaf and flatten into a rectangle about 4 inches long and 2 inches across, making a shallow divot in the middle. Scoop 2 tablespoons of chicken filling and its juices into the divot, leaving a little room on the sides of the dough. Place another ¼ cup dough on top and seal the edges so that no sauce is leaking (feel free to grab a dab of dough to seal).

6. **Fold the tamales:** Fold in the sides of the banana leaf to cover the filling, then fold up the bottom and fold down the top to completely cover the filling. Scoot the package down so that the bottom of the banana leaf is even with the bottom of the corn husk. Fold the sides of the husks in to cover the package, and fold the top down, leaving the bottom open. Center the package in the middle of the foil. Tightly fold in the sides, then tightly roll up the bottom seam of foil to close and roll the top seam down: this will prevent water from entering the tamal during the cooking process. Repeat, making about 12 to 15 tamales.

7. **Cook the tamales:** Pile half of the remaining banana leaves on the bottom of a tall stockpot. Place 2 to 3 tamales in a single layer on the banana leaves. Place another layer of tamales perpendicular to the one underneath, then continue until all tamales are in the pot. Place the remaining banana leaves on top. Fill another large pot about halfway with water and add 1 tablespoon kosher salt. Heat over high heat until hot but not yet simmering. Carefully pour the hot water into the stockpot until it comes about halfway up the stack of tamales. Cover the stockpot, heat over high, and bring to a boil. Reduce the heat to medium-low and steam for 20 minutes. At that point, check the water level by inserting the handle of a wooden spoon into the water: It should still be close to halfway up the stack of tamales; add more hot water if it is not. Cover.

8. Steam for another 20 minutes, then check the water level again, adding more water if necessary.

9. Steam for a final 20 minutes (so that the tamales steam for a total of 1 hour) and check the tamales. Carefully remove one tamal, open the wrapper, and check the dough: It should stick together. If it crumbles apart, the tamales need more steaming time.

10. Remove all the tamales from the pot and lay in a single layer to cool slightly, at least 10 minutes. Unwrap and discard the foil and corn husks.

11. To serve, place the banana leaf packages on serving plates, unwrap the leaves, and serve the tamales warm on the banana leaves, with Rosa's sauce.

Note: To store leftovers, refrigerate or freeze any tamales that you do not eat within a few hours. Store in the refrigerator for 24 hours, or in the freezer for up to 1 month. Thaw in the refrigerator, remove the foil, and heat in the microwave.

Rosa's Green Sauce

ACCOMPANIMENT

I adapted this Peruvian green sauce recipe from Rosa Carhuallanqui. I combine serrano chiles and fresh parsley with the huacatay (black mint) paste, which you can omit if you can't find it. While Rosa adds water, I prefer the sauce without it: This results in a sauce thick enough to scoop up with Tostones (page 32).

MAKES ABOUT ½ CUP

- 1 cup roughly chopped fresh parsley leaves and tender stems (about 2 ounces)
- 4 fresh serrano chiles, roughly chopped
- 1 tablespoon jarred huacatay paste (I like Inca's Food brand), optional, but recommended
- Kosher salt
- ¼ cup fresh lime juice (about 2 limes)
- 1 tablespoon neutral oil

In a small blender or food processor, pulse the parsley, serrano chiles, huacatay paste, and 1 teaspoon kosher salt to roughly combine. Add the lime juice and oil and puree until emulsified, adding a few tablespoons of water if you prefer a thinner sauce. Add more salt to taste.

MEAT

Saltimbocca di Casa Mia

BEEF ROLLED WITH PROSCIUTTO, PECORINO, AND SAGE

Saltimbocca—traditionally, thinly sliced veal layered with prosciutto and sage before being pan-fried—is quintessentially Italian, simple to make, and a rustic yet elegant dish. The word *saltimbocca* means "jump in the mouth." In this version, I forgo veal for beef and add pecorino before neatly rolling each piece into a roulade. My friend Beatrice Tosti di Valminuta, the chef and owner of the East Village restaurant Il Posto Accanto, taught me this method of adding pecorino and rolling up the ingredients into a beautiful package, which also keeps the meat moist. Serve this at a dinner party with roast potatoes and/or sautéed spinach. You will need kitchen string, butcher's twine, or toothpicks for this recipe.

SERVES 4

8 thin slices top round beef (2½ ounces each), 8 to 10 inches long and about 3 inches wide (see Notes)
Fine sea salt and freshly ground black pepper
8 slices prosciutto
8 batons young pecorino (see Notes), measuring about 2 inches long and ½ to ¾ inch thick
8 to 16 fresh sage leaves, plus more for the sauce, if you like
¼ cup extra-virgin olive oil
1 cup white wine

1. Cover a cutting board or tray with parchment paper and lay the beef slices in a single layer. Sprinkle lightly with salt and pepper. Lay one slice of prosciutto over each slice of beef: If the prosciutto is bigger than the meat, fold it over. Place a baton of pecorino on the widest end of the meat. Place 1 or 2 sage leaves next to the cheese. Season with a few grinds of black pepper. Starting from the end closest to the cheese, roll each up in a bundle, tucking the sides in so that the cheese is hidden. Secure with kitchen string, butcher's twine, or toothpicks.
2. In a large sauté pan or Dutch oven, heat the olive oil over medium heat until shimmering. Add the beef rolls and sear on all sides until just golden, 5 to 8 minutes. Deglaze the pan with the white wine, scraping up the bits on the bottom. Sprinkle with a pinch of salt, reduce the heat to medium-low, and simmer until the wine reduces by half, about 3 minutes. Transfer the saltimbocca to a dish and remove the string or toothpicks.
3. For a more intense flavor, you can add more fresh sage to the sauce. Simmer for just a few minutes. Add salt to taste. Drizzle the sauce over the top. Serve immediately.

Notes:

If you have access to an Italian butcher, they often carry top round in thin slices labeled as braciola. Or look for "top round minute steak" and pound it thin to the dimensions listed.

Young pecorino is often labeled as "fresh pecorino" or Pecorino Toscano. Or substitute another cheese that will melt, such as Gruyère, Swiss, or mozzarella.

You can roll the saltimbocca up to 24 hours in advance. Cover and refrigerate; bring to room temperature before sautéing.

STAUB

Chile Verde

PORK IN GREEN CHILE AND TOMATILLO SAUCE

I've been cooking on the *Today* show for more than two decades, and this warming, hearty pot of stew might have been my biggest hit with both the hosts and the crew (a couple of cameramen even anointed it their favorite on-air dish ever). While "Chile Verde" refers to the whole dish, it's the salsa verde—a blended sauce of green chiles and tomatillos, great on its own with tortilla chips—that gives the dish its vibrant, verdant color. This dish is perfect for crisp fall nights or feeding a crowd at a Super Bowl party and couldn't be easier to make: Blend up a batch of sauce, brown some ground pork, open a can of beans, let everything simmer for a bit, and voilà. Go ahead and double the recipe—it freezes beautifully.

SERVES 4 TO 6

3 tablespoons extra-virgin olive oil
2 medium garlic cloves, sliced
2 small yellow onions, diced (about 2 cups)
1 tablespoon dried oregano, preferably Mexican
1 tablespoon sesame seeds
1 teaspoon cumin seeds
1 teaspoon red chile flakes
Kosher salt
1½ pounds ground pork
1 shot glass (3 tablespoons) tequila
Salsa Verde (recipe follows)
1 (15.5-ounce) can cannellini beans, drained and rinsed
2 cups Essential Chicken Broth (page 54) or store-bought chicken broth or stock
Lime wedges, for squeezing

1. In a heavy soup pot, heat the olive oil over medium heat. Add the garlic and sauté for just 1 minute. Add the onions, oregano, sesame seeds, cumin seeds, chile flakes, and a pinch of kosher salt and sauté, stirring frequently, until the onions are glassy, 4 to 5 minutes.
2. Mix in the ground pork and sauté until no longer pink, about 6 minutes.
3. Add the tequila to the pork mixture and stir. Stir in the salsa, beans, broth, and ½ teaspoon kosher salt. Bring to a gentle boil, reduce the heat to medium-low, and simmer, stirring often, until the color goes from pastel to olive green, the chile thickens slightly, and the flavors marry, about 30 minutes. Add more salt to taste. Serve warm, with a squeeze of lime juice.

Salsa Verde

ACCOMPANIMENT

In Mexico, where this originates, a wide variety of green chiles is used, varying by region. Here I use jalapeños, which are easy to find in American supermarkets.

MAKES 3½ CUPS

2 medium avocados, halved and pitted
1 pound tomatillos, husked, rinsed, and halved
4 medium jalapeños, halved
1 cup fresh cilantro
¼ cup fresh lime juice (about 2 limes)
2 tablespoons white wine vinegar
1 tablespoon sesame seeds
2 medium garlic cloves, peeled but whole
2 teaspoons extra-virgin olive oil
Kosher salt

Scoop the avocado flesh into a blender or food processor. Add the tomatillos, jalapeños, cilantro, lime juice, vinegar, sesame seeds, garlic, olive oil, and 2 teaspoons kosher salt. Puree until smooth.

Schnitzel

FRIED VEAL CUTLETS

I've adapted this schnitzel from Julian Kegel, the fourth-generation owner of Kegel's Inn in Milwaukee, which has been serving up Austrian and German food for more than a hundred years. While breaded and fried meat may sound heavy, this dish is surprisingly light: Pounding the meat results in thin cutlets that fry quickly, making them extra crisp and airy. I make schnitzel at home regularly, especially when we have little kids as guests: I've never met a kid who didn't love it. Bonus—they also love helping to crush the crackers that give the crust its distinct texture. If you're a purist, you can leave out my very untraditional suggestions of cayenne, amchur, and smoked paprika. But they add a punch of flavor that's hard to beat.

SERVES 4 TO 6

2 pounds veal scaloppine, pounded 1/8 inch thick
Kosher salt and freshly ground black pepper
1 cup all-purpose flour
2 teaspoons cayenne pepper, plus more to taste
2 teaspoons amchur (dried mango powder; optional)
2 teaspoons smoked paprika (optional)
4 large eggs
2 cups fine dried bread crumbs
1 cup coarsely crushed saltines (12 to 16 crackers)
Neutral oil, for frying
Lemon wedges, for serving

1. Season the veal on both sides with pinches of kosher salt and freshly ground black pepper.
2. Line a sheet pan with parchment paper. Set up a dredging station in three shallow bowls: In one, whisk together the flour, cayenne, 4 teaspoons kosher salt, amchur (if using), and smoked paprika (if using). In a second bowl, beat the eggs. In a third, mix the bread crumbs with the crushed saltines.
3. Using one hand for dry and one hand for wet, dredge each veal cutlet on both sides, first in the flour, then in the egg, then in the bread crumbs, shaking off the excess. Place in a single layer on the sheet pan.
4. Line a plate with paper towels and set it near the stove. Have extra paper towels handy. In a large skillet, heat ¼ inch of the oil over medium-high heat until shimmering. Working in batches, use tongs to lift the veal cutlets from the sheet pan, gently shaking off the excess bread crumbs, and add to the skillet. Fry until the crust is deep golden brown on both sides and the veal is cooked through, about 2 minutes per side. Transfer the veal to the paper towel–lined plate. Cover with another paper towel.
5. Pour more oil into the pan, if necessary. Repeat with additional cutlets, placing each on top of a paper towel so that you build a stack of alternating cutlets and paper towels.
6. Serve warm, with lemon wedges.

Ropa Vieja

BRAISED BEEF

In the late '90s I spent four months living in Cuba while shooting a movie there. At the time, Cuba was still reeling from the fall of the Soviet Union. Many Cubans were experiencing economic insecurity and looking for creative ways to make ends meet. Enter the "paladar," mini restaurants within people's homes, where families served home-cooked meals for a modest fee. I loved eating in paladares—not only was the food usually delicious, but I got to meet and speak with so many Cubans. There was always lively discussion around the dinner table. It was the best four months of my twenty-something life. Just a taste of ropa vieja, the classic Cuban braised-beef dish full of umami and subtle sweetness, transports me back there. This version has dried apricots, which many recipes do not, but I find that the sweetness is lovely. While I can't bring you to a paladar, I can give you this perfect dinner party dish that just gets better as it sits. Make it a day or two before you plan to serve it and warm it through via a gentle stovetop simmer just before your guests arrive.

SERVES 6

- 1 teaspoon cumin seeds
- 1 teaspoon coriander seeds
- 3 whole cloves
- 2 tablespoons neutral oil, plus more if necessary
- 2 pounds flank steak, cut into four pieces against the grain
- Kosher salt and freshly ground black pepper
- 2 medium yellow onions, sliced (about 2½ cups)
- 1 teaspoon dried oregano
- 8 large garlic cloves, minced (about ¼ cup)
- 4 bell peppers (any color; I use green and red), sliced (about 6 cups)
- 2 tablespoons tomato paste
- 1 teaspoon Spanish smoked paprika
- 1 teaspoon red chile flakes
- ½ teaspoon ground allspice
- 1 cup red wine
- 1 cup pimento-stuffed Manzanilla olives, drained
- 2 bay leaves, preferably fresh
- 1 (28-ounce) can good-quality crushed tomatoes, such as San Merican Tomato
- ¼ cup apple cider vinegar
- 5 dried apricots, chopped

1. Preheat the oven to 350°F.
2. In a small dry sauté pan, toast the following spices over medium heat individually, transferring each to the same mortar and pestle or spice grinder after they are done: cumin seeds until they are fragrant and start to brown, about 90 seconds; coriander seeds until browned, about 30 seconds; and cloves until fragrant, about 30 seconds. Coarsely grind the spices.
3. In a large Dutch oven, heat the oil over high heat until it shimmers. Generously season the steak with salt and pepper. Working in batches, sear the steak until browned, about 5 minutes per side. Place on a plate.
4. Reduce the heat to medium. Add more oil to the pan if necessary. Add the onions and stir, scraping up the bits on the bottom, about 1 minute. Add a healthy pinch of kosher salt, partially cover, and cook, stirring often, until the onions are softened and slightly browned, about 10 minutes.
5. Stir in the oregano, partially cover, and cook, stirring occasionally, until the onions are various shades of brown, about 3 minutes. Add the garlic and stir to combine for about 30 seconds. Add the bell peppers and stir well for 2 minutes. Mix in 1 teaspoon of the toasted spice mixture and 1 teaspoon kosher salt and cook, stirring frequently, until the peppers are pliable and their skin rises slightly from the edges, about 5 minutes.
6. Add the tomato paste and cook, stirring frequently, until the tomato paste darkens and evenly coats all the vegetables, about 3 minutes. Stir in the smoked paprika, chile flakes, allspice, and 2 teaspoons kosher salt.

Cook, stirring frequently, scraping the bottom and sides of the pan, reducing the heat if necessary, until the peppers are very soft and coated with the dark brown onions, about 8 minutes.

7. Pour in the red wine to deglaze, scraping the bottom of the pot, and stir in the olives and bay leaves. Reduce the heat to medium-low and simmer uncovered, stirring occasionally, for 10 minutes to combine the flavors.

8. Add the tomatoes, vinegar, apricots, and 3 cups water and stir well. You can also add more of the spice mixture if desired here and stir. Nestle the meat into the sauce, submerging it as much as possible, pouring in any juices from the plate. Bring to a gentle simmer, cover, and braise until the beef is very tender and pulls apart easily, about 2½ hours. (You can leave the lid ajar for the last hour of cooking, if the sauce looks watery.) Remove from the heat.

9. Use tongs to transfer the beef to a bowl and use two forks to shred the beef.

10. Return the sauce to medium heat and reduce until it's thickened as much as you'd like, 5 to 10 minutes. Add the shredded beef to the pot and mix with the sauce. Serve hot.

Note: Advieh is a Persian spice blend, available at Persian markets and specialty spice shops. You can also make your own. Naz recommends mixing 2 teaspoons ground cinnamon, 2 teaspoons ground dried rose petals, 1 teaspoon ground cumin, 1 teaspoon ground cardamom, 1 teaspoon ground nutmeg, and 1/2 teaspoon ground coriander.

Maheecheh

BRAISED LAMB SHANKS

As a ten-year-old Iranian exile who was occasionally taunted and called "little terrorist," Naz Deravian discovered the soft diplomacy of after-school playdates that drifted into home-cooked feasts. I first encountered her work when I was asked to judge a cookbook tournament, the Piglet Prize, for Food52. Once I started cooking through Naz's book, *Bottom of the Pot,* I read it cover to cover, like a novel. Ultimately, I took a week and crammed my fridge with her food. She won the Piglet Prize. These lamb shanks are a showstopper that will leave the heady aromas of clove and saffron perfuming your kitchen. I encourage you to rest the shanks for a full 24 hours once you've applied the rub. Traditionally, this dish is served with bagali polo (Persian fava bean and dill rice), but it's also fantastic with Yogurt Tahdig (page 120) and Sabzi (page 84).

SERVES 4 TO 6

- 1 teaspoon ground turmeric
- Kosher salt and freshly ground black pepper
- 3½ pounds lamb shanks (3 to 4 large shanks), fat trimmed
- ¼ teaspoon saffron threads
- 1¼ teaspoons orange blossom water, plus more to taste
- 3 tablespoons neutral oil
- ¼ cup white wine
- 2 small yellow onions, chopped (about 2 cups)
- 4 large garlic cloves, chopped (about 2 tablespoons)
- 3 tablespoons tomato paste
- 1½ teaspoons advieh (Persian spice blend; see Note)
- Grated zest of 1 large orange (1½ to 3 teaspoons)
- ½ cup fresh orange juice (about 2 oranges)
- Grated zest of 1 lime (about 1 teaspoon)
- 1 tablespoon plus 2 teaspoons fresh lime juice, plus more if needed (about ½ lime)
- Fresh green herbs (optional), such as mint or parsley, for garnish

1. In a small bowl, combine the turmeric, 2 teaspoons kosher salt, and 1 teaspoon black pepper. Rub the lamb shanks evenly with the seasoning. Cover and refrigerate for at least 2 hours and up to 24 hours. Bring to room temperature before cooking.
2. Grind the saffron using a mortar and pestle and add 2 tablespoons hot water and the orange blossom water and set aside.
3. In a large pot or Dutch oven, heat the oil over medium-high heat. Set a baking sheet next to the stove. When the oil is hot but not smoking, add the shanks and sear until browned on all sides, a few minutes per side. You might have to do this in batches so you don't overcrowd the pot. The shanks will release from the pot when ready. Be patient; don't force it. Transfer the shanks to the baking sheet and set aside.
4. Carefully pour all but 3 tablespoons of fat out of the pot. Add the white wine, scraping up any stuck-on bits and pieces, and reduce the heat to medium. Add the onions and 1 teaspoon kosher salt and sauté, stirring constantly, until glassy, 6 to 8 minutes.
5. Add the garlic and sauté until softened, about 2 minutes. Stir in the tomato paste and advieh and cook until fragrant, adding a tablespoon of water if the tomato paste is too thick, and watching carefully so the tomato paste does not burn, 1 to 2 minutes. Add the orange zest, orange juice, lime zest, lime juice, saffron/orange blossom water, 2 teaspoons kosher salt, and ¼ teaspoon black pepper and stir to incorporate.
6. Return the shanks to the pot. Pour in 2 cups water and bring up to a gentle boil. Reduce the heat to low, cover, and simmer until the shanks are tender, 2 to 3 hours. (Alternatively, you can transfer the pot to a 325°F oven and oven-braise for 2 to 3 hours.) Check every 20 minutes or so; if the sauce sticks on the bottom, add ½ cup additional water at a time and scrape with your spoon.
7. Remove the shanks and place them on a serving platter. Skim any fat off the sauce. Taste and add more salt, pepper, a squeeze of lime, or a drop of orange blossom water, to taste. Pour the sauce over the shanks, garnish with the herbs (if using), and serve warm.

HAMID

There's still morning dew on the windshields of the cars parked along Westwood Boulevard when my crew and I pull up to Shamshiri Grill. A "Tehrangeles" institution since 1981, it's a gathering place where Iranian Americans can eat the food of a homeland many have not seen for half a lifetime, if ever.

My producers warn me that owner and executive chef Hamid Mosavi seems somewhat shut down, shy and monosyllabic at best. My stomach drops. This is my first day filming my new show, *Taste the Nation*. I'm not a journalist, and beyond a few short interviews I've conducted at book and food festivals, I'm usually on the other side of the mic.

Inside the restaurant, I scan the room for Hamid. Orange flames flicker on the brown faces firing up the grill in a glass-enclosed kitchen in the back. I turn just as a large figure appears in the doorway, blocking all light. A broad-shouldered gun safe of a man steps into the dining room.

Up close, Hamid also looks uneasy—we are both on unsure footing. The first few minutes are unbearably awkward. I press Hamid repeatedly about his experience with xenophobia during the Iranian hostage crisis, but he doesn't divulge much. Later, I can see I expected him to tell a certain story and so I tried to push him toward that story. It's only when I start following the story as *he* tells it, rather than try to lead, that I learn to truly listen. Hamid teaches me how.

Hamid arrived in LA in the summer of 1976. He left behind an Iran where afternoons were spent playing Frisbee with the American kids outside the US consulate, Led Zeppelin was the best seller at his uncle's record shop, and young women couldn't get enough of the miniskirts his mother sewed at her bespoke clothing boutique. Just sixteen, he planned to go to the US to finish high school, attend college, and then return to Iran.

A natural athlete, Hamid was quickly recruited to the varsity water polo team at Glendale High School. People were friendly, even if they didn't seem to get that Persians weren't Arabs. But the loneliness floored him. He had studied English for years but understood almost nothing once he arrived, struggling with the speed and the slang. He would lie awake at night, so stressed he couldn't sleep. When he wasn't alone in his room, he was helping at his uncle's kebab shop, washing dishes until his arms ached.

When the Shah fled Iran in January 1979, Hamid didn't pay the situation much mind. He had never been religious or political. Few could see what was really coming. It was almost impossible to predict the speed with which a relatively secular country would be transformed into a totalitarian theocracy. Hamid couldn't know that his life was being split into two parts: a "Before" he would never be able to revisit and an "After" in which he would be permanently marooned.

That November, fifty-three Americans were taken hostage in the US Embassy in Tehran. Not long after in Los Angeles, a mob of frenzied men stormed his uncle's restaurant, baseball bats in hand. "You fucking Iranians, go back to your country," one of them yelled. As if in a trance, Hamid walked toward them carrying a 14-inch chef's knife. They scattered.

Slowly, Hamid began to grapple with the knowledge that the Iran he knew was gone. The future he had imagined for himself gone with it. Barely on the cusp of adulthood, he watched as his parents were rendered powerless. Unable to process the enormity of what was happening, cut off from the world he had known, and confronting open hostility on the streets of Los Angeles, he turned further inward. Hamid's sense of isolation gave rise to a "crazy rage" inside him. He felt ashamed of his country, his people. He stopped watching the news. In time, he began to work twenty-hour shifts and nap on the benches in the restaurant's dining room. A few years later, after being shot in a restaurant robbery, he retreated into drugs and alcohol.

In exile, the kitchen became his refuge, a place where he could lose himself. From his uncle, he learned the secrets of making the prized barg kebab, delicate skewers of shaved rib eye. By the end of 1981, Hamid had opened Shamshiri Grill.

HOOD
800-613-1210

He has gone through much in the intervening decades to quell his demons. But always, the kitchen grounded him. He cooks seductive, mouthwatering food that tastes of home. People love his food. Through this exchange, Hamid makes peace with all that he has lost, all that he never got to choose.

In listening, we give others the space to be vulnerable. My conversation with Hamid, its shape and textures, becomes a cherished touchstone I return to as I film *Taste the Nation* over the next few years. Hamid shows me that so often, the "real" story is not about what happens without, but what happens within.

Later that first day, Hamid shows me how he makes koobideh, or ground meat kebabs. The meat feels silky and rich under my fingers. It is kept cool on an ice table to ensure that the fat will melt only once on the grill, rendering the meat succulent and tender. When the kebab is ready, going from pink to juicy brown with blackened edges, Hamid fills half a plate with rice. He picks up the kebab and pinches the meat off the skewer in one clean motion. Lastly, he drops a grilled Anaheim pepper on the plate, too—his own California touch.

Soon his wife, a Thai citizen, appears with their two little ones. The sound of children brings a new energy to the empty restaurant. Hamid tells me he made sure the children had both American and Thai passports, "in case, if something happens." I ask him if he is still nervous about being displaced again after all these decades. He shrugs his shoulders. These days he has learned the art of detachment. "I'm a Buddhist now."

Hamid shows me that so often,
the "real" story is not about what happens
without, but what happens within.

Beef Koobideh

GROUND BEEF KEBABS

In Iran, koobideh are a popular street food. And with good reason: They are delicious. With just four ingredients, these kebabs might seem simple to make, but they're one of the harder recipes to get right. Their success depends entirely on the meat you use. You'll want to make this when you have the time to visit a good butcher, who will freshly grind the beef from just one cut of meat. If you're feeling chummy, ask them what millimeter their grinding blade is, and cross your fingers that it's not much more than 4 millimeters. Then, go straight to your kitchen, refrigerate the meat, and make sure to use it that day so it doesn't lose its juice. It's important to keep the meat cold so that the fat melts only on the grill. You'll need six 1-inch-wide flat metal skewers, which are usually at least a foot long. If you don't have the traditional koobideh skewers, these can also be prepared as 10 oval patties 6 inches long and 2 inches wide.

SERVES 6

2 small yellow onions
2 pounds high-quality freshly ground beef (no leaner than 80/20), such as shoulder or chuck
Kosher salt and freshly ground black pepper
Mast-o Khiar (recipe follows), for serving

1. Quarter the onions and puree with a few teaspoons of water, if needed. You should end up with about ⅔ cup puree. Set aside.
2. Fill a large bowl with ice. Place a medium bowl inside. This will keep the meat cold as you knead it with your hands. Set a bowl with ice water to the side for dipping your hands in. Have a sheet pan handy.
3. Add the beef, onion puree, 1 tablespoon kosher salt, and 1 tablespoon black pepper to the medium bowl. Knead the onion into the meat until well combined and sticky, 2 to 4 minutes. Divide the mixture into 6 equal portions in the bowl and shape them into ovals.
4. Dip your hands into the ice water. Place an oval of meat in the palm of one hand. Lay the top end of a skewer lengthwise onto the center of the oval of meat. Press the skewer down into the meat so the skewer is covered by meat on all sides, using your fingers to close any gaps. You want to end up with an even 10-inch-long log. Gently crimp the meat every ½ inch down the skewer, using your thumb and middle finger to make shallow divots. Pinch to make sure the meat is sealed tightly at both ends so that it sticks to the skewer and stays in place. (See photo on page 242.) Place the skewer on the sheet pan. Repeat with remaining skewers. Transfer to the fridge to chill until ready to grill.
5. Preheat a grill to high or a grill pan over high heat.
6. If grilling, oil the grates. Place the skewers on the hot grill or grill pan. Carefully flip the skewers as soon as the meat easily releases from the hot surface, about 3 minutes. Then flip every 1 to 2 minutes until the meat is charred and cooked through, 6 to 8 minutes total.
7. Using tongs, gently but firmly slide the meat off from the bottom of the skewer to the top in one motion. Serve immediately with the mast-o khiar.

(Continued)

Mast-o Khiar

ACCOMPANIMENT

YOGURT-CUCUMBER SAUCE

Every kebab, Persian or not, can benefit from this easy, tangy, herby yogurt sauce.

MAKES ABOUT 2 CUPS

- 2 cups whole-milk Greek yogurt or labneh
- 1 large shallot, finely diced (about 1/4 cup)
- 1 small garlic clove, minced (about 1 teaspoon)
- Kosher salt and freshly ground black pepper
- 1 Persian (mini) cucumber, peeled and diced (about 1/3 cup), plus more for garnish (optional)
- 2 tablespoons chopped toasted walnuts (see Notes), plus more (optional) for garnish
- 1 teaspoon dried mint, plus more (optional) for garnish
- 1 teaspoon dried dill, plus more (optional) for garnish
- Pinch of dried rose petals (optional), for garnish
- Extra-virgin olive oil, for drizzling

1. In a medium bowl, mix the Greek yogurt, shallot, garlic, 1 teaspoon kosher salt, and ½ teaspoon black pepper. Stir in the cucumber, walnuts, mint, and dill. If desired, garnish with cucumbers, walnuts, mint, dill, and rose petals.
2. Just before serving, drizzle with olive oil.

Notes:

I use Persian cucumbers here because they contain less water and fewer seeds than other cucumbers. It's fine to use a regular cucumber as long as you seed it.

You can toast walnuts in an oven at 350°F, stirring occasionally, until darkened and fragrant, 10 to 12 minutes.

Passover Brisket

My dear friend Esther Fein's beautiful home is filled with books; it has the atmosphere of a cozy salon. Esther is a great conversationalist: Talking with her about politics, literature, or really *anything* is always informative and entertaining. She's become my phone-a-friend when I need feedback on a piece of writing or some Jewish intel to help me celebrate my daughter's Ashkenazi heritage. Esther, like many Ashkenazi Jews, makes brisket every Passover, the spring holiday that marks the Jewish exodus from Egypt and that for many symbolizes rebirth and renewal. She adapted her recipe both from her mother and from Joan Nathan, the author and grand dame of Jewish cooking in America—and, in turn, I adapted my recipe from Esther's. Like many Ashkenazi dishes, brisket is like a warm comforting hug, best served on a cool, crisp day surrounded by friends and family. Though it's definitely not traditional (or kosher), I highly recommend serving brisket with Blackened Corn with Suya Spice (page 88) and Coconut Rice (page 124). For a more traditional approach, serve with roasted potatoes.

SERVES 6 TO 8

3 large garlic cloves, halved
1 (4-pound) first cut beef brisket (also known as the flat), trimmed of excess fat
Kosher salt and freshly ground black pepper
2 tablespoons neutral oil
2 medium yellow onions, finely chopped (about 3 cups)
4 large celery stalks, chopped (about 2 cups)
1 (6-ounce) can tomato paste
3 cups red wine
1 (14.5-ounce) can diced or crushed tomatoes
¼ cup soy sauce
¼ cup apple cider vinegar
1 to 3 sprigs fresh rosemary, to taste
4 to 6 sprigs fresh thyme, to taste
4 bay leaves, preferably fresh
1 tablespoon light brown sugar
1 tablespoon Spanish smoked paprika
1 teaspoon red chile flakes
8 large carrots, peeled and cut on the bias into 1-inch slices (about 4 cups)
¼ cup chopped fresh parsley leaves

1. Preheat the oven to 325°F.
2. Rub the garlic cloves all over the brisket, then reserve the garlic for sautéing with the onions and celery. Season the brisket with 1 tablespoon kosher salt and several healthy grinds of black pepper.
3. In a large Dutch oven, heat the oil over high heat. Add the brisket and sear on both sides until dark brown, 3 to 4 minutes per side. Remove the meat to a plate.
4. Reduce the heat to medium. Add the onions and sauté for 1 minute. Add a pinch of salt and sauté until glassy, about 4 minutes. Add the celery and the reserved garlic halves and sauté until softened, about 3 minutes.
5. Stir in the tomato paste until it coats the vegetables and darkens slightly, about 1 minute. Stir in 1 cup water, the red wine, diced tomatoes, soy sauce, vinegar, rosemary, thyme, bay leaves, brown sugar, smoked paprika, and chile flakes and scrape the bottom of the pot. Submerge the seared brisket, pour in any juices that have accumulated on the plate, cover the pot, and transfer to the oven.
6. Bake for 2½ hours, checking every 30 minutes or so to ensure that the brisket is almost entirely covered in liquid. Add water if needed.
7. Uncover the pot. Flip the meat, add the carrots, parsley, and 1 teaspoon kosher salt, stir, and bake uncovered until a meat thermometer inserted into the thickest part reaches 195°F, 1 to 1½ hours.
8. Remove the brisket from the sauce and place on a cutting board. Remove any thyme or rosemary stems. Let the meat stand for at least 15 minutes before slicing against the grain. If the sauce is too thin for your liking, place the Dutch oven over medium heat and reduce to your desired consistency. If the sauce is too thick, add water, ¼ cup at a time. Taste the sauce. Add more kosher salt if needed. Serve the sauce over the meat.

Sisig

PORK WITH CHICKEN LIVERS

Sisig started life as a salad, which is hard to imagine given today's meaty incarnation of the Filipino dish. The word *sisig* means "to make sour" in Tagalog, and the old-school, salad version of sisig was dressed with vinegar. The modern dish was born during the almost fifty-year-long American occupation of the Philippines, which lasted from 1898 until 1946. The US Army served its soldiers plenty of pork but discarded the pigs' heads. Ingenious and resourceful Filipino cooks saw a culinary opportunity, and added the meat from the discarded pigs' heads, along with chicken livers, to sisig salad, long before the "nose-to-tail" movement. I came face-to-face (quite literally) with what it takes to butcher a pig's head when making sisig with Francis Ang of Abacá, a modern Filipino restaurant in San Francisco. It was an experience I'll never forget, intensely grisly and uncomfortable for me. But, I eat meat. I should face where my meat comes from and what it takes for that meat to reach my plate. That said, I don't think it's realistic to ask you to buy a whole pig's head and butcher it at home, so this sisig is centered around pork butt and chicken livers. Francis makes sisig fried rice at his restaurant, but at home, I serve the unctuous meat over plain steamed rice. White vinegar cuts the fattiness, and I recommend adding additional acidity with Pineapple Salsa (page 250), Pickled Onions (page 173), or Chowchow (page 42).

SERVES 6 TO 8

- 1 (3-pound) boneless pork butt, cut into 4 chunks
- 2 carrots, roughly chopped
- 1 medium yellow onion, quartered, plus 1 large yellow onion, minced (about 2 cups)
- 4 large scallions, white and light-green parts trimmed and left whole, dark green top chopped and kept separate
- 3 garlic cloves, 2 left whole, 1 minced (about 2 teaspoons)
- Kosher salt
- 2 tablespoons unsalted butter
- 1 teaspoon chopped fresh ginger
- 4 ounces chicken livers, rinsed and roughly chopped
- 1 cup distilled white vinegar
- 3 tablespoons soy sauce
- 2 tablespoons fish sauce (I like Red Boat 40°N brand)
- 1 serrano chile, thinly sliced
- 1 tablespoon sugar, preferably turbinado
- 1/2 teaspoon freshly ground black pepper
- Steamed basmati or jasmine rice, for serving

1. In a large soup pot, combine the pork butt, carrots, quartered onion, the white and light-green scallion pieces, the whole garlic cloves, and 1 teaspoon kosher salt. Pour in enough tap water to fully submerge the meat, about 4 quarts. Bring to a boil over high heat. Reduce the heat to maintain a low simmer, partially cover, and simmer just until the meat is tender, 1½ to 2 hours, adding more hot tap water as needed to keep the meat covered.

2. Position a rack in the middle of the oven and preheat the broiler on high. Line a sheet pan with foil.

3. Remove the pork butt from the liquid and place on the prepared sheet pan. (Cool the broth in the pot and save for another use.) Broil the pork until slightly charred, watching closely to prevent burning, about 5 minutes. Cool the meat until it can be handled, about 10 minutes. Transfer the meat to a cutting board and chop into bite-size pieces.

4. In a large skillet, melt the butter over medium-high heat until bubbling. Add the minced onion and sauté until it starts to soften, about 2 minutes. Add the minced garlic and ginger, reduce the heat to medium, and sauté for just 1 minute. Add the chicken livers and cook, stirring frequently, until they go from red to pink, 1 to 2 minutes.

5. Add the chopped pork, vinegar, soy sauce, fish sauce, serrano chile, sugar, and 1 teaspoon kosher salt and bring to a simmer. Reduce the heat to medium-low, cover, and cook, stirring occasionally, until the flavors are combined, about 10 minutes. Stir in the black pepper.

6. Serve warm over rice, garnished with the scallion greens.

Pernil

ROAST PORK WITH CRISPY SKIN

I often make pernil for my family on Christmas Day. Even though none of us are Christian, we do all have the day off—and we spend it together, often in matching onesies, playing parlor games, exchanging gifts, and sipping The Company Cocktail (page 301) while lounging around. And yes, it may sound odd, but my Hindu family, who used to be entirely vegetarian, loves this slow-roasted pork that is the centerpiece of any Puerto Rican holiday table. But it was only after I went to Puerto Rico to film *Taste the Nation* that I learned how to take my pernil from good to great, thanks to chef Maria Mercedes Grubb. The skin on her pernil was shockingly crisp, shattering dramatically with every bite. Maria taught me the secret to achieving this Olympic-level crispiness: poking the skin all over with a sharp paring knife or needle, while taking care *not* to poke too deep, so that the fat does not render up into the skin and remains instead in a single layer. When you taste the results, you will agree that the effort is well worth it. I have never looked back, and I thank Maria for upping my pernil game.

Note that making this recipe requires advance planning: For best results, you want to marinate the pork for 2 days before cooking it, then oven-roast it low and slow for a full day. It's great with Congri / Moros y Cristianos (page 123), Zucchini with Sun-Dried Tomatoes (page 87), and so many other dishes.

SERVES 8

- 12 medium garlic cloves, peeled but whole
- Grated zest and juice of 3 limes (about 1 tablespoon zest, 6 tablespoons juice)
- Grated zest and juice of 1 orange (1 to 2 tablespoons zest, 1/4 cup juice)
- 1 tablespoon dried oregano, preferably Mexican or Dominican
- Kosher salt
- 1 (9- to 10-pound) bone-in, skin-on pork butt, rinsed well and patted dry
- Pineapple Salsa (recipe follows), for serving
- Pickled Onions (page 173), for serving

1. In a small food processor or blender, combine the garlic, lime zest, lime juice, orange zest, orange juice, oregano, and 1 tablespoon kosher salt and blend until well combined.
2. Line a large bowl with sheets of plastic wrap, letting the ends of the sheets hang over the sides of the bowl. Place the pork butt on a cutting board. Use a paring knife or a sterilized safety pin to puncture shallow (about ⅛-inch-deep) holes in the pork skin, spacing the holes about ½ inch apart. Avoid poking too deep into the layer of fat: You want that to stay intact. Score the pork skin with ⅛-inch-deep cuts in a wide crisscross pattern, 4 inches apart, which will allow you to cut the pork into individual portions without cutting through and shattering the crispy skin; this makes for an impressive presentation later. Again, do not cut too deeply.
3. Turn the pork skin-side down and use the paring knife to puncture 1-inch-deep slits all over the meat on its underside. Place the pork on top of the plastic wrap in the bowl, skin-side up.
4. Pour the garlic-citrus marinade over the meat and rub all over, turning the meat in the bowl and using your fingers to push the marinade into the slits in the meat at the bottom. Let sit at room temperature for 20 minutes.
5. Turn the meat skin-side up and pat the skin dry. Gather up the edges of the plastic wrap and wrap them around the meat portion of the pork butt, leaving the skin uncovered (this will result in crispier skin). Refrigerate for about 48 hours.
6. Position a rack in the middle of the oven and preheat the oven to 300°F.

(Continued)

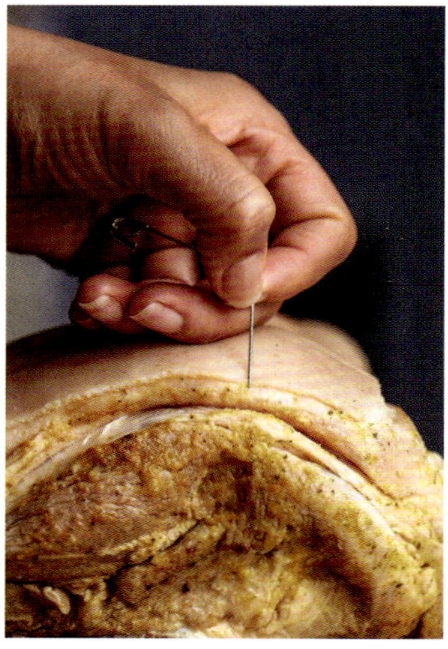

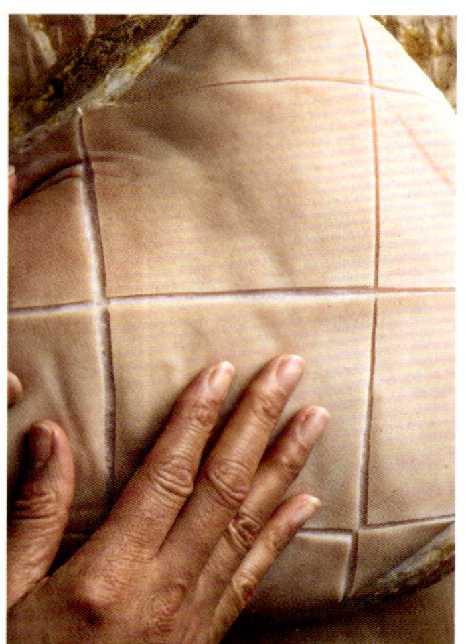

7. Cover a sheet pan with foil. Place a rack on top and cover the rack with parchment paper. Place the pork on the parchment, skin-side up. Wipe the skin clean with a paper towel. Cut a large piece of foil and lightly oil one side. Create a tent over the pork with the foil, oil-side down, and crimp around the edges of the pan. Cover with additional foil as needed.
8. Roast the pork for 5 hours.
9. Remove the foil cover and continue roasting until the meat pulls away easily, the juices run clear, and the internal temperature comes to at least 185°F, 2 to 4 hours longer. Start checking the meat for doneness at about the 2-hour mark (when the pork has been in for a total of 7 hours).
10. Rest the pork at room temperature for 30 minutes. Meanwhile, preheat the oven to 500°F, using a convection setting if available.
11. Roast the pork for 3 minutes. Rotate the pan and roast until the skin is puffed up, another 2 to 4 minutes. (If your oven does not reach 500°F, set the rack on the lowest rung and broil on high just until the skin puffs up.) Rest for at least 15 minutes before serving.
12. Serve with pineapple salsa and pickled onions.

Pineapple Salsa

ACCOMPANIMENT

This salsa lends a bright punch of flavor to grilled fish and seafood, and is a counterpoint to rich meats, such as Jerk Chicken (page 206) and Pernil (page 249). A great way to repurpose extra pineapple, it's so easy to make and delightful to have on hand; try a spoon of it with Mushroom Tacos Campesinos (page 35) or alongside some skewers of Beef Koobideh (page 241) and pita.

MAKES 1 CUP

1 cup ¼-inch-diced fresh pineapple
2 tablespoons coarsely torn fresh mint leaves
2 tablespoons fresh lime juice
½ to 1 teaspoon cayenne pepper or Kashmiri chile powder, to taste
Kosher salt

In a small bowl, stir together the pineapple, mint, lime juice, cayenne, and ½ teaspoon kosher salt.

Qabuli Pulao

LAMB AND RICE PILAF

The cooks at Shamim Popal's childhood home in Kabul would shoo her away any time she tried to enter the kitchen. But after fleeing Afghanistan in the wake of the Soviet invasion in 1979, she settled in Washington, DC, and began cooking Afghan food herself. She wanted her children to remain close to their culture, and like so many immigrants, she found that food was one of the most direct ways to preserve that connection. Though she didn't even know how to make rice when she first came to America, today, Shamim is the executive chef of Lapis, a cozy bistro with a menu full of the food that Afghans of her generation grew up eating at home. The star of the menu is this spiced braised lamb and rice pilaf topped with a tangle of cardamom-flecked carrots and sweetened raisins, which Shamin kindly taught me how to make. I've adapted it here. This aromatic and sumptuous dish is definitely a crowd-pleaser for a dinner party, worthy of any special occasion meal.

SERVES 4

- 1/3 cup neutral oil
- 1 1/2 pounds boneless lamb shoulder or shank, cut into about 3-inch chunks
- Kosher salt and freshly ground black pepper
- 2 small yellow onions, finely chopped (about 2 cups)
- 2 teaspoons minced fresh ginger
- 2 teaspoons minced garlic
- 1 teaspoon ground turmeric
- 2 teaspoons cardamom seeds, roughly ground in a mortar with a pestle
- 1 teaspoon ground cumin
- 1 teaspoon ground cinnamon
- 1/4 teaspoon ground cloves
- 2 cups basmati rice (buy the longest grain you can find; Shamim likes Zafarani brand), rinsed until the water runs clear
- 1 tablespoon unsalted butter or ghee
- 3 cups matchstick-cut or shredded carrots (about 5 large carrots)
- 1/2 cup dark raisins, rinsed
- 1 teaspoon light brown sugar

1. In a large Dutch oven with a tight-fitting lid, heat the oil over high heat until shimmering. Season the lamb on all sides with about 2 teaspoons kosher salt and several grinds of black pepper. Working in batches, sear the lamb on all sides until dark brown, 2 to 3 minutes per side. Transfer to a plate.
2. Reduce the heat to medium, add the onions and 1 teaspoon kosher salt, and sauté, stirring frequently and covering in between stirs, until the onions are deep brown, 15 to 20 minutes.
3. Add the ginger and garlic and stir until combined, about 30 seconds. Stir in the turmeric, 1 teaspoon of the cardamom, the cumin, cinnamon, cloves, 1 teaspoon kosher salt, several grinds of black pepper, and 2 cups hot tap water.
4. Add the seared lamb (the meat will not be submerged in the liquid), cover the pot, and bring to a simmer. Reduce the heat to low and braise until the lamb is tender and falls apart when pierced with a fork, about 2 hours. Stir occasionally to avoid sticking, maintaining a saucy consistency the entire time, and adding water, ½ cup at a time, if the sauce starts to dry up. Remove the pot from the heat, transfer the meat to a plate, cover the pot, and set aside.
5. In a large bowl, cover the rice with cold tap water and soak for 10 to 15 minutes.
6. Meanwhile, in a large skillet, melt the butter over medium-low heat. Add the carrots, raisins, the remaining 1 teaspoon cardamom, the brown sugar, ¼ teaspoon salt, and ½ cup water and cook, stirring frequently, until the liquid has evaporated and the carrots are tender, 6 to 8 minutes. Remove from the heat and set aside.
7. Add 12 cups water to a wide pot and bring to a boil over high heat. Place a fine-mesh colander in the sink. Drain the rice in the colander, carefully transfer the rice to the boiling water, and add ½ teaspoon salt. Return to a boil, then reduce the heat to medium and simmer until the rice is parcooked: It should be soft but with a hard center, just 4 to 6 minutes.

(Continued)

8. Drain the parcooked rice well. Return the lamb braising liquid to medium heat. Bring to a simmer. Stir the rice into the meat sauce. Mix gently with a spatula to keep the grains intact. Place the meat on top of the rice in an even layer. Push the handle of a wooden spoon through to the bottom of the pot in 5 spots, making narrow divots to allow the steam to come through it (liquid should pool in the divots). Cover the pot, set over medium heat, and steam until the rice is tender, 7 to 10 minutes. Uncover and let rest for at least 15 minutes before serving.
9. To serve, place the meat on a large platter. Heap the rice over the meat. Top with the carrots and raisins. Serve warm.

Note: There are a lot of moving parts in this recipe, so it is imperative to chop and measure everything before you begin cooking. Great pilafs feature fluffy, separate, intact grains of basmati rice; to make sure that's the outcome here, be careful not to overcook the rice when parboiling it.

Me and Shamim Popal at Lapis in Washington, DC

SWEETS

Sholeh Zard

RICE PUDDING WITH SAFFRON AND ROSE

The trio of cardamom, saffron, and rose water always takes me back to the Indian desserts of my childhood. In speaking with friends from Iran, Afghanistan, and Pakistan, it's clear we share the nostalgia. This recipe was inspired by a single serving of sholeh zard, a Persian rice pudding I ate with delight at the Tehran Market in Los Angeles. The ideal rice pudding starts by boiling rice until the grains collapse and the texture becomes thick and porridgy. Saffron and freshly ground cardamom impart a delicate spiced aroma. Rose water can be very perfumy—be careful when adding it and trust me, a teaspoon is more than enough. Garnishing with dried rose petals makes this not only a yummy dessert but a pretty one, too.

SERVES 6

1 cup jasmine or basmati rice, rinsed until the water runs clear
½ teaspoon saffron threads, ground in a mortar with a pestle
1½ cups sugar, preferably turbinado
1 teaspoon freshly ground cardamom
Kosher salt
1 teaspoon rose water
Rose petals (optional), for garnish
Fresh raspberries (optional), for garnish

1. In a large pot, bring 11 cups water to a boil over high heat. Add the rice, bring back to a boil, and cook until the grains start to disintegrate and the mixture resembles a loose porridge, at least 1 hour. Stir often so that the rice doesn't stick to the bottom of the pot, and add more water if necessary.
2. Meanwhile, dissolve the saffron in 2 tablespoons hot water.
3. When the rice is done, stir in the saffron water, sugar, cardamom, and a pinch of salt and cook uncovered for 5 minutes to blend the flavors. Remove from the heat and stir in the rose water.
4. Serve warm or chilled. If desired, garnish with rose petals and fresh raspberries.

SAIPIN

In Tamil, my first language, there is a saying: *Avaalodu kai ki oru vasanai iruku.* In English, you might translate it as "Her hand has an aroma." It's a way to describe the magic of an especially talented cook. A shorthand for the fact that everything they touch will taste good, simply because of the power of their hands.

Saipin Chutima has always had that touch. I'm guessing I first heard about Saipin through the gospel of Jonathan Gold, who named Saipin's Las Vegas restaurant, Lotus of Siam, "the single best Thai restaurant in North America" way back in the August 2000 issue of *Gourmet.* I don't really know, though, because Saipin has been lauded by every critic and outlet possible over the last two decades. All I know is that when we filmed *Top Chef* in Las Vegas in 2009, I had to make a pilgrimage to this temple of northern-style Thai cuisine.

In the late aughts, Lotus was a sight to behold. Back then, the restaurant was situated in a desolate strip mall far from the neon paradise of luxury casinos and resorts. The only sign of life was the long line of people waiting outside the restaurant to get in. Though I had been infatuated with Thai food since first tasting it at age thirteen, by the time of my first trip to Lotus of Siam, I no longer found it particularly exciting. That all changed the moment I opened the take-out bag back in my hotel room. Every bite was an addictive swirl of salty and sour, without any of the sweet edge I associated with Thai dishes.

Despite eating so much on set every day, almost every night I would get takeout from Lotus. I didn't know when, if ever, I'd get to eat food like it again. And I was dazzled by Saipin. As I waited in the crowded reception area for my bag of takeout, I would watch her—she was all business and so in command, shifting seamlessly between chef, host, and waitress. She had no idea who I was and couldn't have cared less, too busy to schmooze with tourists who seldom came to that part of town anyway. What a boss.

So, when we settled on exploring Las Vegas's Thai community for an episode of *Taste the Nation,* I knew we had to pay Saipin a visit. Even though so much had been written about her restaurant and her skills as a chef, as far as I could find, no one had told her personal story. No one had asked her not just how Lotus of Siam had come to be, but how she had learned to cook like that. How she had *dared* to cook like that in a country whose familiarity with Thai cuisine could have arguably been said to start and stop with pad Thai.

I would come to learn that Saipin has been defying expectations almost her entire life. Speaking in Thai, with her daughters Penny and Sabrina translating, Saipin described a childhood in the countryside of Lamphun Province in Northern Thailand, not far from Laos and Burma (now Myanmar). The oldest of seven siblings, she grew up in a grass-roofed wooden hut, and her family farmed rice; grew and foraged fruits, vegetables, and herbs; and hunted wild boar in the jungle that started in their backyard. At just five years old, she began cooking with her grandmother. Under her grandmother's tutelage, Saipin mastered a broad repertoire of Northern Thai dishes.

At age twelve, she began living and working in the home of a wealthy, aristocratic family in Chiang Mai. She was meant to serve as a sort of lady's maid for the elderly matriarch of the Chutima family. The Chutimas lived in an elaborate compound that housed ten to twenty relatives at any given time. They frequently put on feasts for fifty to a hundred guests and had a kitchen staff of twenty. When the king of Thailand came to stay at the Northern Palace in the mountains near Chiang Mai, Saipin told me, the elderly matriarch of the house, a formidable chef herself, would help the royal cooks from Bangkok source and prepare foods, with Saipin at her side. She quickly recognized Saipin's talent and intuitive ability in the kitchen.

"I learned very quickly," Saipin told me. By age fifteen, she was budgeting, planning menus for feasts, selecting ingredients at the market, and cooking the food. She became a favorite of the

LOTUS OF SIAM

From left to right: Sabrina, me, Saipin, and Penny at Lotus of Siam

elderly Madame Chutima's, who treated her as a culinary heir. Her own grandmother had taught her the earthy cuisine of the rural areas, relying on the plants and animals of the jungle. In the Chutima kitchen, Saipin learned a more subtle cuisine, with careful combinations of flavors and attention to presentation influenced by Royal Thai Cuisine. Saipin learned to apply such exacting approaches to northern city recipes.

In this upstairs-downstairs environment, Saipin caught the eye of Suchay—who now goes by Bill—one of the sons of the household. When Saipin was eighteen, Bill told her he wanted to marry her. In a society sharply divided by class, his mother disapproved, shipping him off to the United States to earn a degree in business. Promising to come back, he began writing letters to Saipin. He continued to write them for ten years. Finally, a decade after his departure, Bill asked Saipin to join him. He picked her up at the Los Angeles airport and shortly after, for the sum of $52 (the cost of the marriage license), they were married. The Chutimas disowned their son. Saipin and Bill were on their own.

It was Saipin's idea to open a restaurant. She had faith in her cooking and felt she needed to help make ends meet. Their first restaurant was in a suburban neighborhood in the San Fernando Valley. Eventually they moved to Vegas and opened Lotus of Siam in 1999. Saipin built the menu for Lotus using her own northern recipes, imbued with the spirit of the Thai grandmothers who had trained her. On this hot summer weeknight, more than two decades later, the restaurant is packed, but Saipin emphasizes how tough those early years were. At first the restaurant was empty. No one wanted to pay more for her elevated, sophisticated food and its complexity of flavors. They expected cheap take-out prices and large portions. They were not interested in nuance or regionality. In those days Saipin was the cook and the dishwasher—she did everything, including keeping two young children in tow in the back.

Today, Saipin presides over a far more upscale Lotus of Siam, and she no longer washes the dishes. The new location is *big,* easily several times the size of the original. Despite that, wait times often reach an hour and a half. Cushy booths line the dining rooms. The lighting is soft and intimate. A custom mural depicting Thai village life spans one long wall. Saipin flits through the restaurant smiling, joking, stopping at tables here and there, saying hello to regular customers.

Seeing her now, it is hard to believe what Penny tells me about those early years: "She cried every day." But, Saipin says, she was never afraid. When I ask her why not, she holds up her hands. "I have ten fingers and two hands. I'm never afraid."

Women like Saipin are a study in bravery. Women who must leap into the abyss with nothing but faith in themselves. Not knowing if those first steps toward their future will bear fruit. So often, it's women who are the carriers of the flavors and culture of their homeland. It's through their hands that traditions and identities get passed on. It's through their hands that they will a whole new life, in a new land, into existence.

It's through their hands that traditions and identities get passed on . . . that they will a whole new life, in a new land, into existence.

Khao Niao Mamuang

STICKY RICE WITH MANGO

There are so many dishes to choose from at Lotus of Siam, but I always finish with this delightful sweet treat. This recipe is based on my taste memory of the version I have there. The simplicity of the sweetened, creamy coconut sticky rice, juxtaposed with chunks of sweet-tart mango, makes this a lovely, light dessert to end any meal. The textural contrast of the chewy rice and tender, juicy mango is especially wonderful. Here the rice is steamed rather than boiled to keep it intact. Just remember to soak the rice the night before and to seek out ripe mangoes. Pallid, flavorless fruit won't cut it here. And Saipin would not approve.

SERVES 4

- 1½ cups Thai glutinous (sticky) rice, rinsed until the water runs clear
- 1 (13.5-ounce) can unsweetened coconut milk, preferably full-fat
- ½ cup sugar, preferably turbinado
- Kosher salt
- ½ teaspoon almond extract
- 2 mangoes, chopped (about 2 cups)

1. In a large bowl, combine the rinsed rice and cold water to cover by at least 1 inch. Cover the bowl and soak the rice overnight at room temperature.
2. In a medium pot, bring 1 to 2 inches of water to a simmer over medium heat. Drain the rice in a heatproof fine-mesh sieve and rinse. Set the sieve of rice on top of the pot, making sure the water does not touch the bottom of the sieve. Wet a paper towel and place over the rice in the sieve, folding the edges if needed so it doesn't stick out. Cover the pot and sieve with a tight-fitting lid. Steam the rice until tender and cooked through, periodically checking and adding more water if the pot runs dry, about 1 hour.
3. Meanwhile, in a small saucepan, combine the coconut milk, sugar, and ¼ teaspoon salt and bring to a boil over medium heat. Stir until the sugar has dissolved, about 2 minutes. Remove the pan from the heat and stir in the almond extract. Cover to keep warm.
4. Transfer the cooked rice to a large bowl. Stir in two-thirds of the coconut milk mixture, reserving the rest. Cover the bowl and let the rice stand until it has absorbed all the liquid, about 30 minutes.
5. When ready to serve, divide the rice among four serving bowls and drizzle with the remaining coconut milk mixture. Top each serving with the mango.

Mysore Pak

BUTTERY SWEET CHICKPEA SQUARES

Mysore pak, a South Indian treat that's similar to rich, melt-in-your-mouth shortbread cookies, always made an appearance during special occasions or religious holidays like Diwali. Mysore pak contains just three ingredients—sugar, ghee, and besan flour—but it is a very tricky recipe that is notoriously difficult to make well. My aunt Bhanu makes the best Mysore pak in the world; perfecting this recipe took several rounds of videoconferencing with her. She tutored me patiently through every step. No surprise—when I was a child, Bhanu tutored me in math, showing the same incredible patience.

Mysore pak is very much about timing, so it is crucial to lay out all your ingredients and equipment in advance. Make sure that your ghee is fresh. Make sure that you do not skip sifting or whisking your besan flour; smoothing out its inevitable clumps is key to this process. Be prepared to be patient and to stir. Resist the urge to increase the heat too much. Know that even imperfect versions of this dessert are pretty darn good. Aim for a crumbly square that's slightly soft in the center. Remember to show yourself some grace, because at the end of the day, it's just cooking after all.

SERVES 10 TO 12

2 cups sugar, preferably turbinado
1¼ cups besan flour, sifted through a fine-mesh sieve and/or whisked to eliminate clumps
1½ cups ghee, melted, at room temperature

1. Have a long-handled spoon and an ungreased 9-inch round nonstick cake pan ready.
2. In a wide nonstick pot, nonstick skillet, or wok, combine the sugar and 2 cups water. Set over medium heat and use a long-handled spoon to stir constantly until the sugar dissolves. Bring to a gentle boil. Stir frequently until the sugar reaches a "one-string" consistency (when you drip the syrup off a spoon, a long strand should follow the last drop), and about 220°F on a candy thermometer, about 20 minutes. **Remove from the heat.**
3. Sift or whisk the besan again, then immediately stir it into the sugar until the mixture is as smooth as possible, with only small lumps remaining, which will take about 2 minutes. Add the ghee and stir well with a spoon to eliminate any lumps (the mixture will not be emulsified).
4. **Return the pan to medium-low heat** and stir constantly, scraping the bottom to avoid sticking. The mixture will thicken into what looks like dense peanut butter, then it will become bubbly throughout. At this point, slide your spoon under one edge of the dough and fold it toward the middle. Keep doing this constantly on all sides, while it thickens into a rough, shaggy, pockmarked dough. If you see parts of the dough browning, reduce the heat to low. Stir just until the dough becomes a single, solid putty-like mass (the whole mass will move as one when you stir). This process should take 15 to 25 minutes.
5. Carefully pour the mixture into the nonstick cake pan and use a flat or offset spatula to smooth it on top and all the way to the edges. Wait about 5 minutes for the mixture to harden just a little. Cut into 1- to 1½-inch squares or diamonds using short, piercing cuts with a long knife: Do not drag the knife or you won't achieve a clean cut. Wait another 5 to 10 minutes for it to harden further, then cut again along the same lines. Cool completely and carefully separate into pieces. Store in an airtight container.

Decolonized Halo-Halo

TROPICAL FRUIT AND CRUSHED ICE SUNDAE

This Filipino dessert, a textural kaleidoscope of crushed ice, ice cream, fruit, and any other sweet item your heart desires, appeals to the little girl in me; not just because of the frenzy of textured treats, but also because I know how refreshing it is on a hot summer day. Halo-halo, which means "mix-mix" in Tagalog, is supposed to be an indulgence. This is not the time to worry about what has less sugar—Cinnamon Toast Crunch or Frosted Flakes. You can and should use whatever "guilty parent" cereal you want, depending on your threshold for so-called bad parenting. (Krishna loves this dessert because she otherwise never gets to eat Frosted Flakes.) You can add the crumbs from the bottom of a cookie tin. You can crush up some salty pretzels. Mix and match and alter amounts to your preference: It's the comingling of different flavors and textures that is essential. My version focuses on tropical ingredients, including bright violet ube (purple yam) ice cream and mango sorbet for contrasting flavors and visual appeal—the purple and orange look fantastic together. I mix chewy tapioca pearls (boba) with condensed milk to balance the sweetness in the dessert. Finally, I leave out the traditional flan—who needs the colonial influence?—but do use similarly soft coconut jelly. The amounts are approximate: Let your guests decide how they'd like to mix their own.

SERVES ABOUT 6

COCONUT GELATIN

1 (13.5-ounce) can unsweetened coconut milk
1 (5-ounce) can coconut cream
2 (0.25-ounce) envelopes unflavored gelatin powder
1/4 cup sugar, preferably turbinado
1/2 teaspoon pure vanilla extract
A few drops any food coloring (optional)

HALO-HALO

1 (8.8-ounce) package tapioca pearls (boba), black sugar flavor
About 1/2 cup sweetened condensed milk
About 2 cups ice, sealed in a plastic bag and pounded until crushed
1 to 2 cups each of about three types of tropical fruit, such as chopped mango, pineapple, kiwi, papaya, or quartered lychees
1 pint ube ice cream
1 pint mango sorbet
2 cups toasted coconut flakes
2 cups Frosted Flakes, or your cereal of choice
Other options include (but are not limited to) sweetened red beans, jackfruit, and palm seeds

1. **Make the coconut gelatin:** In a small pot, bring the coconut milk to a boil over medium heat.
2. Meanwhile, pour the coconut cream into a heatproof medium bowl and sprinkle the gelatin over the top. Let it bloom for 1 minute.
3. Add the hot coconut milk, sugar, vanilla, and a few drops of food coloring (if using) to the bowl and whisk until the sugar is completely dissolved, about 2 minutes. Pour into an 8-inch square pan and refrigerate until firm, at least 3 hours. Cut into small cubes.
4. **Prepare the halo-halo:** Cook the tapioca pearls according to the package directions, then immediately soak in ice water after cooking. Drain, transfer to a small bowl, and mix with the sweetened condensed milk.
5. Arrange a dessert bar with bowls of the following (these are in the order that I usually use when assembling): crushed ice, fruit, ube ice cream, mango sorbet, boba, coconut gelatin cubes, toasted coconut, and Frosted Flakes.

(Continued)

6. Provide each guest with a tall glass and a long spoon and let everyone build their own dessert. I like to scoop 1 to 2 heaping tablespoons of ice on the bottom of a tall glass, then add 1 to 2 tablespoons of each fruit, ¼ cup ube ice cream, 1 heaping tablespoon of mango sorbet, ¼ cup boba with condensed milk, and a few cubes of coconut gelatin. I sprinkle a handful of toasted coconut and 1 tablespoon of Frosted Flakes over the top.

Black Sesame Maple Ice Cream

This dessert is the result of the long days I spent in the kitchen during the pandemic, experimenting with whatever we had in the house. One day, I wanted to make ice cream, and I spotted a bottle of maple syrup and a jar of sesame seeds in my pantry. The combination of maple and nutty sesame is reminiscent of the sesame brittle that many of us Asian kids grew up eating. Black sesame seeds look particularly stunning against pale ice cream. While throwing in a couple of cloves may seem superfluous, I guarantee that it's crucial. They add complexity and a nuance of flavor that truly elevates the dessert.

MAKES ABOUT 1 QUART

2 cups heavy cream
2 cups whole milk
2 whole cloves
1/4 teaspoon ground cinnamon
4 egg yolks
1/4 cup sugar, preferably turbinado
3/4 cup pure maple syrup
1 teaspoon pure vanilla extract
3 tablespoons white sesame seeds
Kosher salt
1/4 cup black sesame seeds

1. In a heavy-bottomed medium pot or saucepan, heat the cream, milk, cloves, and cinnamon over medium heat, stirring often to prevent a skin from forming on the top, until the cinnamon dissolves and the cream starts to bubble around the edges, 6 to 9 minutes. Remove from the heat. Let cool slightly.
2. In a small bowl, beat the egg yolks, sugar, maple syrup, and vanilla until smooth. Slowly pour in about ¼ cup of the warm cream, whisking constantly so that the eggs don't curdle. Whisk all of that mixture into the saucepan of cream and milk, being careful to prevent curdling. Place over medium-low and stir constantly until the mixture has thickened slightly, taking care not to boil it, about 5 minutes.
3. Strain through a fine-mesh sieve into a bowl. Cool the bowl by immersing it in an ice-water bath for at least 1 hour, or cover and store in the refrigerator until cold.
4. Meanwhile, heat a small dry pan over medium-high heat. Add the white sesame seeds and 1 teaspoon salt, reduce the heat to medium, and toast, stirring frequently, until the seeds are light brown and smell nutty, about 5 minutes. Transfer to a plate.
5. In the same dry pan, toast the black sesame seeds over medium heat, stirring frequently, just until the seeds start to pop, about 2 minutes. Transfer to the plate with the white seeds and allow to cool completely.
6. Pour the cream mixture into an ice cream maker and churn according to the manufacturer's instructions. Once the ice cream starts to thicken up, gradually sprinkle in the sesame seeds so they are evenly distributed throughout the ice cream. If added too early, they'll sink to the bottom. Continue churning, then transfer to an airtight container and chill in the freezer until firm.

Level Up: If you make and have any Mysore Pak (page 268), crumble it on top for a textured garnish. Trust me—whenever my aunt Bhanu comes to visit from Chennai, she brings a bag full. Krishna and I devour the chunks and are eventually left with a bunch of crumbs that happen to make the perfect topper for whatever ice cream we have around.

Ruiz's Pieces

PEANUT BUTTER–MESQUITE TREATS

While learning about Indigenous foodways in Arizona, I met natural foods curandera (healer) and activist Felicia Cocotzin Ruiz, whose work is deeply rooted in the healing properties of earth medicines. She helps Native communities heal from health issues related to a diet of non-Indigenous foods—or, as Felicia calls it, a colonized diet. Felicia's nutritious little sweets are especially fun to make with children who are too little to use a knife or stove. Mesquite flour can be ordered online easily and is essential here for its unique flavor and texture. While these treats can be stored in the refrigerator for up to 2 weeks, they usually disappear much more quickly.

MAKES ABOUT 12

½ cup no-stir creamy peanut butter
3 tablespoons raw mesquite flour
4 tablespoons pure maple syrup
2 tablespoons coconut oil, melted
¼ cup raw cacao powder
½ cup pumpkin seeds
Fine sea salt

1. In a small bowl, use a spoon to mix the peanut butter, mesquite flour, and 2 tablespoons of the maple syrup into a crumbly dough.
2. In another small bowl, mix the coconut oil, cacao powder, and the remaining 2 tablespoons maple syrup. Stir until smooth, making sure there are no lumps. Set aside.
3. In a small blender or food processor, combine the pumpkin seeds and ½ teaspoon salt and pulse into a coarse meal. Place on a baking sheet or large plate.
4. Using a small-portion scoop, spoon, or your hands, roll 2 teaspoons of peanut butter dough into 1-inch balls. Set aside in a single layer.
5. Working in batches, gently place the balls in the cacao coating. Use a spoon (or your hands) to gently roll the balls in the mixture until evenly coated.
6. After the balls are coated with cacao mixture, place them on the pumpkin seed mixture and lightly roll to coat. Hold the balls gently, like a hot potato, being careful not to squash them. Place on a tray.
7. Immediately cover and refrigerate until firm, at least 1 hour. Serve chilled.

Eric Nam's Quick Hotteok

SWEET PANCAKES STUFFED WITH NUTS AND CINNAMON

Keep a can of biscuit dough in your refrigerator and you can have your hands on a freshly made, decadent treat in no time. In Korea, these sweet, filled pancakes are traditionally made from yeasted dough and sold on the street; singer Eric Nam taught me his quick at-home hack when we filmed in Koreatown, Los Angeles. His are filled with a simple brown sugar and roasted seed mixture that melts and turns delightfully gooey, but you could swap in any kind of sugar or even jam; you can also use any kind of seed or nut.

MAKES 8 HOTTEOK

2 tablespoons packed light brown sugar
1/2 teaspoon ground cinnamon
1 (16.3-ounce) can/8 ct biscuits (I used Pillsbury Grands! Buttermilk)
About 2 tablespoons unsalted roasted sunflower seeds
About 2 tablespoons unsalted roasted pumpkin seeds
Neutral oil, for pan-frying

1. In a small bowl, mix the brown sugar and cinnamon together.
2. Place a biscuit on a cutting board. Flatten to about a ¼-inch thickness. Place 1 teaspoon of the brown sugar cinnamon mix in the center. Top with about ½ teaspoon sunflower seeds and about ½ teaspoon pumpkin seeds. Carefully gather up the sides of the biscuit over the topping, pinch shut to seal, then smash down into a ¼-inch-thick disc as evenly flat as possible. Use a rolling pin if needed. Repeat with all the biscuits and fillings. Let sit for 10 to 15 minutes to bring the dough to room temperature. (This will help ensure that the pancakes cook all the way through.)
3. Line a plate with paper towels and set it near the stove. In a large nonstick skillet, heat about 2 tablespoons of oil over medium heat.
4. Once the oil is shimmering, reduce the heat to medium-low. Working in batches, gently pan-fry the pancakes, pressing them down in the pan with an oiled heavy wide spatula, burger press, or bottom of a cup, until deep golden brown on both sides, 2 to 3 minutes per side, adding more oil if necessary. It's important to smash them while in the pan to ensure that they're evenly cooked. Serve warm.

POPS OPEN

Banana Lumpia

SWEET FRIED SPRING ROLLS

While I rarely make dessert, I love spring rolls, I love bananas, and I *love* a good carnival snack. The joy that I experienced biting into one of these the first time I made them, combined with the big toothy grins they instantly produced on the faces of my friends, was enough for me to begin making them regularly. Not only is it fun to roll lumpia, it's also easy to include kids in the process—and bonus, it is not a time-intensive project. These are a great way to use up leftover spring roll/lumpia wrappers that you might still have in the freezer, and the finished rolls themselves freeze beautifully, to be broken out the next time you need to cheer up a kid who took a spill, fell off their bike, or had a bad day at school. Or an adult, for that matter.

MAKES 20 SPRING ROLLS

¼ cup light or dark brown sugar
½ teaspoon ground cinnamon
Small pinch of ground cloves
5 large firm-ripe bananas (yellow with only a few brown spots)
½ teaspoon flour (optional; see Notes)
20 (8-inch-square) frozen spring roll or lumpia wrappers, thawed
Neutral oil, for frying
Powdered sugar, for dusting

1. In a small bowl, mix the brown sugar, cinnamon, and cloves.
2. Cut each banana in half crosswise. Then halve each piece lengthwise. Each quarter should be no more than about 4 inches long. If the bananas are small, double the amount and only cut them crosswise.
3. **Set up a rolling station:** Place a cutting board in front of you and a small bowl of water nearby. Add flour to the water (if using) and mix. Place a lumpia wrapper on the cutting board so that one corner faces you. Dip your finger in the water and wet all the edges of the wrapper. Scoop about ¼ teaspoon spiced sugar in a horizontal line in the middle of the lower third of the wrapper. Place the banana on top of the brown sugar and cover with another ¼ teaspoon spiced sugar. Roll up the bottom of the wrapper over the banana, then tightly fold the left and right corners of the wrapper in. Then roll the log away from you into a sealed package. Repeat with the rest of the banana pieces and wrappers.
4. Place a wire rack over a baking sheet and set it near the stove. Pour about ¾ inch of oil into a deep sauté pan or pot and heat over medium until the oil reaches about 350°F on a deep-fry thermometer.
5. Working in batches, fry the lumpia on both sides until the skin is browned and crisp, 90 seconds to 2 minutes per side. Using tongs, remove to the wire rack and dust with powdered sugar. Serve warm. Freeze any extra; they will last 2 weeks.

Notes:

If your spring roll or lumpia wrappers are on the thick side, you may want to double the amount of bananas. Ideally you want much more banana than wrapper.

I sometimes add a dash of flour to my bowl of water (see pictures) to help with sealing the lumpia wrapper edges.

Blackberry Slump-ish

FRUIT DESSERT WITH CORNMEAL DUMPLINGS

I couldn't get enough of the blueberry slump that pioneering linguist Jessie Little Doe Baird made for me when I visited Massachusetts to learn about the ongoing efforts to preserve the language and culture of the Wampanoag people. Jessie's slump, made with blueberries, comes from a centuries-old Wampanoag recipe, which she understandably wants to keep in her family. The culinary producer of *Taste the Nation*, Anthony Jackson, mentioned that his mother, Carole, used to make a slump all the time using blackberries, so—inspired by Jessie—I adapted Mrs. Jackson's recipe for this homey dessert. I preserve as much berry juice as possible by cooking the berries on the stovetop, then I finish the dish in the oven to bronze the tops of the corn dumplings. Slumps are often cooked entirely on the stove—hence, the slump-ish.

SERVES 6

1½ pounds blackberries (5 to 6 cups), fresh or frozen
½ cup sugar, preferably turbinado
½ teaspoon grated lemon zest
½ teaspoon ground cinnamon
2 teaspoons instant tapioca (such as Kraft Minute), ground in a mortar with a pestle or spice grinder

BISCUITS

1 cup all-purpose flour
½ cup fine-grind cornmeal
2 tablespoons sugar, preferably turbinado
1 tablespoon baking powder
½ teaspoon ground cinnamon
½ teaspoon kosher salt
6 tablespoons (3 ounces) unsalted butter, cut into small pieces
1 cup heavy cream
1 tablespoon demerara sugar (optional), for topping

FOR SERVING

Ice cream

1. Position a rack in the center of the oven and preheat the oven to 375°F.
2. In a 9- or 10-inch cast-iron skillet, combine half of the blackberries, the sugar, lemon zest, and cinnamon. Set over medium heat, cover, and cook, stirring occasionally, to let the berries soften and release their juices, about 5 minutes. Use a potato masher or wooden spoon to mash the berries well.
3. Mix in the remaining blackberries and the tapioca, reduce the heat to medium-low, cover the skillet, and simmer, stirring and scraping the bottom of the pan frequently, to allow the berries to soften, about 5 minutes. Taste and add more sugar, if you like.
4. **While the berries are cooking, make the biscuits:** In a food processor (or in a bowl), combine the flour, cornmeal, sugar, baking powder, cinnamon, and salt. Scatter the butter pieces evenly over the flour and pulse to cut in the butter. (If using a bowl, use a fork or pastry cutter to cut in the butter until it resembles a coarse meal.) Pour in ¾ cup plus 2 tablespoons heavy cream and pulse or stir until just combined.
5. Divide the dough into 6 equal portions (about ⅓ cup dough each) and shape each portion into a patty. Place 5 patties in a circle on top of the fruit, then place the sixth patty in the middle. Brush the biscuits with the remaining 2 tablespoons heavy cream and sprinkle with demerara sugar, if using.
6. Place the skillet in the oven and bake until the biscuits are golden brown, 25 to 30 minutes. Serve warm, with ice cream.

Strawberry-Cardamom and Cream Cake

The recipe for this stunning cake was inspired by a cake the late, great Sylvia Weinstock made for my wedding. We first developed the recipe for the 100th anniversary issue of *Better Homes & Gardens*. Cardamom is a spice used in many Indian desserts and pairs well with fresh strawberries. The pound cake and cream cheese frosting make this an irresistible showstopping dessert.

SERVES 12

3½ cups chopped strawberries, plus more whole strawberries (optional), for garnish
⅔ cup plus 2 teaspoons granulated sugar, preferably turbinado
Softened butter, for the pans
4 cups plus 2 tablespoons all-purpose flour
1 tablespoon ground cardamom
2 teaspoons baking powder
1 teaspoon baking soda
1½ teaspoons kosher salt
8 tablespoons (1 stick/ 4 ounces) unsalted butter, at room temperature
½ cup neutral oil
⅔ cup packed light brown sugar
4 teaspoons pure vanilla extract
4 large eggs, at room temperature
Grated zest of 2 lemons
1½ cups buttermilk
8 ounces cream cheese, at room temperature
2 cups powdered sugar, sifted
2 cups heavy cream

1. In a small bowl, combine 2 cups of the strawberries and 2 teaspoons of the granulated sugar. Set aside.
2. Preheat the oven to 350°F. Butter three 8-inch round cake pans and line the bottoms with rounds of parchment paper.
3. In a medium bowl, whisk together 4 cups of the flour, the cardamom, baking powder, baking soda, and kosher salt.
4. In a stand mixer fitted with the paddle, combine the butter, oil, remaining ⅔ cup granulated sugar, the brown sugar, and 2 teaspoons of the vanilla. Beat on medium-high speed, occasionally scraping down the sides of the bowl with a spatula, until light and fluffy, about 5 minutes. Add the eggs one at a time, scraping down the sides of the bowl in between, until well incorporated. Add in the lemon zest.
5. Reduce the mixer speed to low and add half of the flour mixture, then half of the buttermilk. Repeat with the remaining flour and buttermilk, beating until just incorporated.
6. In another medium bowl, toss together the remaining 1½ cups strawberries and the remaining 2 tablespoons flour. Fold the strawberries into the batter. Divide the batter evenly among the prepared pans.
7. Bake until the cake springs back when touched and a toothpick inserted in the center of each comes out clean, about 30 minutes.
8. Let cool in the pans for about 10 minutes. Run a knife around the edge of the pans and transfer the layers to a wire rack to cool completely before frosting.
9. In a stand mixer fitted with the whisk, mix the cream cheese and powdered sugar to combine. Slowly add the heavy cream and continue to mix until the mixture thickens, like medium-peak whipped cream, 2 to 3 minutes. Mix in the remaining 2 teaspoons vanilla.
10. Use a serrated knife to cut the domed tops from the cakes so they are flat and level. Place one cake layer on a cake stand or serving tray and scoop one-third of the whipped frosting on it and spread evenly. Use a slotted spoon to top with half of the strawberries, leaving most of the juices in the bowl. Place the second cake layer on top, bottom-side up. Top with another one-third of the frosting and the remaining strawberries. Place the last layer of cake, bottom-side up, and spread the rest of the frosting on top, coating the sides with a thin layer, if desired. Garnish with whole strawberries, if desired.

DRINKS

Rose Water Limeade

Growing up in India, I drank a lot of nimbu pani—a limeade or lemonade, accented with sugar and pink or black salt. Often, we'd add a few drops of Rooh Afza, Pakistani rose syrup, which would impart a lovely pink hue, making it our version of pink lemonade. My grandmother would also often stir a bit of the same rose syrup into milk to get me to drink it. I eventually realized that rose *water* was a gentler, purer way of flavoring drinks, and in turn created this limeade, pink hue optional.

SERVES 4

- ½ cup fresh lime juice (about 4 limes)
- 2 tablespoons plus 2 teaspoons sugar, preferably turbinado
- 1 teaspoon rose water
- 1 teaspoon Himalayan pink salt or sea salt
- Red food coloring (optional)

In a pitcher, mix 5 cups room-temperature water, the lime juice, sugar, rose water, and pink salt together until the sugar is dissolved. If using the food coloring, stir in a few drops until the drink reaches your desired color. Serve immediately over ice, or chill before serving.

Note: It's important that your water be room temperature so that the sugar dissolves.

Chicha Morada

ICED PURPLE CORN TEA

Chicha morada, a tart, fruity, and refreshing Peruvian drink, gets its distinctive color from purple corn, which grows in the Andes mountains. People there have been drinking some version of chicha morada since pre-Columbian times. This version is sweetened to my liking, but you can add more sugar if you prefer. Try a glass with Amazonian Tamales (page 218). It's also lovely spiked with some tequila or vodka for a gorgeous cocktail!

MAKES ABOUT 2 QUARTS

- 1 (15-ounce) bag maíz morado (dried purple corn), rinsed
- Rind and core of 1 pineapple, plus ½ cup finely diced pineapple
- 3 Granny Smith apples, cored and quartered, plus another ½ apple, peeled, cored and diced (about ½ cup)
- ½ pound dried sour cherries
- 2 large cinnamon sticks
- 1½ teaspoons whole cloves
- 2 tablespoons sugar, preferably turbinado, or to taste
- ½ cup fresh lime juice (about 4 limes), plus more if you like

1. In a 6- to 8-quart soup pot, combine the corn, pineapple rind and core, quartered apples, dried cherries, cinnamon sticks, and cloves. Add 4 quarts water and bring to a boil over high heat. Boil uncovered until the kernels begin to burst, 45 minutes to 1 hour.
2. Remove from the heat and cool slightly. Strain the liquid through a fine-mesh sieve into a bowl (discard the solids). While the mixture is still warm, add the sugar, increasing it to your taste if needed. Stir until the sugar is dissolved.
3. Pour into a large pitcher and stir in the lime juice, the diced pineapple, and diced apple. Refrigerate to chill. Serve chilled, with a little bit of the fruit in each glass.

Note: You can find dried purple corn (maíz morado) at most Latin supermarkets, but it is also easy to order online.

Horchata

SWEET RICE AND ALMOND MILK

I cannot hit up a taqueria without ordering a sweet, milky, and refreshing horchata. I'm a sucker for anything with cinnamon, too. While slurping some Spicy Noodles (page 150), I found myself intensely craving a glass of horchata. It made me realize that there was no need to wait until my next taco outing to down a cooling glass of one of my favorite drinks. Simple to mix up, horchata is a crowd-pleaser, especially for children. This recipe is easiest to make with a high-powered blender, such as a Vitamix. If your blender is not that powerful, soak the rice and almonds for a few hours, or overnight, before blending. Enjoy horchata with any spicy dish, especially if you're setting out a jar of Salsa Macha (page 103).

MAKES ABOUT 7 CUPS

1 cup jasmine rice, rinsed until the water runs nearly clear
1 cup blanched slivered almonds
3/4 cup sugar, preferably turbinado
2 1/2 teaspoons ground cinnamon, preferably Mexican, plus more (optional) for garnish
1/4 teaspoon kosher salt
2 whole cloves or 1/4 teaspoon ground cloves (optional)
2 cups whole milk

1. Pour 3 cups water into a blender. Add the rice, almonds, sugar, cinnamon, and salt. (At this point, if desired, you can let the mixture soak for a few hours, which will make it easier to blend.) Blend until the rice and almonds are finely ground, 2 to 3 minutes.

2. Pour into a large bowl or pitcher. Add 1 cup water to the blender, blend again (to dislodge the sludge that may remain in the bottom), and pour all of that into the bowl or pitcher. Add the cloves (if using). Cover and soak overnight at room temperature.

3. Strain the liquid through a fine-mesh sieve into a bowl (discard the cloves and solids). (For a smoother horchata, line the sieve with cheesecloth, or strain twice.) Stir in the milk. Refrigerate until ready to serve.

4. Stir well before pouring each glass, to prevent separation. Serve over lots of ice.

Masala Chai

SPICED TEA

First: *Chai* is the word for "tea" in many Indian and other languages. So, when you're asking for "chai tea" at your local coffee shop, you're saying "tea tea." Second: I realize that chai in the West typically suggests a heavily spiced, heavily sweetened black tea, but technically, this type of chai would correctly be called masala chai, because *masala* means "spice" or "blend of spices" in Hindi. Having said all of that, there are many ways to make this comforting drink, and each family has its own recipe that uses their preferred combination of spices in differing proportions. Here is a simple one that's great for every day. Use whatever green cardamom you have on hand: Feel free to swap out the cardamom seeds with ¼ teaspoon ground cardamom (make sure it's fresh) or 1 teaspoon cardamom pods. There's nothing better than a warm cup of masala chai and some hot, crispy Pakori (page 28) on a rainy day.

SERVES 4

1 teaspoon chopped fresh ginger or 1-inch knob unpeeled ginger, thinly sliced
½ teaspoon cardamom seeds, roughly crushed in a mortar with a pestle
2 black peppercorns
1 tablespoon loose Darjeeling or Assam tea
1 tablespoon sugar, preferably turbinado
1 cup whole milk

1. In a medium saucepan, combine the ginger, cardamom, peppercorns, and 4 cups water and bring to a rolling boil over high heat. Add the tea leaves. Bring back to a boil. As soon as the water darkens, add the sugar and milk.

2. Reduce the heat to medium-low, bring to a simmer, and stir constantly until the sugar is dissolved and the chai is the medium tan color of peanut brittle, about 1½ minutes. Strain through a fine-mesh sieve into cups and serve hot.

Hot Toddy Tea

When I'm nursing a cold and need a soothing drink, this is what I make. I like to use rooibos tea, which is (1) caffeine-free and won't keep me up and (2) technically not a tea at all but a shrub, but feel free to use any kind of black tea you like.

SERVES 1

1 thin slice fresh ginger
1 tea bag: English breakfast or Earl Grey for actual tea, or rooibos or chamomile for herbal tea
2 tablespoons bourbon
1 to 2 teaspoons honey, to taste
Pinch of ground cinnamon
Squirt of fresh lemon juice

1. In a small saucepan, combine the ginger and 1 cup water and bring to a boil over high heat.
2. Remove the saucepan from the heat, add the tea bag, and steep for 2 to 3 minutes, depending on how strong you want the tea.
3. In a mug or glass, combine the bourbon, honey, and cinnamon and stir well. Pour in the tea, discarding the ginger and the tea bag. Add the lemon juice and drink immediately.

Red Chile Hot Chocolate

Krishna has quite the hot chocolate habit, especially in the winter months, and she cannot fathom why I don't derive the same amount of pleasure from that sugar bomb in a cup. Meanwhile, she regards me with dismay while I indulge my own vice, a bar of dark, *dark* chocolate with sea salt and chile. "I'm sure you'd like hot chocolate if you made it with that bitter stuff," she told me. I explained to her that the Mayans used chocolate as a savory ingredient, so my way of eating it was closer to the original. At that point, she realized she had inadvertently walked into my TED Talk on the history of chocolate and tuned out. And *I* decided to create this grown-up drink that I can enjoy after sledding or a snowball fight with her, maybe with a side of Eric Nam's Quick Hotteok (page 276) or Banana Lumpia (page 279).

SERVES 4

5 cups whole milk
1/4 cup unsweetened cocoa powder
2 ounces bittersweet chocolate, finely chopped or grated
2 tablespoons sugar, preferably turbinado, plus more to taste
1 teaspoon pure vanilla extract
1 teaspoon ground cinnamon
1/2 teaspoon kosher salt
1/4 teaspoon cayenne pepper (or Kashmiri chile powder for less heat)

In a medium pot, heat the milk over medium-low heat. Whisk in the cocoa powder, bittersweet chocolate, sugar, vanilla, cinnamon, salt, and cayenne. Bring to a simmer. Pour into mugs and serve hot.

Emergency Mojito

RUM AND SPRITE COCKTAIL

Even at Christmas, it's sweltering in Miami. To keep cool, I drank a copious number of these mojitos while shooting our Noche Buena episode of *Taste the Nation* in chef Monica "Mika" León's backyard. Mika's uncle Pedro "Cha Cha" Garcia makes this twist on the classic Cuban cocktail for all their family gatherings. Back at home, I asked Mika for the recipe. To my surprise, I discovered that instead of soda water, Cha Cha uses Sprite. He also forgoes tradition and uses dark rum in place of light or "white" rum. Of course, I follow his lead. Once when all that was at a friend's home was some Sprite, I remembered Cha Cha's drink, hence the name of this cocktail. Muddling the mint leaves to extract all of their oil compensates for the fact that this drink is based on, well, a can of soda.

MAKES 1 COCKTAIL

5 mint leaves, plus 1 sprig of mint, for garnish
½ ounce fresh lime juice
Ice
2 ounces dark rum
4 ounces Sprite

In a rocks glass, muddle the mint leaves and lime juice. Fill the glass with ice. Pour in the rum, then add the Sprite to fill the glass. Stir and garnish with a sprig of mint.

The Company Cocktail

SPICY TEQUILA-CITRUS PUNCH

In college, tequila and I had a falling-out that took days to recover from, so I left it behind for twenty years. Then Susan Sarandon walked into my life. We were at a benefit dinner, and I was complaining about feeling sleepy, and she brought me a tequila on the rocks. By the time the glass was empty, I was no longer down and drowsy. Since then, both my friendship with Susan and my love of tequila have deepened considerably. I first made this drink in our office kitchen—hence its name—at the end of a long day of recipe testing. We had all sorts of leftover bits and bobs on hand, including a bottle of fresh grapefruit juice and an empty jar of pickled jalapeños, cloudy with bright green brine. Today, I use Chile Vinegar (page 99)—which I always have on hand—for a spike of briny heat instead of pickled jalapeño liquid, and a combination of citrus juices for balance. This cocktail would make an excellent start to a dinner where you're serving Pernil (page 249).

MAKES 1 COCKTAIL

2 ounces fresh tangerine juice
2 ounces fresh grapefruit juice
3 ounces tequila blanco or reposado
1 ounce fresh lime juice
1 ounce Chile Vinegar (page 99) or pickled jalapeño brine
2 ounces club soda

Fill a tall glass or tumbler with ice. Add the tangerine juice, grapefruit juice, tequila, lime juice, and chile vinegar and use a long spoon to stir. Top with the club soda.

Note: Yes, I realize this is an 11-ounce drink. But after a long day at work, you'll appreciate it. Cheers.

I never had to leave the country
to taste the world's flavors.
Wherever you live, come along with me.

FEASTS

FEAST 1 (page 50)

Pickled Peanuts (page 15)
Tostones (page 32)
Asun (page 45)
Blackened Corn with Suya Spice (page 88)
Jollof Rice (page 128)
Rosa's Green Sauce (page 221)
Emergency Mojito (page 298)

FEAST 2 (page 80)

Aushak (page 20)
Butternut Squash Bolani (page 23)
Red Onion Chutney (page 24)
Aash (page 74)
Sholeh Zard (page 260)

FEAST 3 (page 116)

Sabzi (page 84)
Fatteh Batinjan (page 112)
Beef Koobideh (page 241)
Mast-o Khiar (page 243)
Qabuli Pulao (page 253)

FEAST 4 (page 162)

Plum Chaat (page 10)

Pakori (page 28)

Mint and Cilantro Chutney (page 31)

Sambar (page 59)

Podimas (page 101)

Dosas (page 155)

Coconut Chutney (page 160)

Masala Chai (page 294)

FEAST 5 (page 188)

Cabbage Poriyal (page 91)

Spicy Noodles with
Sesame Chutney and Mint (page 150)

Amok Trei (page 178)

Khao Niao Mamuang (page 266)

FEAST 6 (page 222)

Zucchini with
Sun-Dried Tomatoes (page 87)

Crab Fried Rice (page 137)

Sweet and Sour Shrimp with
Cherry Tomatoes (page 185)

Jerk Chicken (page 206)

The Company Cocktail (page 301)

FEAST 7 (page 244)

Braised Leeks (page 93)

Yogurt Tahdig (page 120)

Fried Shallots (page 204)

Fesenjan (page 213)

Maheecheh (page 235)

Mast-o Khiar (page 243)

FEAST 8 (page 256)

Kale-Pomegranate Salad (page 9)

Calabaza con Mojo (page 94)

Peruvian Ceviche (page 171)

Pickled Onions (page 173)

Pernil (page 249)

Pineapple Salsa (page 250)

FEAST 9 (page 284)

Kuku Sabzi (page 19)

Tomato Basil Sauce (page 142)

Arroz Caldo (page 203)

Banana Lumpia (page 279)

Rose Water Limeade (page 288)

ACKNOWLEDGMENTS

So many people encouraged, advised, listened, assisted, tested, tasted, edited, read, held my hand, wiped my tears, and more while I've been creating this cookbook. This has never been just a cookbook, but a quest to show the beauty, bounty, and heart of America, to find myself in the faces of all the people I've met on the road, with whom I've laughed and cried, and who've generously shared so much of their lives with me.

First and foremost, thank you to my daughter, **Krishna,** for her patience as I roamed the country, city by city, instead of making samosas for the school food fair, and to her father, **Adam Dell,** who jumped in while I was out on the road. I am thankful to **Luke Janklow,** who first suggested the idea of a book on immigrant food, and to **Daniel Halpern** for seeing this book's possibilities before it became the show *Taste the Nation*. Thank you to **Maya Mavjee, Lexy Bloom, Deb Wood, Kelly Blair,** and **Rob Shapiro** at Knopf; to **Shubhani Sarkar** for her great design taste; to **Elisa Ung** for her assistance in shopping, prepping, testing, and recording all that I did in the kitchen; to **Megan Litt** for checking my work on recipes; and to **Robin Shulman** for listening to all the initial details on late-night calls after a long day's shooting. Thank you to **Charity Burggraaf** for her quiet brilliance with a camera and to **Frances Boswell** and **Young Gun Lee** for expertly wielding their mighty wooden spoons. And to **Nadine Page** and **Mallory Lance** for props. A special thanks to my guardian angels **Libby Edelson** and **Susan Roxborough** for their years of friendship and for always having my back. Thank you to my muse **Jason Comis,** and to **Francine Prose, Susan Sarandon,** and **Gloria Steinem** for their keen and sage mentorship. Thanks to **David Shadrack Smith;** he and I had much help on *Taste the Nation* as well: **Sarina Roma, Rachel Tung, Hunter Hampton,** and all our camera operators, as well as **Dimitri Tisseyre, Sue Pelino, Lauren Budabin, Elizabeth Leiter, Divya Chungi, Nosa Garrick,** and all my field and line producers, as well my Hulu and Disney family: **Belisa Balaban, Jill Chapman, Beth Osisek, Dane Joseph, Trisha Choate, Sabrina Walker, Rob Mills,** and **Dana Walden**. Thank you to **Rekha Malhotra** for a kick-ass theme song. I am grateful for the artistry of **Albert Mendonca, Jeanie Syfu, William Scott, Fatimot Isadare, Matin Maulawizada, Joeri Rouffa, Reyna Garcia, Rachel Wirkus, Natalie Cruz, Luke Nero, Bennett Soloman,** and **Adele Vasilyeva**. Thank you to **Ariel Boles, Doneen Arquines, Thi Nguyen, Austin Sipes, Sandee Birdsong, Rebecca Boswell,** and so many more on both crews of our shows. Thank you to our nanny, **Tashi Dolma,** without whom I could not have done *Top Chef* all those years. Thank you to **David Krinztman, Kristi Eddington, Strand Conover,** and **Anthony Bonsignore**. Thank you to my agent **Ben Levine, Chris Andrews,** and **my whole team at CAA**. Thank you to **Gary Mantoosh** and **Christina Papadopoulos** for their yearslong diligence and friendship. Thank you to **Peach Perkins, Claire Mosteller,** and **Caitlin Stone** for wielding that iPhone wherever I went. Thank you to **Terrance Hayes** for holding my hand. And finally, thank you to **Anthony Jackson,** who has been by my side through it all for a decade. This journey is as much yours as it is mine. We did it!!!!

INDEX

(Page references in *italics* refer to illustrations.)

A

Aash (Hearty Noodle Soup), 74–6, *75*
aash noodles, xxx
Abacá, San Francisco, 247
accompaniments, xxi
  Chile Vinegar, 99
  Chowchow (Pickled Garden Vegetables), 42
  Coconut Chutney, 160, *160*
  Dumpling Sauce, 49
  Garlic Yogurt Sauce, 78
  Green Sauce, Rosa's, 221, *221*
  Grits, 98
  Mast-o Khiar (Yogurt-Cucumber Sauce), 243, *243*
  Mint and Cilantro Chutney, 31
  Pickled Onions, 173
  Pineapple Salsa, 250, *251*
  Ramp Salt, 12
  Red Onion Chutney, 24
  Salsa Macha (Chile Oil with Nuts and Seeds), 103, *103*
  Salsa Verde, 230
  Savory Minced Meat Sauce, 77
  Sesame Chutney, 152
  Shallots, Fried, 204
acids, xx
advieh spice blend, making your own, 234
Afghan food:
  Aash (Hearty Noodle Soup), 74–6, *75*
  Aushak (Leek and Scallion Dumplings), 20, *21*
  Butternut Squash Bolani (Stuffed Flatbread), *22*, 23–4, *25*
  Garlic Yogurt Sauce, 78
  Qabuli Pulao (Lamb and Rice Pilaf), *252*, 253–5
  Sabzi (Sautéed Greens), 84, *85*
  Savory Minced Meat Sauce, 77
Agave Glaze, 200
agave syrup, xxx
Aleppo pepper flakes, xxv
Almond and Rice Milk, Sweet (Horchata), 292, *293*
Alpern, Liz, 104
Amazonian Tamales (Tamales Stuffed with Chicken), 218–21, *219*
amchur, xxv
Amok Trei (Coconut Curry Fish), 178–9, *179*
anchos, xxv
Ang, Francis, 247
Apache food traditions, 194–200
  Desert Chicken (Chicken Thighs with Sumac and Agave), 200, *201*
appetizers:
  Chicken Larb (Ground Chicken with Herbs), 192
  Muhammara (Roasted Red Pepper and Walnut Spread), 13
  Peruvian Ceviche (Fish Marinated in Citrus and Onion), *170*, 171–2
  Tuna Larb (Tuna with Herbs), 166, *167*
apple cider vinegar, xxxi
Arroz Caldo (Chicken and Rice Porridge), *202*, 203
asafoetida powder, xxv
Ashkenazi food:
  Holishkes (Sweet and Sour Stuffed Cabbage), 104–7, *105*, *106*
  Latkes (Fried Potato Pancakes), *38*, 39
  Passover Brisket, 246
Asun (Spicy Goat Bites), *44*, 45
Attara, Kamal, 13, 108–11, *109*, *110*
Aushak (Leek and Scallion Dumplings), 20, *21*
Avgolemono (Chicken Lemon Soup), 79
avocados, in Salsa Verde, 230

B

Baird, Jessie Little Doe, 280
balsamic vinegar, xxxi
Banana Lumpia (Sweet Fried Spring Rolls), *278*, 279
barberries, xxx
basmati rice, xxx
bay leaves, xxv
bean(s):
  Black, Rice and (Congri, or Moros y Cristianos), 123
  Pinto, Homemade, Breakfast Burritos with, H&H-Style, 102–3
  White, and Vegetable Stew (Ribollita), *70*, 71
  see also chickpea(s)
beef:
  Brisket, Passover, 246
  Koobideh (Ground Beef Kebabs), *240*, 241–3, *242*
  Ropa Vieja (Braised Beef), 232–3, *233*
  Sach Ko Jakak (Kreung-Infused Beef Skewers), 43
  Saltimbocca di Casa Mia (Beef Rolled with Prosciutto, Pecorino, and Sage), 226, *227–9*
Beet and Vegetable Soup (Tomorrow's Borsch), *64*, 65
besan flour, xxx
biscuit(s):
  Blackberry Slump-ish (Fruit Dessert with Cornmeal Dumplings), 280, *281*
  dough, in Eric Nam's Quick Hotteok (Sweet Pancakes Stuffed with Nuts and Cinnamon), 276, *277*
Black Beans, Rice and (Congri, or Moros y Cristianos), 123
Blackberry Slump-ish (Fruit Dessert with Cornmeal Dumplings), 280, *281*
Blackened Corn with Suya Spice, 88, *89*
black garlic, xxvi
black lentils, xxix
black mustard seeds, xxvi
black peppercorns, xxvi
Black Sesame Maple Ice Cream, 273
black vinegar, xxxi
blenders, xxiii
Bolani, Butternut Squash (Stuffed Flatbread), *22*, 23–4, *25*
Borsch, Tomorrow's (Beet and Vegetable Soup), *64*, 65
Bottom of the Pot (Deravian), 120, 235
Breakfast Burritos with Homemade Pinto Beans, H&H-Style, 102–3

Brisket, Passover, 246
Brock, Sean, 150
broths:
Chicken, Essential, 54, *55*
Tomato Rasam (Spicy Tomato Broth), 57
Vegetable, 56
Bujadham, Nikki, 176
Burritos, Breakfast, with Homemade Pinto Beans, H&H-Style, 102–3
Butternut Squash Bolani (Stuffed Flatbread), *22*, 23–4, *25*
Buttery Sweet Chickpea Squares (Mysore Pak), 268, *269*

C

cabbage:
Poriyal (Stir-Fried Cabbage), 91
Red, Peppery Sweet and Sour, 90
Spicy Coleslaw, 36, *37*
Sweet and Sour Stuffed (Holishkes), 104–7, *105*, *106*
Cake, Strawberry-Cardamom and Cream, *282*, 283
Calabaza con Mojo (Roasted Squash in a Citrus-Garlic Sauce), 94, *95*
Cambodian food:
Amok Trei (Coconut Curry Fish), 178–9, *179*
Nam Banh Chuk (Fish and Noodle Soup), 181
Sach Ko Jakak (Kreung-Infused Beef Skewers), 43
Carbonara, Spaghetti alla (Pasta with Eggs and Pancetta), *148*, 149
cardamom:
black and green, xxvi
Strawberry and Cream Cake, *282*, 283
Carhuallanqui, Rosa, 214–17, *215*, *216*, 218
Cassadore, Twila, 194–7, *195–9*, 200
Ceviche, Peruvian (Fish Marinated in Citrus and Onion), *170*, 171–2
Chaat, Plum (Spicy Fruit Snack), 10, *11*
Chai, Masala (Spiced Tea), 294, *294*
chana dal, xxix
Chang, David, 72
Chicha Morada (Iced Purple Corn Tea), *290*, 291
chicken, 191–221
Adobo (Braised Chicken in Coconut and Vinegar), 205
Amazonian Tamales (Tamales Stuffed with Chicken), 218–21, *219*
Arroz Caldo (Chicken and Rice Porridge), *202*, 203
Avgolemono (Chicken Lemon Soup), 79
Broth, Essential, 54, *55*
Desert (Chicken Thighs with Sumac and Agave), 200, *201*
Fesenjan (Braised Chicken with Pomegranate and Walnuts), 213
Jerk (Spicy Marinated Chicken), 206, *207*
Larb (Ground Chicken with Herbs), 192
Tagine-Inspired (Spiced Chicken Stew with Lemon, Apricots, and Olives), *210*, 211–12
Tikka Masala (Chicken in a Creamy Spiced Tomato Sauce), 208–9
Yogurt, 193
Chicken Livers, Pork with (Sisig), 247
chickpea(s):
Roasted Eggplant Layered with Yogurt, Pita and (Fatteh Batinjan), 112–15, *113*, *114*
Squares, Buttery Sweet (Mysore Pak), 268, *269*
chile(s), xx, xxv
green, in Salsa Verde, 230
Oil with Nuts and Seeds (Salsa Macha), 103, *103*
Vinegar, 99
Chile Verde (Pork in Green Chile and Tomatillo Sauce), 230
Chinatown, San Francisco, *16–17*
Chinese food:
Pork Dumplings with Water Chestnuts and Dates, 46, *47*, *48*
Rice "Stuffing" with Chinese Sausage and Shiitake Mushrooms, 138, *139*
Tomato Egg Drop Soup, 62, *63*
chipotle peppers in adobo, xxv
Chocolate, Hot, Red Chile, 296, *297*
chopping vegetables, xx
Chowchow (Pickled Garden Vegetables), 42
Chutima, Saipin, 262–5, *263*, *264*
chutneys:
Coconut, 160, *160*
Mint and Cilantro, 31
Red Onion, 24
Sesame, 152
Cilantro and Mint Chutney, 31
coconut:
Braised Chicken in Vinegar and (Chicken Adobo), 205
Chutney, 160, *160*
Curry Fish (Amok Trei), 178–9, *179*
Decolonized Halo-Halo (Tropical Fruit and Crushed Ice Sundae), *270*, 271–2, *272*
Gelatin, 271
Milk, Rice Porridge with Shrimp and (Southeast Asian–Inspired Risotto), 126–7
Rice, 124
coffee grinders, xxiii
Coleslaw, Spicy, 36, *37*
The Company Cocktail (Spicy Tequila-Citrus Punch), *300*, 301
Congri, or Moros y Cristianos (Rice and Black Beans), 123
cooking times, xx
Corn, Blackened, with Suya Spice, 88, *89*
Cornmeal Dumplings, Fruit Dessert with (Blackberry Slump-ish), 280, *281*
Couscous, Sriracha Butter, Krishna's Upma-Style, *140*, 141
Crab Fried Rice, *136*, 137
Crepes, Savory Fermented (Dosas), *154*, 155–6, *158–9*
Cuban food:
Calabaza con Mojo (Roasted Squash in a Citrus-Garlic Sauce), 94, *95*
Congri, or Moros y Cristianos (Rice and Black Beans), 123
Emergency Mojito (Rum and Sprite Cocktail), 298, *299*
Ropa Vieja, 232–3, *233*
Cucumber-Yogurt Sauce (Mast-o Khiar), 243, *243*
cumin, xxvi
curries:
Amok Trei (Coconut Curry Fish), 178–9, *179*
Saag and Grits (Greens and Grits), 96–9
curry leaves, xxvi

D

dal, xxix
see also lentil(s)
Decolonized Halo-Halo (Tropical Fruit and Crushed Ice Sundae), *270*, 271–2, *272*
Dennis, BJ, 98, 130–2, *131–5*, 186
Deravian, Naz, 120, 235
Desert Chicken (Chicken Thighs with Sumac and Agave), 200, *201*
desert pack rat (gloscho), 194–197, 200
Dosas (Savory Fermented Crepes), *154*, 155–6, *158–9*
Podimas (Potatoes with Turmeric and Fried Lentils) as filling for, *100*, 101
drinks, 287–301
Chicha Morada (Iced Purple Corn Tea), *290*, 291
Emergency Mojito (Rum and Sprite Cocktail), 298, *299*
Horchata (Sweet Rice and Almond Milk), 292, *293*
Hot Toddy Tea, 295, *295*
Masala Chai (Spiced Tea), 294, *294*
Red Chile Hot Chocolate, 296, *296–7*
Rose Water Limeade, 288, *288–9*
dumpling(s):
Cornmeal, Fruit Dessert with (Blackberry Slump-ish), 280, *281*
Leek and Scallion (Aushak), 20, *21*
Pork, with Water Chestnuts and Dates, 46, *47*, *48*
Sauce, 49

E

egg(s):
- Drop Soup, Tomato, 62, *63*
- Kuku Sabzi (Herbed Frittata), *18*, 19
- "Noodles" in Tomato-Basil Sauce (Uova in Trippa), 142–4, *143–5*
- Pasta with Pancetta and (Spaghetti alla Carbonara), *148*, 149

Eggplant, Roasted, Layered with Chickpeas, Yogurt, and Pita (Fatteh Batinjan), 112–15, *113, 114*
Elémi Restaurant, El Paso, Tex., 103
Emergency Mojito (Rum and Sprite Cocktail), 298, *299*
Emiliano Marentes, 35
Eric Nam's Quick Hotteok (Sweet Pancakes Stuffed with Nuts and Cinnamon), 276, *277*
Estupiñan, Lupita, 123

F

Fatteh Batinjan (Roasted Eggplant Layered with Chickpeas, Yogurt, and Pita), 112–15, *113, 114*
Feast 1, *50–1*, 305
Feast 2, *80–1*, 305
Feast 3, *116–17*, 305
Feast 4, *162–3*, 306
Feast 5, *188–9*, 306
Feast 6, *222–3*, 306
Feast 7, *244–5*, 307
Feast 8, *256–7*, 307
Feast 9, *284–5*, 307
Fein, Esther, 246
fennel seeds, xxvi
fenugreek leaves, xxxi
Fesenjan (Braised Chicken with Pomegranate and Walnuts), 213
Filipino food:
- Arroz Caldo (Chicken and Rice Porridge), *202*, 203
- Chicken Adobo (Braised Chicken in Coconut and Vinegar), 205
- Decolonized Halo-Halo (Tropical Fruit and Crushed Ice Sundae), *270*, 271–2, *272*
- Sisig (Pork with Chicken Livers), 247

fish:
- Amok Trei (Coconut Curry Fish), 178–9, *179*
- Nam Banh Chuk (Fish and Noodle Soup), 181
- Pad Thai (Tamarind Steamed Fish with Spinach), 176, *177*
- Peruvian Ceviche (Fish Marinated in Citrus and Onion), *170*, 171–2
- Shoyu Poke (Rice and Tuna Bowl), 173
- Simmered with Potatoes and Lemon, 180
- Tuna Larb (Tuna with Herbs), 166, *167*

fish sauce, xxxi
Flatbread, Stuffed (Butternut Squash Bolani), *22*, 23–4, *25*
fleur de sel, xxx
food processors, small, xxiii
foraging, 194–7
fried:
- Banana Lumpia (Sweet Fried Spring Rolls), *278*, 279
- Potato Pancakes (Latkes, or Biracial Latkes), *38*, 39
- Rice, Crab, *136*, 137
- Schnitzel (Fried Veal Cutlets), 231
- Shallots, 204
- Tostones (Fried Green Plantains), *32, 33*

Frittata, Herbed (Kuku Sabzi), *18*, 19
Fritters, Vegetable (Pakori), 28, *29, 30*
Fruit Snack, Spicy (Plum Chaat), 10, *11*
frying spices and leaves in oil (tempering), 69

G

galangal, xxvi
garam masala, xxvi
Garcia, Pedro "Cha Cha," 298
garlic:
- black, xxvi
- Yogurt Sauce, 78

Gefilte Manifesto: New Recipes for Old World Jewish Foods, The (Alpern and Yoskowitz), 104
Gefilteria, New York, 104
German food:
- Peppery Sweet and Sour Red Cabbage, 90
- Schnitzel (Fried Veal Cutlets), 231

Gladkovitser, Lyudmila, 65
Glaze, Agave, 200
gloscho (desert pack rat), 194–197, 200
Goat Bites, Spicy (Asun), *44*, 45
gochugaru, xxv
gochujang, xxv
grains, 119–38
- Coconut Rice, 124
- Congri, or Moros y Cristianos (Rice and Black Beans), 123
- Crab Fried Rice, *136*, 137
- Dosas (Savory Fermented Crepes), *154*, 155–6, *158–9*
- Grits, 98
- Jollof Rice (Rice with Roasted Tomatoes and Peppers), 128–9
- Rice "Stuffing" with Chinese Sausage and Shiitake Mushrooms, 138, *139*
- Southeast Asian–Inspired Risotto (Rice Porridge with Shrimp and Coconut Milk), 126–7
- Yogurt Tahdig (Rice with a Crispy Top), 120–2, *121*

Greek food:
- Avgolemono (Chicken Lemon Soup), 79
- Fish Simmered with Potatoes and Lemon, 180

Green Burrito, La Puente, Calif., 102
Green Papaya Salad (Som Tum), *4*, 5
greens:
- and Grits (Saag and Grits), 96–9
- Sautéed (Sabzi), 84, *85*

Green Sauce, Rosa's, 221, *221*
Grits, 98
- Saag and (Greens and Grits), 96–9
- Shrimp and, 186, *187*

Grubb, Maria Mercedes, 249
Gullah Geechee foodways:
- BJ Dennis and, 98, 130–2, *131–5*, 186
- Crab Fried Rice, *136*, 137
- Grits, 98
- Shrimp and Grits, 186, *187*
- West African jollof rice and, 128

H

Halo-Halo, Decolonized (Tropical Fruit and Crushed Ice Sundae), *270*, 271–2, *272*
H&H Car Wash and Coffee Shop, El Paso, Tex., 102
H&H-Style Breakfast Burritos with Homemade Pinto Beans, 102–3
Hawaiian poke, 173
Hazan, Marcella, 149
Herbed Frittata (Kuku Sabzi), *18*, 19
herbs, xxv–xxviii
Himalayan pink salt, xxx
Holishkes (Sweet and Sour Stuffed Cabbage), 104–7, *105, 106*
Horchata (Sweet Rice and Almond Milk), 292, *293*
Hot and Sour Soup with Shrimp (Tom Yum Goong), 66, *67*
Hot Chocolate, Red Chile, 296, *296–7*
Hotteok, Eric Nam's Quick (Sweet Pancakes Stuffed with Nuts and Cinnamon), 276, *277*
Hot Toddy Tea, 295, *295*
Hwang, Yoonjin, 72

I

ice cream:
- Black Sesame Maple, 273
- Decolonized Halo-Halo (Tropical Fruit and Crushed Ice Sundae), *270*, 271–2, *272*

immersion blenders, xxiii
Indian dried red chiles, xxv
Indian food:
- Biracial Latkes (Fried Potato Pancakes), *38*, 39
- Cabbage Poriyal (Stir-Fried Cabbage), 91

Indian food *(continued)*:
Chicken Tikka Masala (Chicken in a Creamy Spiced Tomato Sauce), 208–9
Coconut Chutney, 160, *160*
Dosas (Savory Fermented Crepes), *154*, 155–6, *158–9*
Krishna's Upma-Style Sriracha Butter Couscous, *140*, 141
Masala Chai (Spiced Tea), 294, *294*
Mussels with a Rasam Vibe (Mussels Simmered with Tomatoes and Spices), 182, *183*
Mysore Pak (Buttery Sweet Chickpea Squares), 268, *269*
Pakori (Vegetable Fritters), 28, *29*, *30*
Podimas (Potatoes with Turmeric and Fried Lentils), *100*, 101
Spicy Noodles with Sesame Chutney and Mint, 150–2, *151*
Sweet and Sour Shrimp with Cherry Tomatoes, *184*, 185
Tadka Dal (Yellow Lentil Soup), 68–9
Tomato Rasam (Spicy Tomato Broth), 57
Yogurt Chicken, 193
ingredients:
gathering before starting to cook, xix
see also pantry
Iranian food. *See* Persian food
Italian food:
Ribollita (White Bean and Vegetable Stew), *70*, 71
Saltimbocca di Casa Mia (Beef Rolled with Prosciutto, Pecorino, and Sage), 226, *227–9*
Spaghetti alla Carbonara (Pasta with Eggs and Pancetta), *148*, 149
Uova in Trippa (Egg "Noodles" in Tomato-Basil Sauce), 142–4, *143–5*

J

jaggery, xxxi
jalapeños, in Salsa Verde, 230
Jamaican jerk chicken, 206, *207*
Jam Rock Jerk truck, New York, 206
jasmine rice, xxx
Jerk Chicken (Spicy Marinated Chicken), 206, *207*
Jollof Rice (Rice with Roasted Tomatoes and Peppers), 128–9, *129*

K

Kale-Pomegranate Salad, *8*, 9
Kari, Homayon, 74, *76*, 77
Karistinos, Anastasios (Taso), 180
Kashmiri pepper, xxv
Katerina's Taverna & Grill, Tarpon Springs, Fla., 79
Kazmi, Katlin and Mohsin, 96, *97*
kebabs:
Ground Beef (Beef Koobideh), *240*, 241, *242*
Mast-o Khiar (Yogurt-Cucumber Sauce) for, 243, *243*
Kegel's Inn, Milwaukee, 231
Khao Niao Mamuang (Sticky Rice with Mango), 266, *267*
kids, sharing cooking with, 23, 147, 279
Kimchi and Pork Soondubu (Soft Tofu and Pork Stew), 72, *73*
kitchen rules, xix–xx
Koobideh, Beef (Ground Beef Kebabs), *240*, 241, *242*
Korean food:
Eric Nam's Quick Hotteok (Sweet Pancakes Stuffed with Nuts and Cinnamon), 276, *277*
Pork and Kimchi Soondubu (Soft Tofu and Pork Stew), 72, *73*
kosher salt, xxx
Kreung-Infused Beef Skewers (Sach Ko Jakak), 43
Krishna's Upma-Style Sriracha Butter Couscous, *140*, 141
Kuku Sabzi (Herbed Frittata), *18*, 19
Kumrar, Thiru, 155

L

lamb:
Maheecheh (Braised Lamb Shanks), *234*, 235
Qabuli Pulao (Lamb and Rice Pilaf), *252*, 253–5
Lapis, Washington, D.C., 84, 253
larb:
Chicken (Ground Chicken with Herbs), 192
Tuna (Tuna with Herbs), 166, *167*
Latkes, or Biracial Latkes (Fried Potato Pancakes), *38*, 39
Lebanese food:
Fatteh Batinjan (Roasted Eggplant Layered with Chickpeas, Yogurt, and Pita), 112–15, *113*, *114*
Kamal Attara and, 13, 108–11, *109*, *110*
Muhammara (Roasted Red Pepper and Walnut Spread), 13
Leche de Tigre, 171–2
leek(s):
Braised, *92*, 93
and Scallion Dumplings (Aushak), 20, *21*
legumes. *See* bean(s); chickpea(s); lentil(s)
lemongrass, xxvi
lemon(s):
Chicken Soup (Avgolemono), 79
preserved, xxx
lentil(s), xxix
Dosas (Savory Fermented Crepes), *154*, 155–6, *158–9*
Fried, Potatoes with Turmeric and (Podimas), *100*, 101
Holishkes (Sweet and Sour Stuffed Cabbage), 104–7, *105*, *106*
Tamarind Stew (Sambar), *58*, 59–60
Yellow, Soup (Tadka Dal), 68–9
Leon, Monica "Mika," 123
Limeade, Rose Water, 288, *288–9*
Llama Inn, Brooklyn, 171
Lo, Buddha, 68
Lofaso, Antonia, 182
Lotus of Siam, Las Vegas, 192, 262, *264*, 265, 266

M

Maheecheh (Braised Lamb Shanks), *234*, 235
makrut lime leaves, xxviii
Mango, Sticky Rice with (Khao Niao Mamuang), 266, *267*
Maple Black Sesame Ice Cream, 273
Marantes, Emiliano, 103
Masala Chai (Spiced Tea), 294, *294*
masoor dal, xxix
Mast-o Khiar (Yogurt-Cucumber Sauce), 243, *243*
meat, 225–55
Beef Koobideh (Ground Beef Kebabs), *240*, 241–3, *242*
Chile Verde (Pork in Green Chile and Tomatillo Sauce), 230
Maheecheh (Braised Lamb Shanks), *234*, 235
Minced, Sauce, Savory, 77
Passover Brisket, 246
Pernil (Roast Pork with Crispy Skin), *248*, 249–50
Qabuli Pulao (Lamb and Rice Pilaf), *252*, 253–5
Ropa Vieja (Braised Beef), 232–3, *233*
Saltimbocca di Casa Mia (Beef Rolled with Prosciutto, Pecorino, and Sage), 226, *227–9*
Schnitzel (Fried Veal Cutlets), 231
Sisig (Pork with Chicken Livers), 247
La Mercerie, New York, 6
Mesquite–Peanut Butter Treats (Ruiz's Pieces), 274
Mexican food:
Chile Verde (Pork in Green Chile and Tomatillo Sauce), 230
Horchata (Sweet Rice and Almond Milk), 292, *293*
Salsa Verde, 230
Mexican oregano, xxviii
Microplane graters, xxiii
Milton, Travis, 41
Minced Meat Sauce, Savory, 77
Minero, Charleston, S.C., 150
Mint and Cilantro Chutney, 31
mise en place, xx
Mojito, Emergency (Rum and Sprite Cocktail), 298, *299*

molcajetes, xxiii
morita chiles, xxv
Moroccan Tagine-Inspired Chicken (Spiced Chicken Stew with Lemon, Apricots, and Olives), *210*, 211–12
Moros y Cristianos, or Congri (Rice and Black Beans), 123
mortars and pestles, xxiii
Mosavi, Hamid, 236–9, *237*, *238*
Muhammara (Roasted Red Pepper and Walnut Spread), 13
mushroom(s):
  portobello, in Holishkes (Sweet and Sour Stuffed Cabbage), 104–7, *105*, *106*
  Shiitake, Rice "Stuffing" with Chinese Sausage and, 138, *139*
  Tacos Campesinos, *34*, 35
Mussels with a Rasam Vibe (Mussels Simmered with Tomatoes and Spices), 182, *183*
mustard greens, in Saag and Grits (Greens and Grits), 96–9
mustard seeds, black, xxvi
Mysore Pak (Buttery Sweet Chickpea Squares), 268, *269*

N

Nam, Eric, 276
Nam Banh Chuk (Fish and Noodle Soup), 181
Nathan, Joan, 246
NY Dosas Cart, New York, 155
Nigerian food:
  Asun (Spicy Goat Bites), *44*, 45
  Blackened Corn with Suya Spice, 88, *89*
  Jollof Rice (Rice with Roasted Tomatoes and Peppers), 128–9, *129*
Noguchi, Mark "Gooch," 173
noodle(s), 141–50
  and Fish Soup (Nam Banh Chuk), 181
  Krishna's Upma-Style Sriracha Butter Couscous, *140*, 141
  Pasta all'Amatriciana (Rigatoni and Pork Cheek Pasta), 147
  Soup, Hearty (Aash), 74–6, *75*
  Spaghetti alla Carbonara (Pasta with Eggs and Pancetta), *148*, 149
  Spicy, with Sesame Chutney and Mint, 150–2, *151*
  Uova in Trippa (Egg "Noodles" in Tomato-Basil Sauce), 142–4, *143–5*

O

oil(s), xxix
  Chile, with Nuts and Seeds (Salsa Macha), 103, *103*
Okoyomon, Precious, 128
olive oil, extra-virgin, xxix
onion(s):
  Pickled, 173
  Red, Chutney, 24
  red, in Pakori (Vegetable Fritters), 28, *29*, *30*
oregano, Mexican, xxviii
Orji, Yvonne, 88
Oyefaso, Bethany, 45

P

pack rat, desert (gloscho), 194–197, 200
Pad Thai Fish (Tamarind Steamed Fish with Spinach), 176, *177*
Pakistani Saag and Grits (Greens and Grits), 96–9
Pakori (Vegetable Fritters), 28, *29*, *30*
pancakes:
  Potato, Fried (Latkes, or Biracial Latkes), *38*, 39
  Sweet, Stuffed with Nuts and Cinnamon (Eric Nam's Quick Hotteok), 276, *277*
Pancetta, Pasta with Eggs and (Spaghetti alla Carbonara), *148*, 149
pantry, xxiv–xxxi
  chiles, xxv
  herbs and spices, xxv–xxviii
  lentils/dal, xxix
  oils, xxix
  rice, xxx
  salt, xxx
  sauces, sweeteners, et cetera, xxx–xxxi
Papas a la Huancaína (Potatoes in Ají Amarillo Sauce), *26*, 27
Papaya, Green, Salad (Som Tum), *4*, 5
parboiled rice, xxx
parsley, in Rosa's Green Sauce, 221, *221*
Passover Brisket, 246
pasta:
  all'Amatriciana (Rigatoni and Pork Cheek Pasta), 147
  with Eggs and Pancetta (Spaghetti alla Carbonara), *148*, 149
  see also noodle(s)
Peanut Butter–Mesquite Treats (Ruiz's Pieces), 274
Peanuts, Pickled, 15, *15*
Pecorino, Beef Rolled with Prosciutto, Sage and (Saltimbocca di Casa Mia), 226, *227–9*
Pelaez, Ana Sofia, 94
pepper(corns):
  black, xxvi
  Szechuan, xxviii
  white, xxviii
Peppery Sweet and Sour Red Cabbage, 90
Pernil (Roast Pork with Crispy Skin), *248*, 249–50
Persian food:
  advieh spice blend, making your own, 234
  Beef Koobideh (Ground Beef Kebabs), *240*, 241, *242*
  Fesenjan (Braised Chicken with Pomegranate and Walnuts), 213
  Hamid Mosavi and, 236–9, *237*, *238*
  Kuku Sabzi (Herbed Frittata), *18*, 19
  Maheecheh (Braised Lamb Shanks), *234*, 235
  Mast-o Khiar (Yogurt-Cucumber Sauce), 243, *243*
  Sholeh Zard (Rice Pudding with Saffron and Rose), 260, *261*
  Yogurt Tahdig (Rice with a Crispy Top), 120–2, *121*
Peruvian food and culture:
  Amazonian Tamales (Tamales Stuffed with Chicken), 218–21, *219*
  Ceviche (Fish Marinated in Citrus and Onion), *170*, 171–2
  Chicha Morada (Iced Purple Corn Tea), *290*, 291
  Green Sauce, Rosa's, 221, *221*
  Papas a la Huancaína (Potatoes in Ají Amarillo Sauce), *26*, 27
  Rosa Carhuallanqui and, 214–17, *215*, *216*, 218
pickled:
  Garden Vegetables (Chowchow), 42
  Onions, 173
  Peanuts, 15, *15*
Pilaf, Lamb and Rice (Qabuli Pulao), *252*, 253–5
Pineapple Salsa, 250, *251*
Pinto Beans, Homemade, Breakfast Burritos with, H&H-Style, 102–3
Plantains, Green, Fried (Tostones), *32*, *33*
Plum Chaat (Spicy Fruit Snack), 10, *11*
Podimas (Potatoes with Turmeric and Fried Lentils), *100*, 101
Poke, Shoyu (Rice and Tuna Bowl), 173
pomegranate:
  Braised Chicken with Walnuts and (Fesenjan), 213
  Kale Salad, *8*, 9
pomegranate molasses, xxx
Popal, Shamim, 84, 253, *255*
pork:
  Chile Verde (Pork in Green Chile and Tomatillo Sauce), 230
  Dumplings with Water Chestnuts and Dates, 46, *47*, *48*
  and Kimchi Soondubu (Soft Tofu and Pork Stew), 72, *73*
  Pasta all'Amatriciana (Rigatoni and Pork Cheek Pasta), 147
  Pernil (Roast Pork with Crispy Skin), *248*, 249–50
  Sisig (Pork with Chicken Livers), 247
porridge:
  Rice, Chicken and (Arroz Caldo), *202*, 203
  Rice, with Shrimp and Coconut Milk (Southeast Asian–Inspired Risotto), 126–7

portobello mushrooms, in Holishkes (Sweet and Sour Stuffed Cabbage), 104–7, *105, 106*
Portuguese Goan influence, in Sweet and Sour Shrimp with Cherry Tomatoes, *184,* 185
Il Posto Accanto, East Village, New York, 142, 226
potato(es):
  in Ají Amarillo Sauce (Papas a la Huancaína), *26,* 27
  Fish Simmered with Lemon and, 180
  Pancakes, Fried (Latkes, or Biracial Latkes), *38,* 39
  with Turmeric and Fried Lentils (Podimas), *100,* 101
preserved lemons, xxx
Prosciutto, Beef Rolled with Pecorino, Sage and (Saltimbocca di Casa Mia), 226, *227–9*
Pudding, Rice, with Saffron and Rose (Sholeh Zard), 260, *261*
Puerto Rican food:
  Pernil (Roast Pork with Crispy Skin), *248,* 249–50
  Tostones (Fried Green Plantains), 32, *33*
Pulao, Qabuli (Lamb and Rice Pilaf), *252,* 253–5
Punch, Spicy Tequila-Citrus (The Company Cocktail), *300,* 301
Purple Corn Tea, Iced (Chicha Morada), *290,* 291

Q

Qabuli Pulao (Lamb and Rice Pilaf), *252,* 253–5

R

Ramirez, Erik, 171
Ramp Salt, 12
Ramsay, Radeem, *2,* 2–3, *3,* 5
Rao's, Harlem, New York, 182
rasam:
  powder, 57
  Tomato (Spicy Tomato Broth), 57
  Vibe, Mussels with (Mussels Simmered with Tomatoes and Spices), 182, *183*
reading recipe before cooking, xix
Red Cabbage, Peppery Sweet and Sour, 90
Red Chile Hot Chocolate, 296, *296–7*
Red Onion Chutney, 24
Red Pepper, Roasted, and Walnut Spread (Muhammara), 13
red wine vinegar, xxxi
Ribollita (White Bean and Vegetable Stew), *70,* 71
rice, xxx
  and Almond Milk, Sweet (Horchata), 292, *293*
  and Black Beans (Congri, or Moros y Cristianos), 123
  Crab Fried, *136,* 137
  with a Crispy Top (Yogurt Tahdig), 120–2, *121*
  Dosas (Savory Fermented Crepes), *154,* 155–6, *158–9*
  Jollof (Rice with Roasted Tomatoes and Peppers), 128–9, *129*
  and Lamb Pilaf (Qabuli Pulao), *252,* 253–5
  Porridge, Chicken and (Arroz Caldo), *202,* 203
  Porridge with Shrimp and Coconut Milk (Southeast Asian–Inspired Risotto), 126–7
  Pudding with Saffron and Rose (Sholeh Zard), 260, *261*
  Sticky, with Mango (Khao Niao Mamuang), 266, *267*
  "Stuffing" with Chinese Sausage and Shiitake Mushrooms, 138, *139*
  and Tuna Bowl (Shoyu Poke), 173
  washing, xx
rice flour, xxx
rice vinegar, xxxi
Rigatoni and Pork Cheek Pasta (Pasta all'Amatriciana), 147
Risotto, Southeast Asian–Inspired (Rice Porridge with Shrimp and Coconut Milk), 126–7
roasting whole spices, xx
rodent, eating, 194–197, 200
Romaine Heart Salad with Za'atar and Herbs, 6, *7*
Roman specialties:
  Spaghetti alla Carbonara (Pasta with Eggs and Pancetta), *148,* 149
  Uova in Trippa (Egg "Noodles" in Tomato-Basil Sauce), 142–4, *143–5*
Ropa Vieja (Braised Beef), 232–3, *233*
Rosa's Green Sauce, 221, *221*
rose (water), xxx
  Rice Pudding with Saffron and (Sholeh Zard), 260, *261*
rosemary, xxviii
Rose Water Limeade, 288, *288–9*
Ruiz, Felicia Cocotzin, 274, *275*
Ruiz's Pieces (Peanut Butter–Mesquite Treats), 274
Rum and Sprite Cocktail (Emergency Mojito), 298, *299*
Russ & Daughters, New York, 39

S

Saag and Grits (Greens and Grits), 96–9
Sabzi (Sautéed Greens), 84, *85*
Sach Ko Jakak (Kreung-Infused Beef Skewers), 43
saffron, xxviii
  Rice Pudding with Rose and (Sholeh Zard), 260, *261*
salads, 5–9
  Coleslaw, Spicy, 36, *37*
  Kale-Pomegranate, *8,* 9
  Romaine Heart, with Za'atar and Herbs, 6, *7*
  Som Tum (Green Papaya Salad), *4,* 5
salsa:
  Macha (Chile Oil with Nuts and Seeds), 103, *103*
  Pineapple, 250, *251*
  Verde, 230
salt, xxx
  Ramp, 12
  salting in stages, xx
Saltimbocca di Casa Mia (Beef Rolled with Prosciutto, Pecorino, and Sage), 226, *227–9*
Sambar (Tamarind Lentil Stew), *58,* 59–60
sambar powder, 57
San Carlos Apache reservation, 194
San Francisco's Chinatown, *16–17*
Sangthongkum, Tina, 66
Sarandon, Susan, 301
sauces:
  Dumpling, 49
  Garlic Yogurt, 78
  Green, Rosa's, 221
  Mast-o Khiar (Yogurt-Cucumber Sauce), 243, *243*
  Savory Minced Meat, 77
  Tomato-Basil, 142
sauerkraut, in Holishkes (Sweet and Sour Stuffed Cabbage), 104–7, *105, 106*
Sausage, Chinese, Rice "Stuffing" with Shiitake Mushrooms and, 138, *139*
Savory Minced Meat Sauce, 77
Sawyer, Oywan, 166
Schnitzel (Fried Veal Cutlets), 231
seafood, 165–86
  Amok Trei (Coconut Curry Fish), 178–9, *179*
  Fish Simmered with Potatoes and Lemon, 180
  Mussels with a Rasam Vibe (Mussels Simmered with Tomatoes and Spices), 182, *183*
  Nam Banh Chuk (Fish and Noodle Soup), 181
  Pad Thai Fish (Tamarind Steamed Fish with Spinach), 176, *177*
  Peruvian Ceviche (Fish Marinated in Citrus and Onion), *170,* 171–2
  Shoyu Poke (Rice and Tuna Bowl), 173
  Shrimp, Sweet and Sour, with Cherry Tomatoes, *184,* 185
  Shrimp and Grits, 186, *187*
  Tuna Larb (Tuna with Herbs), 166, *167*
sea salt, xxx
serrano chiles, in Rosa's Green Sauce, 221, *221*
sesame:
  Black, Maple Ice Cream, 273
  Chutney, 152
  oil, toasted, xxix

Shallots, Fried, 204
Shamshiri Grill, Los Angeles, 236–9, *237, 238*
Shiitake Mushrooms, Rice "Stuffing" with Chinese Sausage and, 138, *139*
Sholeh Zard (Rice Pudding with Saffron and Rose), 260, *261*
Shoyu Poke (Rice and Tuna Bowl), 173
shrimp:
  and Grits, 186, *187*
  Hot and Sour Soup with (Tom Yum Goong), 66, *67*
  Rice Porridge with Coconut Milk and (Southeast Asian–Inspired Risotto), 126–7
  shells, making stock with, 171
  Sweet and Sour, with Cherry Tomatoes, *184*, 185
Simply Khmer, Lowell, Mass., 178
Sisig (Pork with Chicken Livers), 247
skewers:
  Beef, Kreung-Infused (Sach Ko Jakak), 43
  Beef Koobideh (Ground Beef Kebabs), *240*, 241, *242*
Slump-ish, Blackberry (Fruit Dessert with Cornmeal Dumplings), 280, *281*
small plates:
  Asun (Spicy Goat Bites), *44*, 45
  Aushak (Leek and Scallion Dumplings), 20, *21*
  Butternut Squash Bolani (Stuffed Flatbread), *22*, 23–4, *25*
  Kuku Sabzi (Herbed Frittata), *18*, 19
  Latkes, or Biracial Latkes (Fried Potato Pancakes), *38*, 39
  Muhammara (Roasted Red Pepper and Walnut Spread), 13
  Mushroom Tacos Campesinos, *34*, 35
  Pakori (Vegetable Fritters), 28, *29, 30*
  Papas a la Huancaína (Potatoes in Ají Amarillo Sauce), *26, 27*
  Pickled Peanuts, 15, *15*
  Plum Chaat (Spicy Fruit Snack), 10, *11*
  Pork Dumplings with Water Chestnuts and Dates, 46, *47, 48*
  Sach Ko Jakak (Kreung-Infused Beef Skewers), 43
  Tostones (Fried Green Plantains), 32, *33*
  Whipped Spam with Toast Points, *40*, 41
Smiley, Keith, 130
Smith, Tobi, 45
smoked paprika, Spanish, xxv
snacks:
  Asun (Spicy Goat Bites), *44*, 45
  Banana Lumpia, 279
  Blackened Corn with Suya Spice, 88, *89*
  Dosas (Savory Fermented Crepes), *154*, 155–6, *158–9*
  Plum Chaat (Spicy Fruit Snack), 10, *11*
  Red Onion Chutney, 24
  Sach Ko Jakak (Kreung-Infused Beef Skewers), 43
Som Tum (Green Papaya Salad), *4*, 5
Soondubu, Pork and Kimchi (Soft Tofu and Pork Stew), 72, *73*
soups, 53–79
  Aash (Hearty Noodle Soup), 74–6, *75*
  Avgolemono (Chicken Lemon Soup), 79
  Borsch, Tomorrow's (Beet and Vegetable Soup), *64*, 65
  Chicken Broth, Essential, 54, *55*
  Nam Banh Chuk (Fish and Noodle Soup), 181
  Tadka Dal (Yellow Lentil Soup), 68–9
  Tomato Egg Drop, 62, *63*
  Tomato Rasam (Spicy Tomato Broth), 57
  Tom Yum Goong (Hot and Sour Soup with Shrimp), 66, *67*
  Vegetable Broth, 56
  see also stews
Southeast Asian–Inspired Risotto (Rice Porridge with Shrimp and Coconut Milk), 126–7
Spaghetti alla Carbonara (Pasta with Eggs and Pancetta), *148*, 149
Spam, Whipped, with Toast Points, *40*, 41
Spanish smoked paprika, xxv
Spiced Chicken Stew with Lemon, Apricots, and Olives (Tagine-Inspired Chicken), *210*, 211–12
Spiced Tea (Masala Chai), 294, *294*
spices, xxv–xxviii
  whole, roasting, xx
Spicy Fruit Snack (Plum Chaat), 10, *11*
Spicy Marinated Chicken (Jerk Chicken), 206, *207*
Spicy Noodles with Sesame Chutney and Mint, 150–2, *151*
Spicy Tequila-Citrus Punch (The Company Cocktail), *300*, 301
Spicy Tomato Broth (Tomato Rasam), 57
spiders, xxiii
spinach:
  Saag and Grits (Greens and Grits), 96–9
  Sabzi (Sautéed Greens), 84, *85*
  Tamarind Steamed Fish with (Pad Thai Fish), 176, *177*
Spring Rolls, Sweet Fried (Banana Lumpia), *278*, 279
Sprite and Rum Cocktail (Emergency Mojito), 298, *299*
Squash, Roasted, in a Citrus-Garlic Sauce (Calabaza con Mojo), 94, *95*
star anise, xxviii
stews:
  Chile Verde (Pork in Green Chile and Tomatillo Sauce), 230
  Pork and Kimchi Soondubu (Soft Tofu and Pork Stew), 72, *73*
  Ribollita (White Bean and Vegetable Stew), *70*, 71
  Sambar (Tamarind Lentil Stew), *58*, 59–60
  Tagine-Inspired Chicken (Spiced Chicken Stew with Lemon, Apricots, and Olives), *210*, 211–12
  see also soups
sticky rice:
  with Mango (Khao Niao Mamuang), 266, *267*
  Thai, xxx
Stir-Fried Cabbage (Cabbage Poriyal), 91
Stock (fish), 171
Strawberry-Cardamom and Cream Cake, *282*, 283
Stuffed Cabbage, Sweet and Sour (Holishkes), 104–7, *105, 106*
Stuffed Flatbread (Butternut Squash Bolani), *22*, 23–4, *25*
"Stuffing," Rice, with Chinese Sausage and Shiitake Mushrooms, 138, *139*
sumac, xxviii
Sundae, Tropical Fruit and Crushed Ice (Decolonized Halo-Halo), *270*, 271–2, *272*
sushi rice, xxx
Suya Spice, Blackened Corn with, 88, *89*
Sweet and Sour Shrimp with Cherry Tomatoes, *184*, 185
Sweet and Sour Stuffed Cabbage (Holishkes), 104–7, *105, 106*
sweets, 259–83
  Banana Lumpia (Sweet Fried Spring Rolls), *278*, 279
  Blackberry Slump-ish (Fruit Dessert with Cornmeal Dumplings), 280, *281*
  Black Sesame Maple Ice Cream, 273
  Decolonized Halo-Halo (Tropical Fruit and Crushed Ice Sundae), *270*, 271–2, *272*
  Hotteok, Eric Nam's Quick (Sweet Pancakes Stuffed with Nuts and Cinnamon), 276, *277*
  Khao Niao Mamuang (Sticky Rice with Mango), 266, *267*
  Mysore Pak (Buttery Sweet Chickpea Squares), 268, *269*
  Ruiz's Pieces (Peanut Butter–Mesquite Treats), 274
  Sholeh Zard (Rice Pudding with Saffron and Rose), 260, *261*
  Strawberry-Cardamom and Cream Cake, *282*, 283
Swiss chard, in Saag and Grits (Greens and Grits), 96–9
Syfu, Jeanie, 203
Szechuan peppercorns, xxviii

T

Tacos, Mushroom, Campesinos, *34,* 35
Tadka Dal (Yellow Lentil Soup), 68–9
Tagine-Inspired Chicken (Spiced Chicken Stew with Lemon, Apricots, and Olives), *210,* 211–12
Tahdig, Yogurt (Rice with a Crispy Top), 120–2, *121*
Tamales, Amazonian (Tamales Stuffed with Chicken), 218–21, *219*
tamarind, xxxi
  Lentil Stew (Sambar), *58,* 59–60
  Steamed Fish with Spinach (Pad Thai Fish), 176, *177*
tea:
  Hot Toddy, 295, *295*
  Spiced (Masala Chai), 294, *294*
Tehran Market, Los Angeles, 260
tempering (frying spices and leaves in oil), 69
Tequila-Citrus Punch, Spicy (The Company Cocktail), *300,* 301
Thai food:
  Chicken Larb (Ground Chicken with Herbs), 192
  glutinous (sticky) rice, xxx
  Khao Niao Mamuang (Sticky Rice with Mango), 266, *267*
  Lotus of Siam and, 192, 262, *264,* 265, 266
  Pad Thai Fish (Tamarind Steamed Fish with Spinach), 176, *177*
  Radeem (Radeem Ramsay) and, *2,* 2–3, *3, 5*
  Saipin Chutima and, 262–5, *263, 264*
  Som Tum (Green Papaya Salad), *4,* 5
  Tom Yum Goong (Hot and Sour Soup with Shrimp), 66, *67*
  Tuna Larb (Tuna with Herbs), 166, *167*
Thai Village, West Covina, Calif., 66
Tikka Masala, Chicken (Chicken in a Creamy Spiced Tomato Sauce), 208, *209*
Tofu, Soft, and Pork Stew (Pork and Kimchi Soondubu), *72, 73*
tomatillos, in Salsa Verde, 230
tomato(es):
  Basil Sauce, 142
  Egg Drop Soup, 62, *63*
  Mussels Simmered with Spices and (Mussels with a Rasam Vibe), 182, *183*
  Rasam (Spicy Tomato Broth), 57
  Roasted, Rice with Peppers and (Jollof Rice), 128–9, *129*
  Sauce, Creamy Spiced, Chicken in (Chicken Tikka Masala), 208–9
Tomorrow's Borsch (Beet and Vegetable Soup), *64,* 65
Tom Yum Goong (Hot and Sour Soup with Shrimp), 66, *67*
tools, xxiii
Tosti di Valminuta, Beatrice, 142, 226
Tostones (Fried Green Plantains), 32, *33*
Tropical Fruit and Crushed Ice Sundae (Decolonized Halo-Halo), *270,* 271–2, *272*
Tsiliclis, Katerina, 79
tuna:
  Larb (Tuna with Herbs), 166, *167*
  Shoyu Poke (Rice and Tuna Bowl), 173
turmeric, xxviii
Tuscan Ribollita (White Bean and Vegetable Stew), *70,* 71
Twitty, Michael, 128

U

Ukrainian borsch (Tomorrow's Borsch, Beet and Vegetable Soup), *64,* 65
Uova in Trippa (Egg "Noodles" in Tomato-Basil Sauce), 142–4, *143–5*
Upma-Style Sriracha Butter Couscous, Krishna's, *140,* 141
urad dal, xxix

V

Veal Cutlets, Fried (Schnitzel), 231
vegetable(s):
  and Beet Soup (Tomorrow's Borsch), *64,* 65
  Broth, 56
  chopping, xx
  Fritters (Pakori), 28–30, *29*
  Garden, Pickled (Chowchow), 42
  and White Bean Stew (Ribollita), *70,* 71
vegetable and legume dishes, 83–112
  Blackened Corn with Suya Spice, 88, *89*
  Braised Leeks, *92,* 93
  Cabbage Poriyal (Stir-Fried Cabbage), 91
  Calabaza con Mojo (Roasted Squash in a Citrus-Garlic Sauce), 94, *95*
  Fatteh Batinjan (Roasted Eggplant Layered with Chickpeas, Yogurt, and Pita), 112–15, *113, 114*
  Holishkes (Sweet and Sour Stuffed Cabbage), 104–7, *105, 106*
  Podimas (Potatoes with Turmeric and Fried Lentils), *100,* 101
  Red Cabbage, Peppery Sweet and Sour, 90
  Saag and Grits (Greens and Grits), 96–9
  Sabzi (Sautéed Greens), 84, *85*
  Zucchini with Sun-Dried Tomatoes, *86,* 87
vinegar, xxxi
  Chile, 99
volume measurements, xx

W

Walnut and Roasted Red Pepper Spread (Muhammara), 13
Wampanoag foodways, 280
Weinstock, Sylvia, 283
Whipped Spam with Toast Points, *40,* 41
White Bean and Vegetable Stew (Ribollita), *70,* 71
white pepper, xxviii
white vinegar, xxxi
white wine vinegar, xxxi
Wong, Ali, *xv, 14,* 15
Wong, Meeling, 138

Y

Yellow Lentil Soup (Tadka Dal), 68–9
yogurt:
  Chicken, 193
  Cucumber Sauce (Mast-o Khiar), 243, *243*
  Roasted Eggplant Layered with Chickpeas, Pita and (Fatteh Batinjan), 112–15, *113, 114*
  Sauce, Garlic, 78
  Tahdig (Rice with a Crispy Top), 120–2, *121*
Yoskowitz, Jeffrey, 104
yuzu juice, xxxi

Z

za'atar, xxviii, 6
  Romaine Heart Salad with Herbs and, 6, *7*
Zucchini with Sun-Dried Tomatoes, *86,* 87